Delia Smith's Cookery Course Part Two

Delia Smith's Cookery Course

Part Two

BRITISH BROADCASTING CORPORATION

This book accompanies the second part of the
BBC Television series *Delia Smith's Cookery Course*.
Part two of this series first broadcast on BBC-2
from January 1980. Producer: Peter Riding.

Edited by Philippa Davenport

Photographs by Bob Komar
Drawings by Ray and Corrine Burrows

Grateful thanks to Elaine Bastable, Linda Blakemore,
Susan Goodman, Elisabeth Ingham, Gwyneth Phillips
and Rosemary Oates for their help in the preparation
of this book. Also to Mr P. Holroyd of Marks and Spencer
Limited for his help with the poultry section.

Acknowledgment is due to Universal Pictorial Press
and Agency for the portrait of Delia Smith on the cover,
to British Meat for the information for drawings on
page 322 and to the British Poultry Meat Association
Limited for the information for drawings on page 395.
The BBC would also like to thank the following for
the loan of equipment and accessories for the photographs:
Debenhams Limited, Oxford Street, London W1
Divertimenti, Marylebone Lane, London W1
Selectasine, Bulstrode Street, London W1
Selfridges Limited, Oxford Street, London W1

Published to accompany a series of programmes prepared in
consultation with the BBC Continuing Education Advisory Council.

Filmset in 12/13 point Baskerville
Printed and bound in Great Britain by W & J Mackay Limited, Chatham

Contents

Conversion tables

All these are *approximate* conversions, which have either been rounded up or down. In a few recipes it has been necessary to modify them very slightly. Never mix metric and imperial measures in one recipe, stick to one system or the other.
All spoon measurements used throughout this book are level unless specified otherwise.

Oven temperatures

Mark 1	275 °F	140 °C
2	300	150
3	325	170
4	350	180
5	375	190
6	400	200
7	425	220
8	450	230
9	475	240

Volume

2 fl oz	55 ml
3	75
5 ($\frac{1}{4}$ pt)	150
10 ($\frac{1}{2}$ pt)	275
15 ($\frac{3}{4}$ pt)	425
20 (1 pt)	570
$1\frac{3}{4}$ pt	1 litre

Measurements

$\frac{1}{8}$ inch	3 mm
$\frac{1}{4}$	$\frac{1}{2}$ cm
$\frac{1}{2}$	1
$\frac{3}{4}$	2
1	2·5
$1\frac{1}{4}$	3
$1\frac{1}{2}$	4
$1\frac{3}{4}$	4·5
2	5
3	7·5
4	10
5	13
6	15
7	18
8	20
9	23
10	25·5
11	28
12	30

Weights

$\frac{1}{2}$ oz	10 g
1	25
$1\frac{1}{2}$	40
2	50
$2\frac{1}{2}$	60
3	75
4	110
$4\frac{1}{2}$	125
5	150
6	175
7	200
8	225
9	250
10	275
12	350
1 lb	450
$1\frac{1}{2}$ lb	700
2 lb	900
3 lb	1 kg 350 g

Introduction

This, the second part of the Cookery Course, continues with the same essential aims that I tried to establish in Part One. That is to say, to explain and demonstrate the basic skills and techniques of cooking and to offer a number of varied recipes in order to exercise those skills. However, I begin this part with one advantage I didn't have when we set out on Part One. I have your overwhelming support and enthusiasm, which has been so encouraging and for which I thank you. I also have the benefit of your suggestions and comments which I've read with interest. In particular there seems to be one aspect of food and cooking which—understandably—concerns a lot of people, and that is the question of health and diet.

It is a concern I have long shared. No-one who reads newspapers or magazines can be in much doubt that there *are* certain health hazards attached to our modern Western diet, but exactly what they amount to is not so clear. Nutritionists often *do* disagree amongst themselves. Nor is it much help to be confronted at one moment with an expensive advertising campaign helping to move a Common Market butter mountain, and at the next another expensive campaign selling tons of polyunsaturated margarine.

In certain areas however, there is a great deal of concensus. Heart disease is responsible for more than one in three deaths among men between 35 and 65 in this country. Originally one of the major causes was said to be over-consumption of animal fats: now the blame has been extended to include some vegetable fats and oils, and we are being advised to cut down our *total* fat consumption by about 25%, which is in fact a very moderate target.

Equally there is no dispute about the problem of obesity, and the contribution made to it by too much sugar. It is a myth that refined sugar is needed for energy: anyone eating a balanced diet has no need of added sugar because carbohydrates naturally convert into sugar when digested. Sugar is a very highly refined food, which deceives both the appetite and the palate. The palate becomes used to over-sweetness and very soon normally sweet foods (like fresh fruits) don't taste sweet any more. And after many years of tasting food I can assure you that sugar is also a flavour-killer, so easily overpowering the natural flavours of food.

Another consequence of our over-refined diet nowadays is lack of fibre—sometimes referred to, not very accurately, as roughage—in our foods, which is singled out on fairly conclusive evidence as a cause of other types of disease. In this book, as in Part One, I touch on the value of foods that are left in their unrefined state such as wholemeal bread, brown rice and wholewheat cereals. I recommend them to you not only for flavour, but for the sake of healthy eating.

She's a bit of a killjoy, you're probably thinking by now. But it is not my belief that anything should be banned outright. I'm convinced that the underlying problem is over-consumption of food *full stop*. It is a tragic irony that when two-thirds of the world lives at or below subsistence level, the rest of us suffer from diseases caused by the effects of over-eating. It is a fact that this nation was never so healthy as during the war years when there was food rationing, and we were eating far less of foods we don't really need. Of course we all need the basic essentials, but not the surplus. And modern technology, and high-powered advertising that invades our homes, and the pull of commercialism have brain-washed us into believing we need to eat more and more of the wrong types of food.

You will find sugar in the recipes that follow, and butter and cream. As a race we have evolved quite naturally on a balanced diet that contains meat and dairy foods, and I cannot for the life of me believe that suddenly we should go vegetarian or that we need to completely replace butter with polyunsaturated margarine. My point is that what we *do* need to do is not be so heavy-handed with butter and other fats, and not eat meat quite so often. And if we want to eat sugary foods like cakes and puddings, rather than deny ourselves completely (which could only make a craving more obsessive), let's give them a more restricted place in our diet.

In my job keeping slim has been an uphill struggle, but I have found that crash diets to repair any damage have simply been an incentive to start all over again. A sensible approach to eating at all times is a much more relaxed way: for me the perfect answer to the sugar problem is only to eat pudding or cake *once a week*. I can therefore look forward to something gooey or chocolatey without guilt, and appreciate it more when I do have it. (And it follows that this is an opportunity not to be wasted by squandering calories on synthetic puds or shop-bought cakes: if I'm going to treat myself, I want to treat myself *well* with good home cooking.)

That's why in this Course, with the more basic recipes I have included some richer and more expensive ones. Responsible—and healthy—eating does not mean cutting out anything that might be 'fattening' once and for all: it means not eating more than we need and finding a sensible balance in our diet *all the time*. It may mean cooking less than we used to, but cooking it well.   *Delia Smith*

Cakes

Including recipes for:

One of the cheapest ways to add a touch of luxury to our everyday eating, I think, is to indulge in a little home baking now and then. Some of the chief contributors to the boredom of our modern synthetic diet are those dull factory-made cakes and flavourless biscuits which come so prettily wrapped on our supermarket shelves. Eating of course is for sustenance—but surely for enjoyment too: and hasn't the sheer blandness of mass production taken away some of the joy?

If you have never done any home baking, or have lapsed for some time, I do hope you'll help revive the art. There's so much personal pleasure in it and a sort of wholesomeness about a kitchen filled with the aroma of baking—a lovely way to make your family feel spoiled.

I've never believed, as some people seem to, that you either have a gift for cake-making or you don't. Confidence is the key and nothing can shake one's confidence like having a failure with a cake into which so much care has gone. So perhaps the first thing we ought to do is to try to understand what is actually happening when a cake is being baked—because any interference with this process could end in the failure we all want to avoid!

What happens when you bake a cake?

When fat and sugar are mixed together—the process is called creaming—little bubbles of air are being trapped in the mixture, each one surrounded by a film of fat (which is why the mixture changes colour during creaming as the trapped air creates a foam). It is this air which produces the lightness in the finished cake, but unless beaten egg is added to the mixture the fat would collapse and the air escape during cooking. The egg white conveniently forms a layer around each air bubble, and as the temperature of the cake rises in the heat of the oven this layer coagulates and forms a rigid wall round each bubble, preventing it from bursting and ruining the texture of the cake.

During the baking the bubbles of air will expand and the cake will 'rise'. At the same time the stretchy gluten in the flour—which has formed an elastic network round the air bubbles—will stretch until, at a higher temperature, it loses its elasticity and the shape of the cake becomes fixed.

But until that moment is reached the expansion process must be allowed to continue uninterrupted. Which is why a) the cake should be baked as soon as it is mixed and b), even more importantly, the oven door should *never* be opened in the early stages of cooking: the temperature will drop suddenly and the air in the cake will stop expanding and actually contract. The whole structure of the cake will then sink back because there's nothing to prop it up. So, remember, never look at a cake until three-quarters of the cooking time has elapsed.

Cake tins

Here we have another possible cause of failure. There are so many differing sizes of cake tin available, and even a half-inch difference all round can often upset both the timing of a recipe and the finished size of the cake. It is therefore *important* to use the correct sized tin. In my recipes I usually try to keep to 7 or 8 inch tins (which metrically is approximately 18 or 20 cms—the difference in volume is minimal). These are fairly standard sizes, though some manufacturers come up with some very strange alternatives in the name of metrication.

Sponge sandwich tins To get a properly risen cake it is most important to use a sponge tin that is at least $1\frac{1}{2}$ inches (4 cm) deep. The cause of many a flat sponge cake is a sponge tin that is too shallow.

Loaf tins These too come in a confusing array of sizes, and again I have kept all my recipes to two sizes—either the 2 lb (900 g) capacity loaf tin, or else a slightly narrower tin with a base measurement of $7\frac{1}{2}$ inches (19 cm) by $3\frac{1}{2}$ inches (8·5 cm).

Non-stick surfaces Normally I use non-stick bakeware simply as an extra aid, never relying on it exclusively. In practice I use it as I would normal bakeware, greasing and lining it by the traditional method. I just find this more reliable.

Cake ingredients

Plain flour Unless yeast is used in a recipe (e.g. *Hot cross buns*, Cookery Course Part One) ordinary soft flour is always best for cake recipes requiring plain flour. This has a lower protein content than strong flour, and therefore produces that finer, shorter texture suitable for cakes, biscuits and scones.

Self-raising flour On those occasions when a raising agent is called for, it is usually more convenient to use self-raising flour since this has a standard amount of raising agent already added to it. From time to time a recipe might need rather more (or less) raising power, in which case plain flour plus the appropriate quantity of baking powder is used.

Wholewheat flour Nowadays most food scientists are agreed about the lack of fibre in our diet, and even the commercial giants are replacing the bran which was milled out of flour in the first place (thus we see 'bran' finding its way into countless breakfast cereals, biscuits and cakes). To meet the problem at home I find it better to switch over completely to wholewheat flour in baking. I'm delighted to report that most of my wholewheat experiments with cakes have been very successful, which I hope some of the following recipes will prove.

Baking powders These are normally a mixture of bicarbonate of soda and another acid-acting chemical, like cream of tartar. Very often, though, one needs far less raising power than these mixtures give—which explains why some recipes require bicarbonate of soda on its own.

Fats Flavour-wise it is said you can't beat butter in baking. And certainly for purists that's probably true—I see one leading chain-store proudly advertises 'made with all butter' on its wrappings! My own opinion is that margarine—now it has improved so much in flavour—is very good for baking, and with the advent of soft margarine and the all-in-one method of making sponges (see recipes), I actually hardly ever use butter for baking. Very occasionally I use lard, as in the *Marmalade cake* recipe (see page 275).

Fats should usually be at room temperature for cake-making. Allow 1 hour to soften butter, block margarine and lard. Soft or whipped margarines can be used straight from the fridge (although in practice I usually allow half an hour at room temperature), but it is vital that any margarine that is high in polyunsaturated fats is always used straight from the fridge.

Sugar I believe caster sugar is worth paying the extra for in baking (especially for sponges), since it does give a finer texture. Some people manage successfully to make granulated sugar into caster sugar in a liquidiser and so save money, but be warned; if you over-do it you can finish up with a powdery 'icing' sugar and won't have saved anything! In wholefood cakes, soft brown sugar (or sometimes demerara) can be used and indeed is preferable.

Eggs As we discussed in Part One, eggs for all cooking purposes should be at room temperature. If they are too cold or used straight from the fridge, they curdle more easily. So remember to remove from the fridge a couple of hours before beginning baking.

Air Yes, another all-important ingredient. Air means lightness in your cakes, and to incorporate it you need (i) large and roomy mixing bowls, and (ii) always to sift the flour, holding your sieve up high to give the flour a good airing on its way to the bowl. Careful folding with a metal spoon, which cuts cleanly into the mixture, enables you to retain the precious air incorporated at the mixing stage.

What went wrong?

I hope you're not reading this section because things *have* gone wrong! It's really here to try to prevent that happening, or at least to reassure you.

Hit or miss One of the primary reasons why cakes sometimes fail is the recipe itself. It might be wrong or simply too vague, like some of grandma's hand-me-downs which never mention details like tin sizes or oven temperatures. Be suspicious of any recipe that does not offer you all the information you need. But if it is precise, then follow it precisely: if it calls for an 8 inch (20 cm) square tin and you've only got a 6 inch (15 cm) round tin, it *does* matter.

Over-anxiety It is always tempting to take a peep in the oven to see how your creation is getting on. As I mentioned before, impatient cooks are inviting disaster.

Curdling If you are using a creaming method (see page 263), it can sometimes happen that the beaten eggs are added to the sugar-and-fat mixture too quickly, causing the whole mixture to separate. This 'breaking up' means that some of the air incorporated at the creaming stage will escape and the finished cake will be slightly heavier. For beginners the way to avoid this is to add the beaten eggs just a teaspoonful at a time, whisking preferably with an electric hand-whisk. If it does curdle, don't worry: the cake won't be as light but it's not a disaster.

Fruit sinking This is usually a fault in the recipe. It means the mixture is too slack (too liquid) to hold the fruit. Fruit cakes need a larger proportion of flour in order to hold the fruit evenly. Glacé cherries and other sugar-coated fruit should be rinsed and dried (and chopped if large) before adding to a cake mixture. Both the size of the fruit and sugar coating can cause sinking.

Over-browning Sometimes the top of a cake becomes brown before the centre is cooked. To prevent this, check the cake three-quarters of the way through the cooking time and, if necessary, fit a protective circle of double greaseproof paper (with a hole about the size of a 50p piece in the centre) over the top of the cake.

But above all, don't be daunted. Always remember the good things that go into a home-made cake, and even if the finished product does happen to have sunk a bit, it will still taste delicious.

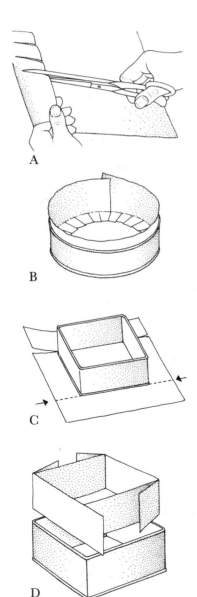

A

B

C

D

Notes on preparation

Lining tins Where a recipe asks you to line a tin, always do so. It may seem like an extra bother, but it only takes a few moments and it makes turning out the cake far easier. Greaseproof paper is used in most cases, but for delicate cakes like sponges I use silicone paper (from good stationers) for a base lining, as it *never* sticks. It is important to allow an extra couple of inches (5 cm or so) so that the lining paper extends above the rim of the cake tin.

For a round tin: cut a strip of paper slightly longer than the circumference of the tin, and fold back about an inch (2.5 cms) along its length. Snip this at intervals with scissors, cutting at a slight angle right up to the fold (A). Grease the tin, then press the paper around the sides. You will find the snipped edge will overlap on the base of the tin to give a snug fit. (B). Finally, cut a circle of paper—using the tin as a template—to fit over the base.

For a square tin: cut a piece of paper to size by measuring the length and width of the tin and adding twice its depth. Centre the tin on the paper, then make four cuts from the paper's edge right up to the corners of the tin (C). Grease the tin and fit the paper inside, folding and overlapping at the corners (D).

Greasing tins In my experience so-called non-stick tins sometimes do! So I recommend that you always grease cake tins regardless. The best thing is to use some of the same sort of fat as is used for the cake mixture. Smear it evenly all over the inside of the tin (making sure you get into the corners) using a piece of absorbent kitchen paper.

Flouring tins Some recipes state that the tins should also be lightly dusted with flour. This is unnecessary unless for some reason the cake needs to be extra crisp at the edges.

How to store cakes

Cake tins are definitely better than plastic boxes for storage, because metal is non-porous. However carefully you wash plastic, smells linger on. The previous occupant of a plastic container can taint the next, and mould can develop. Also never store cakes and biscuits in the same tin, as the moisture from the cake will make the biscuits soggy. For short-term storing an aluminium foil wrapping can be used, but if you're storing a rich fruit cake for a longer period, then use a double layer of greaseproof paper on the inside and foil on the outside—because the acid in the fruit can corrode the foil if it comes into direct contact with it and a mould will develop.

Some different methods of cake-making

Creaming This is the term used when a cake is made with butter or block margarine (soft or whipped margarines are unsuitable). It means that the fat and sugar are beaten together till creamy and pale: the eggs are then beaten into this mixture, bit by bit. This method is explained in the *Classic Victoria sponge* recipe (page 264).

Rubbing-in A cake made by this method starts off with the fat being rubbed into the flour—exactly the same as for shortcrust pastry. Butter, block margarine and lard can all be used. It is a very easy method—see the *Marmalade cake* recipe (page 275).

Boil-and-bake In recipes of this kind the fat and liquid are boiled together before the flour is added. Again, a very straightforward method, as in the *Sticky date cake* recipe (page 274).

All-in-one Exactly as the name suggests, these cakes are mixed all in one go. All the ingredients go into the bowl together and the mixing is done in seconds. Soft margarine is tailor-made for this method.

Sponge cakes

I have to admit that since soft margarine came onto the market and sponge cakes can be made simply by combining all the ingredients in the bowl at once, I very rarely make the classic Victoria sponge, which is a lot more work. However there will probably always be those who prefer cakes made with butter for that bit of extra flavour. Anyway, for those who are new to cake-making or those who would like to experiment, here are my own notes on the differences between the three main methods of sponge-making:

1 Classic (Victoria) sponge Provides a good flavour and, if skilfully made, should have a light texture; but not quite as moist as an all-in-one sponge especially after storing.

2 All-in-one sponge This does have a very light texture—it really melts in the mouth. It keeps better than any other type of sponge I've made. The flavour is slightly less rich than the Victoria.

3 Whisked fatless sponge Extremely light in texture but the absence of fat can give a hint almost of rubberiness. This one must be eaten as fresh as possible: it can become stale by the next day.

There are of course other, rather more complicated sponge recipes, such as a Genoese or an oil-based sponge. But as this is essentially a basic cookery course I have not included them here. Recipes for them can be found in *Delia Smith's Book of Cakes* (Coronet books).

Classic Victoria sponge

I find a four ounce mixture (i.e. 4 oz or 110 g each of flour, sugar and butter to 2 eggs) gives just the right depth and balance between cake and filling, if 7 inch (18 cm) tins are used. However if you like your sponges to have more depth, you can increase this mixture to 6 oz (175 g) each of flour, sugar and butter and use 3 eggs. Allow an extra 5–10 minutes cooking time in that case.

4 oz butter, at room temperature (110 g)
4 oz caster sugar (110 g)
2 large eggs
4 oz self-raising flour, sifted (110 g)

A few drops of vanilla essence
Some hot water, if required

To finish:
jam and sifted icing sugar

Pre-heat the oven to gas mark 3,
325°F (170°C)

Two 7 inch (18 cm) sponge tins at least
1½ inches (4 cm) deep, greased and the
bases lined with greaseproof paper.

In a medium-sized mixing bowl, cream the butter and sugar
together until you get a pale, fluffy mixture that drops off the
spoon easily (an electric hand-whisk speeds this up considerably,
but a wooden spoon will do). Then in a separate jug or bowl beat
the eggs together thoroughly, then add them a little at a time,
beating well after each addition. For a beginner I recommend just
a teaspoonful at a time: if you add it like this, just a little at a time
and beating after each addition, the mixture won't curdle.

When the eggs have been incorporated, stir in a few drops of
vanilla essence, then take a metal spoon (which will cut and fold
the flour in much better than a wooden spoon). Have the flour in a
sieve resting on a plate, then lift the sieve high above the bowl and
sift about a quarter of the flour onto the mixture. Then replace the
sieve on the plate, and lightly and gently fold the flour into the
mixture (if you beat the flour in, you'll lose some precious air).
Then repeat until all the flour is incorporated: lifting the sieve high
above the bowl will ensure the flour gets a good airing before it
reaches the mixture.

Now that the flour has been added you should have a mixture that
will drop off the spoon easily when you tap it on the side of the
bowl (this is what is called a good 'dropping' consistency). If the
consistency is not right, add one or two teaspoons of hot water.

Now divide the mixture equally between the two tins—if you want
to be very precise you could place both tins on balance scales (I've
never bothered, though, because I don't mind if one sponge is
fractionally larger than the other). Place them on the centre shelf
of the oven, and they'll take about 25–30 minutes to cook. When
they are cooked the centres will feel springy when lightly touched
with a little finger-tip and no imprint remains.

When you are satisfied that the sponges are cooked, remove them from the oven, then after about one minute turn them out onto a wire cooling tray, loosening them around the edges with a palette knife first. Then carefully peel off the base papers and leave the cakes to cool completely before sandwiching them together with jam and sifting a little icing sugar over the surface.

Note: for 8 inch (20 cm) sponge sandwich tins, use 6 oz (175 g) each of flour, sugar and butter and 3 large eggs.

All-in-one sponge

For me this is the best sponge of all, and should work even if you've never made a cake before in your life.

4 oz self-raising flour, sifted (110 g)
1 teaspoon baking powder
4 oz soft margarine, at room temperature (110 g)
4 oz caster sugar (110 g)
2 large eggs
2–3 drops vanilla essence

To finish:
Icing sugar, jam and/or fresh cream

Pre-heat the oven to gas mark 3, 325°F (170°C)

Two 7 inch (18 cm) sponge tins, no less than 1½ inches (4 cm) deep.

Lightly grease the tins and line their bases with greaseproof paper (also greased) or silicone paper.

Take a large roomy mixing bowl, and sift flour and baking powder into it, holding the sieve high to give the flour a good airing. Then simply add all the other ingredients to the bowl, and whisk them—preferably with an electric hand whisk—till thoroughly combined. If the mixture doesn't drop off a wooden spoon easily when tapped on the side of the bowl, then add 1 or 2 teaspoonfuls of tap-warm water, and whisk again.

Now divide the mixture between the two prepared tins, level off and bake on the centre shelf of the oven for about 30 minutes. When cooked leave them in the tins for only about 30 seconds, then loosen the edges by sliding a palette knife all round and turn them out onto a wire cooling rack. Peel off the base papers carefully and, when cool, sandwich them together with jam or lemon curd (or jam and fresh cream), and dust with icing sugar.

All-in-one chocolate sponge
Add 1 tablespoon of cocoa powder to the basic ingredients. Omit the vanilla essence.

All-in-one coffee and walnut sponge
Add 2 oz (50 g) of finely chopped walnuts, plus 1 tablespoon of instant coffee mixed with 1 dessertspoon of hot water, to the basic ingredients. Omit the vanilla essence. For filling and topping use *Coffee cream mousseline* (page 269).

All-in-one orange or lemon sponge
Add the grated rind of a medium orange or lemon, plus 1 dessertspoon of the juice, to the basic ingredients. Omit the vanilla essence.

All-in-one orange or lemon layer cake
Use 6 oz (175 g) flour, margarine and sugar to 1½ teaspoons baking powder and 3 large eggs, together with the orange or lemon flavour as above, in two 7 inch (18 cm) tins. Bake for 30 minutes, then when the cakes are cold, slice each one carefully in half horizontally. Use a lemon or orange curd filling (page 269) to sandwich the layers together, and dust the top with icing sugar.

All-in-one wholewheat sponge
This works surprisingly well using 4 oz (110 g) of plain wholewheat flour and adding 2½ teaspoons of baking powder. You could also use soft brown sugar, but I find the texture is better with caster sugar. In short, any recipe for an All-in-one sponge cake can be made with wholewheat flour so long as the extra amount of baking powder is also used.

Whisked fatless sponge

This is a very good recipe for those attempting to cut the fat content in their diets—and one or two slices will not contain a great deal of egg.

3 oz plain flour, sifted (75 g)

½ teaspoon baking powder

3 large eggs
3 oz caster sugar (75 g)

To finish:
A little caster sugar, jam and icing sugar

Pre-heat the oven to gas mark 4, 350°F (180°C)

Two 7 inch (18 cm) sandwich tins, liberally brushed with melted fat and the bases lined with greaseproof paper (also greased).

First separate the eggs, placing the whites in a very large grease-free bowl and the yolks in a separate one. Now add the sugar to the yolks and whisk, either with an electric hand-whisk or by hand, until the mixture is very pale and fluffy and has thickened—about 5 minutes with an electric whisk. Now wash and dry the whisk very thoroughly and use it to beat the whites until stiff but not dry.

Next with the aid of a large metal spoon fold the egg whites into the yolk-and-sugar mixture alternately with the sifted flour and baking powder, starting and finishing with egg whites. Then spoon an equal quantity of the mixture into the prepared tins and bake in the centre of the oven for 20–25 minutes. The sponges are cooked when they feel firm and springy in the centre and have begun to shrink slightly away from the sides of the tins.

Leave to cool in the tins for 3 minutes, then have ready a sheet of greaseproof paper, sprinkled with a little caster sugar. Turn the cakes out onto this before transferring to a wire rack to finish cooling. Then sandwich them together with jam, and dust the top with icing sugar.

Note: it's important to eat a fatless sponge as fresh as possible.

Sponge toppings and fillings

These are an important part of a finished sponge, and while jam in the centre and icing sugar on top are delicious, there are a great many possible alternatives. What starts out as an ordinary sponge can be made into something really special.

One of the little campaigns that runs through my cooking is to try to reduce the amount of sugar in recipes, wherever possible and desirable (for reasons see page vii). Consequently I have avoided those sickly sweet icings and butter creams (which taste even worse made with margarine) in this section. Instead here are several delicious alternatives, that aren't too much bother and taste far better. Quantities are for the standard sponge recipes on the previous pages.

Fresh lemon curd

Home-made lemon curd is so easy a child can make it, and it is a beautifully fresh-tasting filling. The quantity here is enough to sandwich a layer cake.

3 oz caster sugar (75 g)
1 large, juicy lemon (grated rind and juice)
2 large eggs
2 oz unsalted butter (50 g)

Place the grated lemon rind and sugar in a bowl. In another bowl whisk the lemon juice together with the eggs, then pour this mixture over the sugar. Add the butter cut into little pieces, and place the bowl over a pan of barely simmering water. Stir frequently till thickened—about 20 minutes. Then cool the curd and use it to sandwich the sponges together, spreading it thickly.

Note: for *orange curd* replace the lemon with 1 large orange.

Coffee cream mousseline

This is a soft, fluffy, not-too-sweet creamy filling; it goes very well with the *Coffee and walnut sponge* page 267.

5 oz unsalted butter, at room temperature (150 g)
2½ oz caster sugar (60 g)
2 large egg yolks
4 tablespoons water
1 tablespoon instant coffee dissolved in 1 tablespoon hot water

Place the sugar and water together in a small saucepan and slowly bring it to the boil—keep an eye on it and make sure the sugar has dissolved completely before it comes to the boil. Then let it simmer gently for about 10–15 minutes or until the mixture forms a 'thread' when pressed between thumb and forefinger (to do this take some on a teaspoon, cool it a little, and dip your finger in cold water before testing). If you have a cooking thermometer the temperature should be between 218°F (103°C) and 220°F (105°C).

Now whisk the egg yolks in a bowl, place the bowl on a damp tea towel to steady it, then pour the sugar syrup onto the egg yolks in a steady stream, whisking all the time. Then whisk the butter in, about 1 oz (25 g) at a time, till you have a smooth fluffy cream. Now whisk in the dissolved coffee, and use the cream to sandwich the cake together and to decorate the top (along with some walnut halves perhaps). This fills and tops a 7 or 8 inch (18 or 20 cm) sponge.

Chocolate and soured cream filling

This has a sophisticated, dark bitter chocolate flavour and is not at all sweet (should you want it sweeter, add 1 dessertspoon of caster sugar).

5 oz plain dessert chocolate (150 g)
5 fl oz soured cream (150 ml)

Break the chocolate into a basin fitted over a pan of barely simmering water, add the soured cream too, and stir—keeping the heat low until the chocolate has melted. Then remove the pan from the heat and as soon as the mixture has cooled, spread it over the centre and top of a 7 or 8 inch (18 or 20 cm) chocolate sponge. A few walnuts or hazelnuts are nice for decoration.

Chocolate fudge filling and topping

This makes enough to fill and top a 7 or 8 inch (18 or 20 cm) cake.

3 oz granulated sugar (75 g)
1½ oz butter or margarine (40 g)
3 oz unsweetened cooking chocolate, or plain dessert chocolate (75 g)
4 fl oz evaporated milk (100 ml)
2 drops vanilla essence

To start with combine the sugar and evaporated milk in a heavy saucepan. Place the pan over a low heat and allow the sugar to dissolve, stirring frequently. When all the granules of sugar have melted, bring the mixture to the boil and simmer very gently for 6 minutes—this time without stirring.

Take the pan off the heat, stir in the chocolate (broken into small pieces) and keep stirring until the chocolate has melted. Finally stir in the butter and vanilla essence.

Now transfer the mixture to a bowl, cool, then cover with clingfilm and chill for a couple of hours until it has thickened to a spreadable consistency.

Family cakes
In the section that follows I have selected some of my own favourite cake recipes, and have attempted at the same time to cover a variety of cake-making methods.

Oatmeal parkin   One of the fascinating things about this traditional Northern recipe is that it's nothing out of the ordinary when it's freshly made—but if kept in an airtight tin it matures to a lovely chewy consistency. One week's keeping is enough, but two weeks is even better!

6 oz medium oatmeal (175 g)
3 oz self-raising flour, sifted (75 g)
A pinch of salt
4 oz golden syrup (110 g)
1 oz black treacle (25 g)
3 oz margarine (75 g)
3 oz soft brown sugar (75 g)
1½ teaspoons ground ginger
1 small egg, beaten
1 dessertspoon milk

Pre-heat the oven to gas mark 1, 275°F (140°C)

One 6 inch (15 cm) square cake tin, lightly greased.

First weigh a saucepan on the scales, then weigh the syrup and treacle into it. Then add the margarine and sugar to the saucepan and place it over a gentle heat until the margarine has melted down—don't go away and leave it unattended, because for this one you do not want it to boil.

Meanwhile measure the oatmeal, flour and ginger into a mixing bowl, add a pinch of salt, then gradually stir in the warmed syrup mixture until everything is thoroughly blended. Next add the beaten egg and lastly the milk. Now pour the mixture into the prepared tin and bake in the centre of the oven for about $1\frac{1}{2}$ hours or until the centre feels springy to the touch.

Then cool the parkin in the tin for 30 minutes before turning out. Don't worry too much if the parkin sinks slightly in the middle—it sometimes happens in Yorkshire too, I'm told.

Date, apple and walnut loaf

A very easy and deliciously wholesome cake—which I particularly like to make for a picnic or a packed lunch.

1 small cooking apple
4 oz soft margarine (110 g)
6 oz soft brown sugar (175 g)
2 eggs, lightly beaten
4 oz wholewheat flour (110 g)
4 oz plain flour (110 g)
A pinch of salt
$1\frac{1}{2}$ teaspoons baking powder
4 oz walnuts, roughly chopped (110 g)
3 oz pitted dates, roughly chopped (75 g)
3 or 4 tablespoons milk

Pre-heat the oven to gas mark 4, 350°F (180°C)

A loaf tin with base measurements of $3\frac{1}{2} \times 7\frac{1}{2}$ inches (8·5 × 19 cm), well buttered.

Put the margarine, sugar, eggs, flours, salt and baking powder into a large mixing bowl (sifting the flours in) then whisk them together with an electric hand-whisk until thoroughly combined. Next add the apple, peeled and cored and roughly chopped, followed by the walnuts and pitted dates. Finally add the milk, then mix it all well before transferring the mixture to the prepared tin. Spread it out evenly, then bake for 1 hour or until the loaf feels springy in the centre and a skewer inserted in the middle comes out clean.

Let the cake cool for a minute or two in the tin, then turn it out onto a wire tray. Store in an airtight tin as soon as cold.

Squidgy chocolate log

This is a cake that has no flour in it—so it's extremely light and moist. It's also a bit wicked, with its chocolate mousse and whipped cream filling!

5 oz caster sugar (150 g)
6 large eggs, separated
2 oz cocoa powder (50 g)

For the filling:
8 oz plain chocolate (225 g)
2 large eggs, separated
8 fl oz double cream (225 ml)
Icing sugar

Pre-heat the oven to gas mark 4, 350°F (180°C)

A tin 11½ × 7 inches (29 × 18 cm) and about 1 inch (2·5 cm) deep, oiled and lined with greaseproof paper (also lightly oiled).

Begin by making the chocolate filling. Break the plain chocolate in pieces into a basin and add 2 tablespoons of water. Now place the basin over a saucepan of barely simmering water and wait for the chocolate to melt. After that, remove from the heat and beat it with a wooden spoon until smooth. Next separate two large eggs and beat the yolks, first on their own, then into the warm chocolate mixture. Let it cool a bit then whisk the egg-whites till stiff and fold them into the chocolate mixture. Cover the bowl and chill in the refrigerator for about an hour.

Meanwhile you can get on with the cake. First place the egg yolks in a basin and whisk until they start to thicken, then add the caster sugar and continue to whisk until the mixture thickens slightly—but be careful not to get it *too* thick. Now mix the cocoa powder into the egg yolk mixture then, using a clean whisk and bowl, beat up the egg whites to the soft peak stage. Next carefully cut and fold the egg white into the chocolate mixture—gently and thoroughly—then pour the mixture into the prepared tin.

Bake the cake on the centre shelf for 20–25 minutes until springy and puffy. When the cake is cooked, remove it from the oven but leave it in the cake tin to cool (it will shrink quite a bit as it cools but don't worry, that's normal).

Then when the cake is quite cold, turn it out onto an oblong of greaseproof paper which has been liberally dusted with icing sugar. Peel away the cake tin lining paper from the bottom of the cake (which is now facing upwards), then spread the chocolate mousse filling over the cake. Next whip the cream softly and spread it over the chocolate filling. Finally, gently roll up the cake to make a log shape. This will serve 8 people and, although it's unlikely that there will be any left, you can cover any remaining cake with an upturned basin and keep it in the refrigerator. As an alternative, an 11 oz tin of sweetened chestnut purée (crème de marrons) can replace the chocolate mousse.

Note: during the rolling up, the cake will crack, but this is quite normal and looks most attractive.

Sticky date cake

This is an example of what I call 'boil-and-bake'. There's no sugar in it, but the boiled condensed milk gives a lovely dark toffee flavour.

4 oz raisins (110 g)
8 oz chopped dates (225 g)
6 oz sultanas (175 g)
4 oz currants (110 g)
10 oz margarine (275 g)
½ pint water (275 ml)
1 large tin condensed milk
5 oz plain flour (150 g)
5 oz wholemeal flour (150 g)
¾ teaspoon bicarbonate of soda
A pinch of salt
1 generous tablespoon chunky marmalade

Pre-heat the oven to gas mark 3,
325°F (170°C)

An 8 inch (20 cm) square cake tin,
greased and lined.

Place all the fruits in a saucepan, together with the margarine,
water and condensed milk and bring to the boil. Stir frequently to
avoid sticking. Simmer the mixture for exactly 3 minutes and stir
occasionally. Now transfer the mixture to a large mixing bowl and
let it cool for approximately 30 minutes.

While it's cooling, weigh the flours and sift them into a bowl
together with the salt and bicarbonate of soda. (When sieving
wholemeal flour, you frequently find small quantities of bran left
in the sieve; these can be tipped on to the already sieved flour.)

When the fruit mixture has cooled stir into it the flour, salt and
bicarbonate of soda and add a good round tablespoon of
marmalade. Now spoon the mixture into the prepared tin and
bake the cake on the centre shelf of the oven for 2½–3 hours. This
cake does get rather brown on top if not protected. You should
therefore cover it from the beginning of the cooking with a double
square of greaseproof paper (with a hole the size of a 50p piece
in the centre).

After removing the cake from the oven let it cool in the tin for 5
minutes before turning it out onto a wire tray. This is quite a large
cake which will keep well for several weeks in an airtight tin and, I
think, even improves with keeping.

Marmalade cake

It's hard to beat the flavour of this cake,
although it looks quite ordinary when
it's cooked. It's made by the
'rubbing-in' method, which is very easy.

8 oz self-raising flour, sifted (225 g)
4 oz caster sugar (110 g)
2 oz butter, at room temperature (50 g)
2 oz lard, at room temperature (50 g)
1 rounded tablespoon thick marmalade
Grated rind of half a large lemon
Grated rind of half a large orange
1 teaspoon mixed spice

1 teaspoon vinegar
A pinch of salt
6 fl oz milk (175 ml)
4 oz mixed dried fruit (110 g)
1 tablespoon demerara sugar

Pre-heat the oven to gas mark 4,
350°F (180°C)

I like to make this in a loaf tin with a base measurement of $7\frac{1}{2} \times 3$ inches (19 cm × 8·5 cm) greased and base lined with lightly greased greaseproof paper.

First rub the butter and lard into the flour until crumbly then add the sugar, salt, mixed fruit, spice, lemon and orange rinds. Now stir in the milk a little at a time, add the vinegar and mix until the ingredients are well combined. Next stir in the marmalade and now the mixture should be of a good dropping consistency. (This means that when you tap a spoonful of the mixture on the side of the bowl it drops off easily.)

Now spoon the mixture into the prepared tin and spread it out evenly. Sprinkle the surface with the demerara sugar and bake for $1-1\frac{1}{4}$ hours. The cake, when cooked, will have shrunk away from the side of the tin and the centre will be firm and springy to the touch. Leave the cake in its tin for 15 minutes then turn it out onto a wire cooling rack. When cold, store in an airtight tin. I think this cake improves after a couple of days' keeping.

Traditional Dundee cake

This is a really good fruit cake for those who don't like the heavy, rich sort. It does have an excellent flavour and a light crumbly texture.

5 oz butter, at room temperature (150 g)
5 oz caster sugar (150 g)
3 large eggs
8 oz plain flour, sifted (225 g)
1 teaspoon baking powder
6 oz currants (175 g)
6 oz sultanas (175 g)
2 oz glacé cherries, rinsed, dried and cut into halves (50 g)

2 oz mixed whole candied peel, finely chopped (50 g)
2 tablespoons ground almonds
The grated rinds of 1 small orange and 1 small lemon
2 oz whole blanched almonds (50 g)

Pre-heat the oven to gas mark 3, 325°F (170°C)

A 7–8 inch (18–20 cm) round cake tin, greased and then lined with greaseproof paper.

Put the butter and sugar in a mixing bowl and beat with a wooden spoon until light and fluffy—or an electric mixer will do this much more quickly.

Whisk the eggs separately then, a little at a time, beat them into the creamed butter and sugar. Next, using a large tablespoon, carefully *fold* in the flour and baking powder. Your mixture needs to be of a good, soft dropping consistency so, if it seems too dry, add a dessertspoon of milk.

Now carefully fold in the currants, sultanas, cherries, mixed peel, ground almonds, orange and lemon rinds. Then spoon the mixture into the prepared cake tin, smoothing it out evenly with the back of the spoon. Next arrange the whole almonds in circles on top of the mixture, but do this carefully and lightly; if they are pressed in they will sink during the baking.

Place the cake in the centre of the oven and bake for 2–2½ hours or until the centre is firm and springy to the touch. Let it cool before taking it out of the tin. This cake keeps very well in an airtight tin and tastes all the better if kept for a few days before cutting.

Lemon curd butterfly cakes
(makes 12–13 cakes)

These little cakes are baked in small paper baking cases, which can usually be bought at good stationers.

6 oz self-raising flour (175 g)
A pinch of salt
4 oz soft margarine, at room temperature (110 g)

4 oz caster sugar (110 g)
2 large eggs
1 dessertspoon lemon juice
The grated rind of 1 lemon

For the lemon curd filling:

1 quantity of lemon curd (see page 269)

Pre-heat the oven to gas mark 5, 375°F (190°C)

A patty tin, greased, and some paper baking cases.

First of all make up the filling, and leave to get quite cold.

To make the cakes combine all the ingredients together in a bowl and beat till absolutely smooth (1–2 minutes). Then drop an equal quantity of the mixture into the paper cases, and sit the cases in the patty tin—give it two or three light taps to settle the cake mixture. Then bake on the shelf just above the centure of the oven for 15–20 minutes or until the cakes are well risen and golden. Then remove them to a wire rack and leave to cool.

When they're cool, take a sharp knife and cut the top of each at an angle in a circle about ½ inch (1 cm) from the edge of the cake, so that you remove a cone-shaped round, leaving a cavity in the centre. Cut each cone in half (top to bottom) and set aside. Now fill the cavity of each cake with the lemon curd then sit the two cone-shaped pieces of cake on top like butterfly wings.

Scones and biscuits

Including recipes for:
Plain scones
Wholewheat fruit scones
Wholewheat cheese-crusted scones
Wholewheat girdle cakes
Crumpets
Shortbread biscuits
Scottish shortbread
Strawberry shortcake
Wholewheat shortbread
Whole oat crunchies
Oatmeal biscuits
American brownies
Gingernuts
Cheese savouries

In the days when households had such things as 'baking' days, bread and cakes would be baked in batches to last a week or even longer. The kitchen range was brought up to heat and kept topped up all day, and not an inch of space or minute of fuel time was wasted. Girdle cakes or cumpets used the heat on the top of the stove, scones fitted in alongside the bread, and biscuits were dried out at the end of the day as the heat died down in the range. The results, I'm sure, must have been enough to feed an army.

Nowadays few of us have the time or inclination to bake on such an organised scale, and inevitably the main casualties have been those items which form the subject of this chapter. We have come to rely very largely on bakeries and supermarkets for our scones and biscuits, but we are paying very dearly for this convenience (as a quick comparison between the weight and prices of almost any packet of biscuits will confirm). Yet this branch of baking is the easiest of all, using ingredients that most people keep regularly in their store-cupboard. I hope the recipes in this section will inspire you to re-discover some of the pleasures of 'batch' baking, and save lots of money at the same time!

Scones

The modern scone seems to have evolved from something rather similar to the girdle cake (see recipe page 285): it was only when raising agents were introduced to flour that scones began to be oven-baked and well-risen as we know them today. And that straightaway brings me to one of the most persistent queries I get from readers: why don't their scones ever rise to a proper height?

Now some problems are difficult to answer specifically, particularly when you can't see what people are doing wrong. But on the subject of scones I can nearly always put them right by suggesting that perhaps they are rolling the dough out too thinly—the major cause of failure. The dough for a perfect scone should never be rolled out to anything less than $\frac{3}{4}$ inch (2 cm). And there's another minor cause for concern which can be tracked down to the rolling too—that's scones which emerge uneven in shape. This is caused by uneven pressure on the rolling pin, which tends to make the dough (and therefore the scones) slanted. Hardly a disaster, in fact it can be quite appealing by giving them that home-made air in contrast to the clinical perfection of the shop-bought variety!

Right (from top to bottom): All-in-one sponge, page 266; Squidgy chocolate log, page 273; Traditional Dundee cake, page 276; Lemon cheesecake with frosted grapes, page 482.

Plain scones

(makes about 12)

Eat these with butter, home-made jam and, if you can get it, clotted cream.

8 oz self-raising flour, sifted (225 g)
1½ oz butter (or margarine) at room temperature (40 g)
¼ pint milk (150 ml)
1½ tablespoons caster sugar
A pinch of salt
A little extra flour

Pre-heat the oven to gas mark 7, 425°F (220°C)

A baking sheet, greased.

First of all, sift the flour into a bowl and rub the butter into it rapidly, using your fingertips. Next stir in the sugar and salt, then take a knife and use it to mix in the milk little by little. Now flour your hands a little and knead the mixture to a soft dough—adding a drop more milk if it feels at all dry.

Then turn the dough out onto a floured pastry board and roll it out to a thickness of not less than ¾ inch (2 cm) using a lightly floured rolling pin. Take a 1½ or 2 inch (4 or 5 cm) pastry cutter (either fluted or plain) and place it on the dough, then tap it sharply so that it goes straight through the dough—don't twist it or the scones will turn out a peculiar shape! After you have cut out as many scone shapes as you can like that, knead the dough trimmings together again and repeat until you have used it all.

Then place the scones on the greased baking sheet, dust each one with a little extra flour and bake near the top of the oven for 12–15 minutes. When cooked the scones will have turned a crisp golden brown. Cool on a wire rack and eat them slightly warm, still crisp on the outside and soft and light inside. In fact, always eat scones as fresh as possible as they can go stale very quickly.

Wholewheat fruit scones

(makes 7 or 8)

It took several tests and a few brick-like results before I got the right combination of ingredients for these, and I think it is most important to have the oven really hot before you bake them in order to raise them properly.

Left: Plain scones and Wholewheat fruit scones, page 283; Whole oat crunchies, page 291; Shortbread biscuits, page 288; Gingernuts, page 293.

3 oz wholewheat flour, sifted (75 g)
3 oz self-raising flour, sifted (75 g)
1 teaspoon baking powder
½ teaspoon ground cinnamon
1 oz soft brown sugar (25 g)
1 oz butter or margarine at room temperature (25 g)
1½ oz mixed dried fruit (40 g)
1 large egg
2–2½ tablespoons milk
Extra milk and wholewheat flour

Pre-heat the oven to gas mark 8,
450°F (230°C)

A baking sheet, well-greased

In a large mixing bowl, combine the sifted flours, the bran
remaining in the sieve, baking powder, cinnamon and sugar. Then
rub in the fat and mix in the dried fruit. Now beat the egg with 2
tablespoons of milk and add this, mixing it to a smooth dough
using a palette knife. If you need to, add a spot more milk.

Next roll out the dough to ¾ inch (2 cm) thick and, using a 2¼ inch
(6 cm) cutter cut out the scones. Place them on the baking sheet,
brush the tops with milk and dust them with wholewheat flour.
Bake on a high shelf in the oven for 15–20 minutes. Cool on a wire
tray and serve warm, spread with butter.

Wholewheat cheese-crusted scones

(makes 6 to 8)

If you can't think of anything for a quick
snack lunch or late supper, these are
quick to make and quite irresistible
served warm and spread with butter.

3 oz wholewheat flour (75 g)
3 oz self-raising flour (75 g)
1 oz butter (room temperature) (25 g)
1 teaspoon baking powder
2–3 tablespoons milk
3 oz finely grated strong Cheddar cheese (75 g)
1 large egg
½ teaspoon salt

$\frac{1}{2}$ teaspoon mustard powder
2 good pinches cayenne pepper
A little extra milk

Pre-heat the oven to gas mark 7, 425°F (220°C)

A baking sheet, well-greased.

First sift the flours into a mixing bowl, add the bran remaining in the sieve, the mustard powder, salt and one good pinch of cayenne pepper. Mix them together well, then rub in the butter—using your fingertips—until the mixture is all crumbly. Now mix in most of the grated cheese, leaving about 1 tablespoon.

Next, in a small bowl, beat the egg together with 2 tablespoons of milk. Add this to the mixing bowl to make a soft dough—what you are after is a smooth dough that will leave the bowl clean, so add just a few more drops of milk if it is too dry.

Now roll out the dough on a floured surface to a thickness of about $\frac{3}{4}$ inch (2 cm) and use a $2\frac{1}{4}$ inch cutter (6 cm) to cut out the scones. Place the scones on the baking sheet, brush the tops with milk, then sprinkle the remaining grated cheese over the top of each scone, with a faint dusting of cayenne. Bake on a high shelf for 15–20 minutes, cool them slightly on a wire tray, and serve warm.

Wholewheat girdle cakes

(makes about 25)

Unlike oven-baked scones, girdle cakes are cut quite thin and cooked on top of the stove. Traditionally cooked on a heavy iron girdle, we can now make them in a thick-based, heavy frying pan (though iron girdles are still available at good kitchen shops).

4 oz wholewheat flour (110 g)
4 oz self-raising flour (110 g)
1 teaspoon baking powder
3 oz mixed dried fruit (75 g)
3 oz caster sugar (75 g)
1 large egg
$\frac{1}{2}$ teaspoon mixed spice
4 oz butter or margarine, at room temperature (110 g)

Begin by sifting the dry ingredients (except the fruit) together into a mixing bowl, add any bran remaining in the sieve then rub in the butter until the mixture becomes crumbly. Then add the fruit and mix it in thoroughly. Next beat the egg lightly, add it to the mixture, and mix to a dough (if it seems to be a little too dry, you can add a spot of milk).

Transfer the dough onto a lightly floured surface and roll out to a thickness of about ¼ inch (5 mm). Then, using a 2½ inch (6·5 cm) plain cutter, cut the dough into rounds—re-rolling and cutting the trimmings until you have used all the dough.

Now lightly grease your pan and heat it over a medium heat, then cook the girdle cakes, a few at a time, for about three minutes on each side. If they look as if they are browning too quickly, turn the heat down because they must be cooked all through and still be fairly brown and crisp on the outside. Serve warm with lots of butter and perhaps some home-made jam.

Crumpets

(makes about 12)

Although you can buy quite good crumpets, I do think they're fun to make—especially on a cold snowy day when everyone's housebound. Once upon a time you could buy special crumpet rings, but egg cooking rings will do equally well provided you grease them really thoroughly.

½ lb strong plain flour (225 g)
1 teaspoon salt
1 tablespoon dried yeast
1 teaspoon caster sugar
½ pint milk (275 ml)
2 fl oz water (55 ml)

A thick-based frying pan, some egg cooking rings, and a little lard.

First of all heat the milk and water together in a small saucepan till they are hand-hot. Then pour into a jug, stir in the sugar and dried yeast and leave it in a warm place for 10–15 minutes till there is a good frothy head on it.

Meanwhile sift the flour and salt into a mixing bowl, make a well in the centre and, when the yeast mixture is frothy, pour it all in. Next use a wooden spoon to work the flour into the liquid gradually, and beat well at the end to make a perfectly smooth batter. Cover the basin with a tea-towel and leave to stand in a warm place for about 45 minutes—by which time the batter will have become light and frothy.

Then to cook the crumpets: grease the insides of the egg rings well, and grease the frying pan as well before placing it over a medium heat. Arrange the rings in the frying pan and when the pan is hot, spoon one tablespoon of the crumpet batter into each ring. Let them cook for 4 or 5 minutes: first tiny bubbles will appear on the surface and then, suddenly, they will burst leaving the traditional holes. Now take a spoon and fork, lift off the rings and turn the crumpets over. Cook the crumpets on the second side for about 1 minute only. Re-grease and re-heat the rings and the pan before cooking the next batch of crumpets.

Serve crumpets while still warm, generously buttered. If you are making crumpets in advance then reheat them by toasting lightly on both sides before serving.

Biscuits
The origins of the biscuit are described in the word itself. 'Twice-cooked' it means in French, and that goes back to the days when bakers were in the habit of putting slices of newly-baked bread back into the cooling oven, so that they dried out completely. The result was something like a rusk, and was used as ships' biscuits for long voyages.

For a long time housewives continued to dry their biscuits with a second baking: the practice only died out at the beginning of the last century, but when it did the quality and variety of biscuits improved no end. There's almost no limit to the kind of biscuit that can be easily baked at home today. Here are some favourites using a range of basic biscuit ingredients.

Shortbreads
One thing that distinguishes the several 'rules' about making shortbread that have been handed down is their conflicting advice. Thus one old Scottish cookbook of mine suggests that it should be 'browned to taste': a more modern one recommends no colouring at all on the surface. There is a concensus that butter—and only

butter—should be used: yet I have a friend who makes hers with margarine and I have to admit that it tastes very good.

For my part I would say that shortbread mixture should *not* be over-cooked: it ought to be a pale golden colour and not golden brown. And I certainly think that the mixture shouldn't be over-worked, because the heat in your hands can turn the fat oily. To overcome this the method I now use involves beating the fat with a wooden spoon to soften it, then gradually working it into the other ingredients. This way it is only handled at the end. When it is mixed, you can then either just pat and spread the dough straight into a prepared tin, or else roll out the dough and cut the biscuits out. Some say the latter method makes the shortbread tough because it involves extra handling, but I've not found this.

Shortbread biscuits

(makes about 15)

6 oz plain flour (175 g)
4 oz butter or margarine, at room temperature (110 g)
2 oz caster sugar (50 g)
Extra caster sugar for dusting

Pre-heat the oven to gas mark 2, 300°F (150°C)

A baking sheet, lightly greased.

Begin by first beating the butter with a wooden spoon to a soft consistency, then beat in first the sugar and then the sifted flour. Still using the wooden spoon, start to bring the mixture together, then finish off with your hands to form a paste. Now transfer this to a board lightly dusted with caster sugar, then quickly and lightly roll it out to about ⅛ inch (3 mm) thick (dusting the rolling pin with sugar if necessary). Use a 3 inch (7·5 cm) fluted cutter to cut the biscuits out, then arrange them on the baking sheet and bake on a highish shelf in the oven for 30 minutes. Cool the biscuits on a wire rack, dust them with some caster sugar, and store in an airtight tin to keep them crisp.

Scottish shortbread

(makes 12 wedges)

This shortbread is made in one piece in a tin, then cut into wedges after baking. The addition of fine semolina gives it a crunchier texture.

6 oz plain flour (175 g)
6 oz butter or margarine, at room temperature (175 g)
3 oz caster sugar (75 g)
3 oz fine semolina (75 g)

Pre-heat the oven to gas mark 2, 300°F (150°C)

An 8 inch (20 cm) fluted flan tin with a loose base.

First of all beat the butter in a bowl with a wooden spoon to soften it, then beat in the sugar followed by the sifted flour and the semolina. Work the ingredients together with the spoon, pressing them to the side of the bowl, then finish off with your hands till you have a dough that doesn't leave any bits in the bowl.

Next transfer the dough to a flat surface and roll it out lightly to a round (giving it quarter turns as you roll), then transfer the round to the tin. Lightly press the mixture evenly into the tin, right into the fluted edges (to make sure it's even you can give it a final roll with a small glass tumbler). Now you *must* prick the shortbread all over with a fork or it will rise up in the centre while it's baking.

Bake the shortbread for about 1¼ hours on the centre shelf, then using a palette knife mark out the surface into 12 wedges while it's still warm. Leave it to cool in the tin, then remove the rim of the tin, cut the shortbread into wedges and store in an airtight tin.

For *Strawberry shortcake* In the summer a round of shortbread made as above and left whole can be spread with whipped cream, and topped with strawberries just before serving. This makes a really delicious pud for a summer dinner party, or tea in the garden.

Wholewheat shortbread

(makes 12 wedges)

This is similar to the previous recipe, but I've used half wholewheat flour for more of a wheaty flavour, and ground rice in place of semolina for crunchiness.

3 oz wholewheat flour (75 g)
3 oz plain flour (75 g)
2 oz ground rice (50 g)
2 oz caster sugar (50 g)

6 oz butter or margarine, at room temperature (175 g)
A little extra sugar

Pre-heat the oven to gas mark 2, 300°F (150°C)

An 8 inch (20 cm) fluted flan tin with a removable base, lightly greased.

Start by beating the butter in a bowl with a wooden spoon to soften it, then beat in the sugar followed by the flours and ground rice. Work it together as much as you can with the wooden spoon, then finish off with your hands lightly and quickly. Now roll out the dough to approximately an 8 inch (20 cm) round, giving it quarter turns as you roll. Transfer it to the tin and press it evenly into the edges. If it seems uneven on top, just roll lightly over the surface with a glass tumbler.

Now prick the dough all over to prevent it rising, then bake it for 80 minutes on a high shelf. Remove the shortbread from the oven, cut it into 12 portions while it's still warm. Then cool it in the tin, remove the portions and store them in an airtight tin.

Oat biscuits

Oats have long been used in Scotland and the north of England for biscuit-making: they give a lovely crunch to the biscuit as well as a characteristic nutty flavour. Prepared oats come in a variety of forms, all of them suitable for baking.

Oatmeal This means that the oats have been milled, in the same way as wheat is milled into flour. Oatmeal comes in different grades, most commonly as *fine* or *medium* (either of which can be added to bread dough or used for biscuits—see oatmeal biscuit recipe below) or *coarse* which is often used for porridge.

Oat flakes These are also known as *rolled oats* and are the husked grains which have been rolled mechanically into flakes. Very good for porridge and biscuits.

Whole oats Also referred to as *jumbo oats*, these are flakes as well, but large and coarse. They also have more of a nutty flavour and are excellent for biscuits.

Quick cooking oats Or so-called 'instant oats' have been treated in some way and are not really suitable for baking.

Whole oat crunchies

(makes 12)

These are the quickest and easiest biscuits I've ever made: they have a nice crunchy, toffee taste. If you can get hold of jumbo oats from a health food shop so much the better, otherwise all ordinary porridge oat flakes will do.

2 oz whole (jumbo) oats (50 g)
2½ oz porridge oats (70 g)
4 oz margarine (110 g)
3 oz demerara sugar (75 g)

Pre-heat the oven to gas mark 5, 375°F (190°C)

A shallow baking tin measuring 11 × 7 inches (28 × 18 cm), well greased.

First weigh out the oats and sugar, place them in a bowl and mix them together as evenly as possible. Then gently melt the margarine in a saucepan—only just melt it, be careful not to let it brown. Next pour the melted margarine into the bowl with the oats and sugar and mix until everything is well and truly blended.

Now all you have to do is to tip the mixture into the prepared tin and to press it out evenly all over using your hands.

Bake on the centre shelf of the oven for 15 minutes or until it's a nice pale gold colour. Then remove the tin from the oven and cut the mixture into 12 portions while it's still warm. Leave it in the tin until cold and crisp before storing the biscuits in an airtight tin.

Oatmeal biscuits

(makes 24)

I think it's really nice to be able to offer home-made biscuits with cheese and these are lovely with some Stilton or strong Cheddar and crisp celery.

6 oz wholewheat flour (175 g)
2 oz medium oatmeal (50 g)
4 oz butter or margarine, at room temperature (110 g)
4 teaspoons soft brown sugar
1 teaspoon baking powder
½ teaspoon salt

¼ **teaspoon hot curry powder**

About 1 tablespoon milk, for binding

Pre-heat the oven to gas mark 4,
350°F (180°C)

A baking sheet, lightly greased.

Simply combine all the ingredients (except the milk) together in a
bowl, then rub the fat evenly into the ingredients and add just
enough milk to give you a slightly wetter dough than you would
require normally (say, for shortcrust pastry)—since this pastry is
prone to breaking, a little extra moisture is deliberately used to
help to hold it together.

Next, turn the dough out onto a floured working surface and roll
out to about ⅛ inch (3 mm) thick. Use a 2¾ inch (7 cm) cutter to cut
out the biscuit rounds—re-rolling the trimmings and adding a
drop of milk if the dough happens to become a little dry.

Place the biscuits on the baking sheet and bake them for 15–20
minutes until firm and lightly browned. Leave them to cool on the
baking sheet for 5 minutes before transferring them to a wire rack
to cool. Store in an airtight tin.

American brownies
(makes 15 squares)

These are squidgy, nutty chocolate
bars—delicious if you want to be really
self-indulgent once in a while.

**2 oz American unsweetened chocolate
(available at specialised food shops) or plain
dessert chocolate (50 g)**

4 oz butter (110 g)

2 eggs, beaten

8 oz granulated sugar (225 g)

2 oz plain flour, sifted (50 g)

1 teaspoon baking powder

¼ **teaspoon salt**

**4 oz chopped nuts—these can be walnuts,
almonds, hazelnuts or Brazils or a mixture
(110 g)**

Pre-heat the oven to gas mark 4,
350°F (180°C)

An oblong tin measuring 7 × 11 inches (18 × 28 cm) well-greased and lined with greaseproof paper. Bring the paper up a good 2 inches (5 cm) above the rim of the tin.

First of all melt the butter and the chocolate (broken up into small pieces) together in the top of a double saucepan (or else place in a basin fitted over simmering water on a very low heat). Away from the heat, stir all the other ingredients into the butter and chocolate mixture thoroughly, then spread all this in the lined tin.

Bake in the oven for 30 minutes, or until a knife inserted in the centre comes out cleanly (but don't over-cook, it will firm up as it cools). Then leave the mixture in the tin to cool for 10 minutes before dividing into approximately fifteen squares and transferring them to a wire rack to finish cooling.

Gingernuts

(makes 16)

These are, like most biscuits, extremely simple to make at home and you'll wonder why you ever bought them!

4 oz self-raising flour (110 g)
1 slightly rounded teaspoon ground ginger
1 teaspoon bicarbonate of soda
1½ oz granulated sugar (40 g)
2 oz margarine (50 g)
2 oz (or 2 tablespoons) golden syrup (50 g)

Pre-heat the oven to gas mark 5, 375°F (190°C)

One large (or two small) baking sheets, lightly greased.

Begin by sifting the flour, ginger and bicarbonate of soda into a mixing bowl, add the sugar, then lightly rub in the margarine until the mixture is crumbly. Next add the syrup and mix everything together to form a stiff paste.

Now divide the mixture into sixteen pieces about the same size as each other, and roll each piece into a little ball. Place them on the baking sheet(s), leaving plenty of room between them because they spread out quite a bit while they're cooking. Then simply flatten each ball slightly with the back of a spoon and bake just above the centre of the oven for 10–15 minutes, by which time they will have spread out and cracked rather attractively. Cool on the baking sheet(s) for 10 minutes then transfer to a wire rack to finish cooling, and store in an airtight tin.

Cheese savouries

(makes about 30)

I like to make batches of these, cut out quite small, to serve with drinks at a party. They can be sprinkled with different toppings to vary the flavours. Alternatively you can cut out larger biscuits for a lunch box or a picnic.

2 oz wholewheat flour (50 g)
2 oz grated Cheddar cheese (50 g)
2 oz grated Cheshire cheese (50 g)
2 oz butter, at room temperature (50 g)
¼ teaspoon salt
1 pinch cayenne pepper
1 twist ground black pepper

Optional toppings: **garlic salt, celery salt, mild curry powder, or cayenne pepper.**

Pre-heat the oven to gas mark 5, 375°F (190°C)

A baking sheet, lightly greased.

First of all sift the flour and salt into a mixing bowl, and add the cayenne and black pepper. Next add the two cheeses along with the butter and rub the mixture to the crumbly stage, then bring the mixture together—it shouldn't need any liquid, but if it does add just a drop of milk.

Now roll out the dough to a thickness of about ⅛ inch (3 mm) then use a 1 or 1½ inch (2·5 or 4 cm) cutter to cut out the biscuits. Arrange them fairly close together on the baking sheet, sprinkle the selected topping (if any) on them, then bake on a high shelf in the oven for 10–12 minutes, before removing to a wire rack to cool and crisp. Store them in an airtight tin.

Stocks and soups

Including recipes for:

I can recall a time, not so long ago, when home-made soups seemed to be in a period of decline: perhaps the combination of increased affluence after the war and the advent of tinned, dehydrated and instant soups gave us less incentive to make our own. Thankfully I feel that home-made soups are now making a comeback. Where once we could overlook the bland uniformity of a ready-made soup at a price, in these days of world shortages and inflation we've grown more critical. I have long been of the opinion that you can either spend money or time on food, and lately many people are finding they have rather more time than money and (as a result) that thirty minutes preparation can produce a soup at half the cost and with twice the flavour and quantity of a canned one.

Of course economy is not the only reason for making a proper soup. There's something wholesome and comforting about a soup made with care from fresh, natural ingredients. It is filling, satisfying and above all easy. However I would emphasize the word care, because simply throwing together any old hotch-potch of ingredients—however good they may be individually—can result in no real flavour whatsoever.

Stocks are the basis of many soups (and indeed casseroles—see next chapter), and are included in this section. Like soups, home-made stocks have been eclipsed by the huge range of commercial alternatives, and the dilemma facing us is the same. So first let's see what is involved in making stock at home.

Stock

The first thing to say about making basic stock for soups and casseroles is that it is *not* as much bother as it sometimes sounds. For a start a proper stock-pot—the sort that needs endless boiling-up and skimming—isn't really needed in today's family kitchen. What I think is more useful is one occasional stock-making session. Freezer owners (even those like me who only have a small freezer at the top of the refrigerator) can freeze any surplus and use it on another occasion.

All that is actually involved is bones, carcasses or giblets plus a few other ingredients being simmered, totally unattended. A rich brown stock is the only one that requires the bones to be roasted first, and even this doesn't call for any real work. The results will produce goodness and flavour at a minimal cost, and will prove how well spent in these days of chemical flavourings just a few minutes of your own time can be.

Is home-made stock necessary?

Not always. Especially with many vegetable soups, bearing in mind that most vegetables have lots of good fresh flavour of their own, introducing a meat-flavoured stock can be quite contrary and spoil the original vegetable flavour. On the other hand, a meaty stock makes the world of difference to clear-based soups (like *French Onion* or *Minestrone*), and I nearly always use some sort of stock to give body to soups made with dried vegetables and pulses.

Stock cubes

If you were making a soup containing the delicious juices and flavour of, say, a pound of leeks and the same amount of carrots, would you *really* want (or need) to add ingredients like hydrolised protein, ribonucleotides, and monosodium glutamate? These, and several others, are ingredients to be found in the various stock cubes available, and it is my opinion that they are very often totally opposed to the flavour of natural ingredients. Unless you positively happen to like the taste of stock cubes (which as far as I'm concerned never come close to the chicken, beef or whatever they're supposed to be derived from) then I suggest you don't use them. It has been suggested that because of their overpowering flavour, stock cubes need a lot more watering down than is usually recommended—but then why really bother in the first place?

Some principles of stock-making

Simmering An important word in the vocabulary of stock and soup making. Fast boiling can turn a stock very cloudy and murky, or ruin the delicate flavour of a fresh vegetable soup. So always keep everything at a *gentle* simmer.

Skimming When you're boiling bones, giblets or a chicken carcass, a certain amount of scum inevitably rises to the surface. To get rid of this it's important to skim the surface right away. Quite easy to do: just slide a large spoon horizontally across the surface and gently lift off and discard the scum.

Removing fat Marrowbones, oxtails, neck of lamb etc all give off a certain amount of fat while they're cooking, and there are two ways of dealing with this. First, if you allow the stock or soup to settle for about 30 minutes after cooking, you can skim some of the fat from the surface as above. What is also helpful here is to lay a double sheet of absorbent kitchen paper on the surface, to float as it were, and absorb the fat (sometimes it needs two or three lots to remove the fat completely). The other way, and this de-greases *more* thoroughly, is to leave the whole thing to cool overnight, and next morning you'll find the fat has solidified on the top and you can remove it completely.

Reducing If, after straining and de-greasing, you feel your stock needs more concentrated flavour, bring it back to the boil and simmer *without* the lid on so that some of the liquid evaporates. Simmer until the flavour of the stock is as concentrated as you want it to be. One of the great French chefs, Michel Guérard, in his book *Cuisine Gourmande* actually gives some directions for a concentrated jellied fish stock, by reducing $1\frac{3}{4}$ pints (1 litre) of liquid down to seven tablespoonfuls!

Brown beef stock

Butchers will chop up and sell you marrowbones for just a few pence.

3 lb beef marrowbones, in pieces, (approx 1·5 kg)
2 onions, peeled and quartered
2 large carrots, peeled and cut into chunks
3 celery stalks, each cut into three pieces
A few parsley stalks
1 bayleaf
8 whole black peppercorns
1 blade mace
1 teaspoon salt
$\frac{1}{4}$ teaspoon dried thyme
4–5 pints cold water ($2\frac{1}{4}$–3 litres)

Pre-heat the oven to gas mark 8, 450°F (230°C)

Begin by placing the bones in a meat roasting tin, tucking the chunks of carrot, quartered onion and celery in amongst them. Now, without adding any fat, just pop the roasting tin onto a high shelf in the oven and leave it there for 45 minutes, basting with the juices now and then. After that both the bones and the vegetables will have turned brown at the edges. Now transfer them all to the very largest cooking pot you own, add enough cold water just to cover everything, add the rest of the ingredients, then as soon as it reaches boiling point remove the scum and lower the heat. Put the lid on but not completely (leave a little gap for the steam to escape thereby reducing and concentrating the stock). Now simmer very gently for about 4 hours. When the stock is ready, strain it into a clean pan, leave it to become quite cold, then remove the congealed fat from the surface. The stock is now ready for use, or for freezing for later use.

Light beef stock
If you want a pale coloured stock, use the same ingredients as above and follow the same instructions but leave out the initial roasting of the bones and vegetables.

Pressure cooked beef stock

This method, of course, cuts the cooking time down to an incredible 40 minutes. You can't make such a large quantity, but the resulting stock will have a more concentrated flavour and you can dilute it afterwards.

2½ lb beef marrowbones, in pieces (approx 1 kg)
2 pints cold water (just over 1 litre)
1 small onion
1 carrot, cut into chunks
1 celery stalk halved (plus leaves)
1 small bunch parsley stalks
1 bayleaf
5 whole black peppercorns
1 small blade mace
1 teaspoon salt

Place the bones in the pressure-cooker along with the water. Bring to the boil, then remove any scum with a spoon. Now add the remaining ingredients, put the lid on the cooker and bring to pressure. Then place the 15 lb weight on and cook for 40 minutes. Reduce the pressure by allowing the cooker to cool slightly, then place it under cold running water to release. Strain the stock, leave to cool, then remove the fat from the surface.

Chicken giblet stock

This stock is useful not only for soups, but also for chicken casseroles, cooking rice, and making gravies and sauces.

12 oz chicken giblets washed (350 g)
2 pints cold water (1·25 l)
1 carrot, cut into chunks
1 onion, quartered
1 celery stick halved
1 leek, sliced
6 whole black peppercorns
¾ teaspoon salt
A few parsley stalks
2 pinches dried herbs (or sprig of fresh thyme)

The general rule is to use 1 pint of water per set of giblets, or if you're buying frozen giblets (which are a godsend for stock) use 6 oz (175 g) of giblets per 1 pint (570 ml) of water. If you are using fresh giblets and don't need the liver for making a stuffing, do add it to the stock as well—I think it adds a real richness of flavour.

Just put everything into a large cooking pot, bring to the boil, skim the surface to remove any scum, then simmer gently with the lid almost on for 2 hours. After that strain the stock, cool it and remove the fat from the surface before using or freezing.

Chicken carcass stock
Use the same vegetables, herbs and flavourings as in the above recipe, adding them to the cooking pot along with the broken-up carcass of the bird (plus any odd bits of bone and skin). Add enough cold water to cover, then proceed as above.

Pressure-cooked chicken stock
Proceed as above with vegetables, herbs and flavourings and either giblets or carcass, plus 2 pints (1¼ litres) of water. Bring to pressure and cook with 15 lb pressure for 30 minutes.

Fish stock

Use this as the basis for all kinds of fish soup.

1 lb fish trimmings (whatever your fishmonger can rustle up for you)

1 pint water (570 ml)
1 onion, quartered
2 sticks celery, chopped
A few parsley sprigs
1 bayleaf
¼ teaspoon dried thyme
¼ pint dry white wine (140 ml)
Salt and freshly-milled black pepper

Simply place the fish trimmings in a large pan, with the water, wine and the rest of the stock ingredients, season with salt and pepper, then bring up to simmering point. Simmer for about 20 minutes (without a lid on), then strain and reserve the stock.

Soups
Some principles of soup making

Sweating I have found that a better flavour is produced in vegetable soups if the chopped vegetables are stirred into a little melted butter quite thoroughly until they're all glistening and well-coated. Then, with a little salt added, they are placed over the gentlest heat possible and the pan is covered. The heat then draws out the natural juices and the vegetables become softened before the liquid is added. Care is needed for this, because too much heat will cause the vegetables to brown and spoil: so to prevent this you need to take off the lid from time to time and just stir them around. This process is called 'sweating'.

Blending and Puréeing There are several ways to purée a soup. First of all, a good old fashioned sieve will serve you very well: the contents of a soup pan can be pressed through it in a few minutes. Sieves can be difficult to wash, though, and perhaps a more satisfactory method is to whizz the soup to a purée in an electric liquidiser (blender). If you are using one of these, do remember that liquidizing is liable to reduce food to a velvet-smooth consistency. Some people prefer a less uniform texture: this can be achieved if you take care to liquidize food very briefly indeed.

 There is also available a gadget called a vegetable or food mill (see illustration opposite). It can be used to purée fruit and vegetables very finely, to medium thickness or quite coarsely. Useful, but I find it needs rather intricate washing and carefully drying.

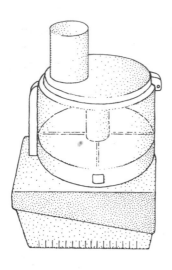

Lastly there is now widely available a machine called a food processor (see illustration), which not only purées but also chops, shreds, slices and does all the work of a mincer. It has one big disadvantage, and that's its price— which is the equivalent of a large freestanding mixer with all its various attachments. Having been asked several times to comment on this particular piece of equipment, my conclusion is that for someone who does a great deal of cooking it is well worth the price, but otherwise probably not.

Rescue operations

Beware of over-seasoning a soup, especially if (a) you are using a stock that's already seasoned and (b) if you are reducing the stock or soup. A concentration of flavour will also mean a concentration of seasoning, and it's very easy to end up with a soup that's too salty. I recommend tasting and seasoning right at the end.

If for these or any other reason you have *over-salted* a soup, you have two possibilities. One is to add more unsalted liquid to dilute the salty flavour, though this way you risk also diluting the overall flavour. The other is to add a couple of raw potatoes cut in half and allow these to cook gently in the soup. They will absorb quite a bit of saltiness which may put things right. Remember to remove the potatoes before serving.

If a soup is *too thin*, removing the lid and allowing it to simmer gently will reduce and thicken it (as described on page 298). Or, if you're short of time, you can make up a paste by mashing together softened butter and flour (say 1 tablespoon of each) then use a balloon whisk to whisk the paste into the soup; when it comes up to simmering point the soup will have thickened. Alternatively you can use arrowroot. This thickens liquid without clouding it—so it is the best choice for thickening a clear soup (see recipe for *Chinese mushroom soup*, page 313).

Another fast way to thicken anything, when you're in a hurry, is to add some ground rice. What is so good about this is that you can just plonk a couple of tablespoons of ground rice into the hot liquid (it won't go lumpy) and whisk with a balloon whisk till sufficiently thickened—and if not, add a bit more.

If on the other hand your soup is *too thick*, you can thin it down with milk or stock, or even plain water.

Having said all this, let me now reassure you that by following the recipes with care you should have none of these problems!

Leek, onion and potato soup

(serves 4–6 people)

I think this has to be my very favourite soup—if possible garnished with some fresh snipped chives and a swirl of cream.

4 large leeks
2 medium potatoes, peeled and diced
1 medium onion, chopped small
1½ pints light chicken stock or water (850 ml)
½ pint milk (275 ml)
2 oz butter (50 g)
2 tablespoons cream or top of the milk
1½ tablespoons fresh snipped chives (or, if unavailable, chopped parsley)
Salt and freshly-milled black pepper

Trim off the tops and roots of the leeks, discarding the tough outer layer. Now split them in half length-ways and slice them up quite finely, then wash them thoroughly in two or three changes of water and drain well.

In a large thick-based saucepan gently melt the butter, then add the leeks, potatoes and onion, stirring them all around with a wooden spoon so they get a nice coating of butter. Season with salt and pepper, then cover and let the vegetables sweat over a very low heat for about 15 minutes.

After that add the stock and milk, bring to simmering point, put the lid back on and let the soup simmer very gently for a further 20 minutes or until the vegetables are soft—if you have the heat too high, the milk in it may cause it to boil over. Now you can either put the whole lot into a liquidiser and blend to a purée, or else press it all through a sieve.

Return the soup to the saucepan and reheat gently, tasting to check the seasoning, and stirring in the chopped chives and adding a swirl of cream just before serving.

Note: the chilled version of this soup is called *Vichyssoise*.

Minestrone soup with rice

(serves 4–6 people)

This soup is really a meal in itself, especially if you have some home-made wholewheat bread to serve with it and perhaps a lump of cheese to follow.

8 oz leeks, washed and finely chopped (225 g)
2 sticks celery, washed and finely chopped
6 oz carrots, washed and finely chopped (175 g)
6 oz cabbage, washed and shredded (175 g)
2 tomatoes, fresh or from a tin
1 medium onion, finely chopped
2 oz streaky bacon, rinds removed and finely chopped (50 g)
1 tablespoon butter
1 tablespoon olive oil
1 clove of garlic, crushed
2½ pints any good home-made stock (1·5 litres)
1 teaspoon dried basil
2 tablespoons rice
1 dessertspoon tomato purée
2 tablespoons chopped parsley
Salt and freshly-milled black pepper
Lots of grated Parmesan cheese to serve with it

First heat up the butter and oil in a large saucepan, then add the bacon and cook this for a minute or two before adding the onion, followed by the celery and carrots and then the tomatoes, also chopped. Now stir in the crushed garlic and some salt and pepper, then cover and cook very gently for 20 minutes or so to allow the vegetables to sweat—give it an occasional stir to prevent the vegetables sticking.

Then pour in the stock along with the basil. Continue to simmer gently (covered) for about 1 hour. After that add the leeks, cabbage and rice and cook for a further 30 minutes.

Finally stir in the tomato purée, cook for another 10 minutes and, just before serving, stir in the parsley. Serve in warmed soup bowls and sprinkle with Parmesan cheese.

Note: in the autumn finely chopped courgettes—instead of the cabbage—make a nice change.

Chilled avocado soup
(serves 6 people)

This makes a lovely first course at a dinner party at any time of the year. It looks very pretty served in glass bowls to show off its pale green pistachio colour.

2 medium-sized, ripe avocado pears
1 clove of garlic, crushed
1 tablespoon lemon juice
½ pint soured cream (275 ml)
1 pint cold chicken stock (570 ml)
Salt, and freshly-milled black pepper

First halve the avocado pears, remove the stones and scoop out all the flesh—it's very important that you take care to scrape out all the very greenest part next to the skins, because this is what makes the soup such a lovely colour. Now chop the flesh roughly, and put it into the goblet of the liquidiser with the garlic, lemon juice, half the chicken stock and some salt and pepper.

Blend at high speed for about 15 seconds, then empty the contents into a soup tureen or bowl. Now stir in the soured cream and the rest of the stock, then whisk it a bit to get it all blended evenly. Cover the soup and chill very thoroughly for several hours. Serve it with one or two cubes of ice stirred in at the last minute.

Note: only make this soup on the day you intend to eat it, because if it's kept too long it tends to discolour.

Gardeners' soup
(serves 6–8 people)

This is a soup for autumn when there's nearly always a glut of tomatoes and the over-ripe ones are sold cheaply; or, as the title suggests, it's helpful for gardeners whose tomato and cucumber crops threaten to overwhelm them.

¾ lb English cucumber, peeled and chopped (350 g)
¾ lb red ripe tomatoes (350 g)
1 medium potato, peeled and chopped
The outside leaves of a lettuce, shredded
1 small onion, finely chopped
1 clove of garlic, crushed

1 pint hot water (570 ml) mixed with 1 teaspoon tomato purée
1 teaspoon dried basil
2 teaspoons freshly-chopped parsley
1 dessertspoon lemon juice
Butter
Oil
Salt and freshly-milled black pepper

First drop the tomatoes into boiling water then, after one minute, slip the skins off and chop the flesh roughly. Now in a thick-based saucepan melt one tablespoon of butter with one tablespoon of oil and soften the onion in it for 5 minutes. Next add the garlic, lettuce, cucumber, tomatoes and potato. Stir everything around, add seasoning and lemon juice, then pop the lid on and, keeping the heat low, let the vegetables sweat for a good 15 minutes.

Then add the basil and the hot water mixed with tomato purée, bring it up to simmering point, cover and simmer gently for a further 20 minutes or until the vegetables are soft.

Now pour the soup into a liquidiser, but only liquidise it for 6–8 seconds (the vegetables should be in very fine bits). Then sprinkle with parsley and serve hot with some fresh, crusty bread.

Smoked bacon and lentil soup

(serves 4–6 people)

This is another very substantial soup and, remember, brown lentils don't need any soaking.

6 oz green-brown whole lentils, washed and drained (175 g)
6 rashers smoked, streaky bacon, de-rinded and finely chopped
2 carrots, chopped
2 medium onions, chopped
2 celery stalks, sliced
8 oz finely shredded cabbage (225 g)
1 × 8 oz tin Italian tomatoes (225 g)
2 cloves of garlic, crushed
3 pints home-made stock (1·75 litres)
1 tablespoon oil
Salt and freshly-milled black pepper
2 tablespoons chopped parsley

Heat the oil in a large cooking pot and fry the bacon in it until the fat begins to run. Then stir in the prepared vegetables (except the cabbage) and, with the heat fairly high, toss them around to brown them a little at the edges. Now stir in the washed, drained lentils plus the contents of the tin of tomatoes followed by the crushed garlic then the stock. As soon as the soup comes to the boil, put a lid on and simmer, as gently as possible, for about 1 hour. About 15 minutes before the end add the cabbage. Taste and season. Just before serving stir in the chopped parsley.

Chilled beetroot consommé

(serves 6 people)

This is a refreshing summer soup which requires no fat for cooking and is, therefore, suitable for slimmers if low fat yoghurt is used at the end. Be sure to use *raw* beetroot.

1½ lb raw beetroot, peeled and chopped (700 g)
10 large spring onions, chopped
2½ pints water (1·5 litres)
1 cucumber
A bouquet garni*
1 tablespoon red wine vinegar
1 tablespoon lemon juice
¼ pint natural yoghurt (150 ml)
2 tablespoons snipped chives to garnish
Salt and freshly-milled black pepper

* Bouquet garni—sprigs of thyme, 1 clove of garlic, parsley, bayleaf and 2 strips of orange zest tied up in a piece of gauze.

Put the prepared beetroot in a large saucepan with the chopped spring onions, the water and the bouquet garni. Bring to the boil and simmer gently, uncovered, for about 1 hour. At the end of this time the beetroot will have lost its redness and have a pale look.

Now peel and dice the cucumber, add it to the soup and simmer for about 10 minutes. Next, have ready a large sieve set over a suitable bowl and pour the soup through the sieve and leave it to drain through. You should now have a good clear soup. Season to taste and add a tablespoon of vinegar and a tablespoon of lemon juice to sharpen the flavour. Chill well and serve with a marbling of yoghurt and a garnish of snipped chives.

Scots broth

(serves 6–8 people)

This soup really needs to be made a day in advance—so that the fat can be lifted off the surface more easily when the soup is cold. Reheat the next day and you'll have one of the best winter 'stomach warmers' I know.

2 lb neck of lamb, cut into even-sized pieces (900 g)
2 oz pearl barley, rinsed (50 g)
1 large carrot
1 medium turnip
1 medium onion
3 leeks
Half a small white cabbage
Chopped parsley
Salt and freshly-milled black pepper

Place the meat in a deep saucepan together with 3 pints (1·75 litres) cold water. Bring to the boil and skim off any scum which appears on the surface, then add the rinsed barley together with a little seasoning. Put a lid on the pan but tilt the lid slightly so that some of the steam can escape, then simmer, very gently, for about 1 hour.

Meanwhile prepare the vegetables: peel the carrot, turnip and onion and cut into $\frac{1}{4}$ inch dice ($\frac{1}{2}$ cm). Now trim the leeks, cutting off the root and leaving about 2 inches (5 cm) of green at the top. Halve lengthways, cut into small pieces, wash thoroughly then drain well. Slice the cabbage thinly and wash and drain that well too.

When the broth has been cooking for 1 hour, add the vegetables. Bring to the boil again, half cover the pan with a lid and simmer gently until the vegetables are tender (about 45–60 minutes). Then remove from the heat and set aside to cool slightly.

Using a draining spoon, take out the meat and place it on a plate. Now separate the flesh from the bones, discard any fat and gristle as well as the bones, and return the meat to the pan. Leave until the soup is cold and the fat has solidified on top; scrape off the fat.

When required, reheat the broth, season to taste and serve piping hot with a sprinkling of chopped parsley on top.

Watercress cream soup

(serves 4–6 people)

This makes an excellent first course at a dinner party and can, if you prefer, be served well chilled.

The white parts of 3 large leeks—approximately 1 lb (450 g), washed and chopped
2 bunches watercress, de-stalked and chopped. Reserve 4 sprigs for garnishing
2 medium potatoes, peeled and chopped
2 oz butter (50 g)
1½ pints very light chicken stock (or water) (850 ml)
¼ pint double cream (150 ml)
Salt and freshly-milled black pepper

Melt the butter in a thick-based saucepan, then add the prepared leeks, potato and watercress and stir them around so that they're coated with the melted butter. Add some salt, cover with a lid and let the vegetables sweat over a low heat for about 20 minutes, giving the mixture a stir about halfway through.

After that, add the stock (or water), bring to simmering point and simmer, covered, for a further 10 to 15 minutes or until the vegetables are quite tender. Remove from the heat and when cool liquidise the soup—but not too vigorously. Return the soup to the saucepan, stir in the cream, season to taste and re-heat gently. When serving, garnish each bowl with a sprig of watercress.

Punchnep soup

(serves 6–8 people)

Punchnep is a Scottish dish of creamed potatoes and creamed turnips cooked separately then whipped together (see Part One page 208). This soup, based on that dish, has a lovely creamy texture and translucent look.

1½ lb turnips, peeled and weighed after peeling (700 g)
1 large potato, peeled—about ½ lb (225 g) after peeling
The white parts of 2 leeks
2 oz butter (50 g)
1 pint milk (570 ml)

1 pint hot water (570 ml)
Freshly-grated nutmeg
2–3 tablespoons double cream
Salt and freshly-milled black pepper

First split the leeks in half lengthways and cut into pieces of about $\frac{1}{4}$ inch ($\frac{1}{2}$ cm), wash well in cold water and drain in a colander. Then cut the peeled turnip and potato into cubes.

Next melt the butter in a thick-based saucepan, add the vegetables and stir them around so that they're well coated with the butter. Season with a little salt and pepper, cover with a lid and, keeping the heat very low, cook gently for 15 minutes, stirring from time to time. Now pour in the hot water and milk, bring to simmering point and simmer, again gently, for approximately 15 minutes or so until the vegetables are absolutely tender.

Then liquidise the soup or rub it through a sieve placed over a large bowl. Rinse the saucepan, return the purée to the pan and re-heat slowly. Season to taste with salt and freshly-milled black pepper and some freshly-grated nutmeg. Make sure the soup is piping hot then stir in a swirl of cream just before serving.

Soupe à l'oignon gratiné

(serves 6 people)

This is so French that I've kept its original title. It's very filling and warming but remember that only fireproof soup bowls can safely go under the grill. To make croûtons of French bread, cut the bread in diagonal slices and bake in a medium oven for 20–25 minutes until golden and crisp.

2 tablespoons butter
2 tablespoons oil
1½ lb onions, thinly sliced (700 g)
2 cloves of garlic, crushed
½ teaspoon granulated sugar
2 pints good beef stock (1·25 litres)
½ pint dry white wine (275 ml)
6 large croûtons of French bread
8 oz Gruyere cheese, grated (225 g)
Salt and freshly-milled black pepper

In a large thick-based saucepan heat the butter and oil together. Add the prepared onions, garlic and sugar and cook over a low heat, stirring occasionally, for approximately 30 minutes or until the bottom of the pan is covered with a nutty brown, caramelized film. (This browning process improves both the colour and flavour).

Next add the stock and wine, bring to the boil and simmer, covered, over a low heat for about 1 hour. Then season to taste and, if you're feeling in need of something extra specially warming, add one or two tablespoons of brandy.

Now spread the croûtons with butter and place one slice in each fireproof soup bowl. Ladle the soup carefully on top and, when the croûtons float to the surface, sprinkle with the grated cheese. Place under a hot grill and when nicely golden brown and bubbling serve immediately.

Eliza Acton's vegetable mulligatawny

(serves 4 people)

Eliza Acton, as I explained in Part One, is one of my very favourite cookery writers and this is another recipe from her cookery book published in 1840.

3 large onions, chopped
4 oz butter (110 g)
1½ lb peeled marrow or unpeeled courgettes (700 g)
½ lb tomatoes, skinned and chopped (225 g)
1 large potato
¾ pint stock or water (425 ml)
1 dessertspoon Worcester sauce
1 teaspoon Madras curry powder
Long grain rice measured to the 3 fl oz level in a measuring jug
Boiling water measured to the 6 fl oz level in a measuring jug
Salt and freshly-milled black pepper

First melt the butter in a large saucepan, add the chopped onions and cook until they're golden brown colour. Meanwhile cut up the marrow into 1 inch (2·5 cm) cubes and peel and dice the potato. Now add these to the onions together with the tomatoes. Season well then let the vegetables cook (covered) over a low heat until soft—about 20–30 minutes.

In the meantime put the rice in another saucepan with some salt, pour on the measured boiling water, bring to the boil, cover and cook gently until all the liquid is absorbed and the rice is tender.

Next, when the vegetables are cooked, turn them into a liquidiser and reduce to a purée. Then pour the purée back into the saucepan, stir in the cooked rice together with the stock, Worcester sauce and curry powder. This soup should have quite a strong flavour so season to taste and add more curry powder if you think it needs it.

Reheat gently, cook for about five minutes more then serve with some crisp croûtons of bread sprinkled in each bowl.

Chilled Spanish gazpacho

(serves 6 people)

This is a truly beautiful soup for serving ice-cold during the summer and it's particularly refreshing when the weather is hot. However, please don't attempt to make it in the winter as the flavourless imported salad vegetables will not do it justice.

1½ lb firm ripe tomatoes (700 g)
One 4 inch piece of cucumber, peeled and chopped (10 cm)
2 or 3 spring onions, peeled and chopped
Half a large red or green pepper, seeded and chopped
2 cloves of garlic, crushed
4 tablespoons olive oil
1½ tablespoons wine vinegar
1 heaped teaspoon fresh chopped basil, marjoram or thyme (depending on what's available)
About ½ pint cold water (275 ml)
Salt and freshly-milled black pepper

For the garnish:
Half a large red or green pepper, seeded and very finely chopped
One 4 inch piece of cucumber, peeled and finely chopped (10 cm)
2 spring onions, finely chopped

1 hard-boiled egg, finely chopped

1 heaped tablespoon fresh chopped parsley

Salt and freshly-milled black pepper

4 ice cubes

Begin by placing the tomatoes in a bowl and pouring boiling water over them; after a minute or two the skins will loosen and slip off very easily. Halve the tomatoes, scoop out and discard the seeds and roughly chop the flesh.

Now place the tomatoes, cucumber, spring onions, crushed garlic and chopped pepper in a liquidiser, adding a seasoning of salt and pepper, the herbs, oil and wine vinegar. Then blend everything at top speed until the soup is absolutely smooth. (If your liquidiser is very small combine all the ingredients first then blend in two or three batches). Taste to check the seasoning and pour the soup into a bowl. Stir in a little cold water to thin it slightly—anything from $\frac{1}{4}$–$\frac{1}{2}$ pint (150–275 ml) then cover the bowl with foil and chill thoroughly.

To make the garnish, simply combine all the ingredients together with a seasoning of salt and freshly-milled black pepper, and hand them round at the table together with small croûtons of bread fried till crisp in olive oil, well drained and cooled. Serve the soup with four ice cubes floating in it.

Chinese mushroom soup
(serves 4–6 people)

This needs a really good well-flavoured chicken stock as a base, then it provides a lovely light soup without too many calories.

$\frac{3}{4}$ lb small flat mushrooms, finely chopped (350 g)

2 medium onions, finely chopped

1 tablespoon oil

3 pints good chicken stock (1·75 litres)

2 tablespoons long grain rice

2 dessertspoons arrowroot

4 spring onions, finely chopped

Salt and freshly-milled black pepper

Begin by melting the oil in a large saucepan then add the chopped onions and fry gently for about 10 minutes. Next add the prepared mushrooms, stir them around in the oil and cook for a minute or two. Now pour in the chicken stock, sprinkle in the rice and bring to simmering point, stirring occasionally to prevent the rice from sticking. Simmer gently, uncovered, for approximately 25 minutes.

Meanwhile, in a small basin, blend the arrowroot (which will thicken the soup) with 2 dessertspoons of water until smooth.

When the soup is ready, add the blended arrowroot together with the spring onions and, stirring continuously, bring back to simmering point and simmer for 1 minute. Season to taste and serve very hot.

Cream of celery soup
(serves 4 people)

Try, if possible, to use crisp *English* celery for this recipe.

¾ lb trimmed celery stalks, save the leaves (350 g)
¼ lb potatoes, peeled and cut into chunks (110 g)
2 medium-sized leeks (whites only), sliced and washed
1 pint chicken stock (570 ml)
¼ pint single cream (150 ml)
¼ pint milk (150 ml)
¼ teaspoon celery seeds
Salt and freshly-milled black pepper
1 oz butter (25 g)

In a largish pan melt the butter over a low heat. Then chop the celery and add it to the pan with the potatoes and drained leeks. Stir well, coating the vegetables with butter, cover with a lid and cook for about 15 minutes.

Then add the stock with the celery seeds and some salt. Bring to simmering point, cover once more and cook very gently for 20–25 minutes or until the vegetables are really tender. Purée the soup by liquidising or sieving, then return to the pan, stirring in the cream and milk.

Bring the soup back to the boil, check the seasoning, adding more salt and pepper if necessary. Then just before serving, chop the reserved celery leaves and stir them into the soup to give it extra colour.

Right: Minestrone soup, page 304; Quick and easy wholewheat bread. Part One page 50; Mixed vegetables à la Grecque, page 433; Watercress cream soup, page 309.

Tomato, apple and celery cream soup

(serves 4 people)

This is one of John Tovey's famous soups, as served at his hotel the Miller Howe in the English Lakes, and it demonstrates his own method of sweating vegetables tightly sealed with greaseproof paper.

1 pint chicken (or turkey) stock—see recipe page 300 (570 ml)
4 oz onions, finely chopped (110 g)
5–6 oz tomatoes, quartered—use the stalks as well (150–175 g)
5–6 oz apples, quartered—use the cores as well (150–175 g)
5–6 oz celery, cut into 2 inch (5 cm) lengths, plus leaves (150–175 g)
2 oz butter (50 g)
2½ fl. oz dry sherry (60 ml)
¼ teaspoon salt
Freshly milled black pepper
Freshly grated nutmeg
1 small pinch ground ginger
Apple slices and snipped fresh chives, to garnish

First melt the butter in a large, heavy pan then add the onion and cook gently until golden (about 10 minutes), taking care that they don't burn or catch on the bottom. Add the sherry, vegetables, fruit, spices and seasoning to the pan, place a double thickness of greaseproof paper (which has been well dampened with cold water first) over the ingredients, and cover the pan with a lid.

Simmer very gently for 1 hour, checking from time to time that nothing is sticking. After that, add the stock to the contents of the pan (first removing the paper!), and stir everything. Now transfer the soup—in two batches—to a liquidiser and blend, then press the soup through a sieve (to remove pips and stalks), and return to a clean pan. Re-heat, check the seasoning, ladle into warmed soup bowls, and garnish each serving with an apple slice and some snipped chives. Serve with croûtons.

Left: Spanish pork with olives, page 338.

Garlicky fish soup

(serves 3–4 people)

This soup always conjures up visions of the south of France for me! You can, of course, cut down on the quantity of garlic if you prefer (but don't leave it out altogether).

1 quantity of fish stock (see page 300)
1 lb fish fillets—haddock, cod, or whiting, skinned and cut into smallish cubes (450 g)
1 × 14-oz tin of Italian tomatoes (400 g)
2 medium potatoes, finely chopped
2 tablespoons fresh chopped parsley
3 cloves of garlic, crushed
$\frac{1}{2}$ teaspoon dried basil
1 tablespoon lemon juice
2 tablespoons olive oil
Salt and freshly-milled black pepper

In a large, heavy saucepan or flameproof casserole heat the oil and add the diced potato and garlic, to cook for about 5 minutes before adding the fish stock, the cubes of fish and the contents of the tin of tomatoes. Then sprinkle in the basil, add a squeeze of lemon juice, and simmer the soup gently for 15 minutes. After that taste to check the seasoning, and sprinkle in the chopped parsley just before serving.

Casseroles and braised dishes

Including recipes for:
Beef in beer
Simple Stroganoff
Hungarian goulash
Boeuf Bourguignonne
Braised steak and onions in stout
Stewed shin of beef with
  mushroom dumplings
Irish stew with parsley dumplings

Lancashire hotpot
Ragôut of lamb
Normandy pork with cream and apples
Pork with apples and cider
Spanish pork with olives
Ossobuco
Sausages braised in red wine
Braised meatballs with peppers
  and tomatoes

Stews, casseroles, ragoûts, hotpots, carbonnades, navarins . . . there are any number of names for what is essentially the same method of cooking meat. All of them spring from that momentous (though unrecorded) moment in history when someone discovered that they could protect their meat from the fierce direct heat of a fire by insulating it in a clay pot. The advantages were soon obvious, I'm sure: the pot could also contain liquid and vegetables and flavouring which the meat could absorb, and the longer slower cooking made the meat more tender, no matter what part of the animal it came from. Nothing has really changed today, except perhaps for the clay pot, which has been replaced by decorative oven-to-table casseroles.

We tend to lump together all recipes that are cooked in a pot and call them casseroles. But strictly speaking, there is a difference. *Stewing* is done on the top of a cooker with heat being applied directly to the underneath of the pot; while *casseroling* takes place inside the oven with heat circulating all around the pot. In both cases the meat is cut up fairly small and cooked in a liquid (stock, wine, water, cider or whatever).

Braising, like casseroling is done in the oven, but the meat is cooked in much larger pieces and only a minimum amount of liquid is added, so that the meat actually cooks in the steam for the most part.

The numerous other names given to meat cooked in a pot refer to specific recipes, or types of recipe (e.g. the hallmark of a good hotpot is a layer of crunchy golden potatoes over the top).

But whatever names we choose to give it, I now feel that the casserole has become one of the cornerstones of British family cooking. What with inflation and more women devoting their time to careers, feeding families of four or more with expensive steaks or chops is not a very practical proposition. Casseroles on the other hand can be prepared (even cooked) ahead. They can be left to simmer slowly without attention from the cook, and costs can be kept down quite a lot by stretching the meat with the addition of vegetables and pulses.

It is for these reasons that it's helpful to have a good collection of casserole recipes, that range from the everyday to those suitable for entertaining. Here is a selection of my own tried and trusted favourites, showing I hope how—with a little bit of imagination— a couple of pounds of stewing meat can be transformed into something really delicious and special.

Choosing the right cuts

It is the forequarter meat on an animal (see chart) that's usually the most suitable for stewing and braising—in other words everything from the waist up. Without becoming too technical, it is the front portion that initiates the movements of the animal and therefore works harder than the back portion. This means there is more muscle there, and more of something called connective tissue, a gelatinous substance which builds up as the animal matures. Conveniently, there is also rather more fat marbling the forequarter meat, so that during the longer, slower cooking that's needed for these cuts, there is a gradual rendering-down of the connective tissue (which provides flavour and body to the sauce), and at the same time an internal basting of the meat fibres by the marbling of fat. This does a splendid job of keeping the meat succulent, and (because there's a good deal of flavour in the fat itself) explains why forequarter meat *develops* flavour as it cooks.

In short, these factors perhaps explain why so often the cheaper cuts of, say, beef given longer cooking have a beefier flavour than the more expensive hind-quarter cuts: why, for instance, a slow-cooked piece of shin can compare so well in flavour with a grilled fillet steak.

I find certain cuts of so-called stewing steak better for some dishes than for others, so that in all my recipes I name the cut—and suggest you always ask for it by name too. Unidentified stewing, or braising, steak can often be a mixture and can cook unevenly, I've found. Below is a list of the cuts that are suitable for braising and stewing; as you can see from the illustration these cuts are always from the same part of the animal's anatomy but, confusingly, the *way* they're cut varies from region to region. The names vary even more—in fact one cut (I call it thick flank) has some 27 different names up and down the country!

Braising beef

My own favourite cut for braising is no. 9 on the chart. Where I live in East Anglia, this is called *chuck* and *blade steak*. In other regions it can be called *shoulder*, which as you can see from the diagram is exactly where it is.

If you want larger pieces of meat rather than cubes, *thick flank* (no. 4) is suitable: actually from the hind-quarters and called *round* or *flesh end* in Scotland or *bedpiece* elsewhere.

Beef skirt is not shown on the chart because its position is internal—below the diaphragm of the animal. It is however an

Beef

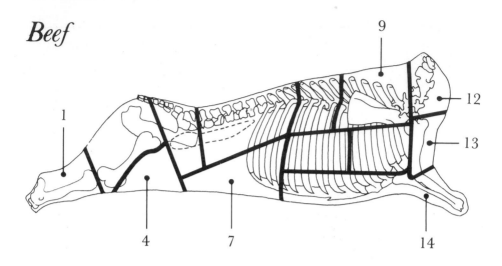

Lamb

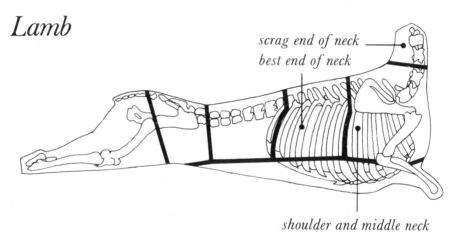

Pork

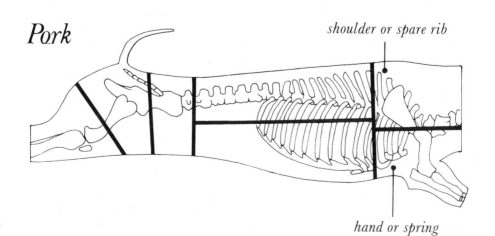

excellent cut for braising and one end can even be grilled if scored across the grain and tenderised by marinating before cooking.

Stewing beef
Next come stewing cuts from the *neck* (no. 12) and *clod* (no. 13). These are accorded some undignified titles such as *sticking*, or in Scotland *gullet*, or in the North *vein* or *sloat*! Also suitable for stewing is *thin flank* (no. 7) sometimes just called *flank*.

Both the *leg* (no. 1) and the *shin* (no. 14) provide excellent stewing meat, with an exceptionally good flavour. But because of the extra amount of connective tissue these cuts need much longer stewing than any of the other cuts of beef I have mentioned, and they are not suitable for braising.

Lamb
For stewing, *middle neck* or *scrag end of neck* are generally used as the bones impart delicious juices to the liquid. Also *best-end of neck chops* are ideal for braising (as in *Lancashire hotpot*). In Scotland these are called *single loin chops* and in the Midlands simply *cutlets*.

Pork
Pork for braising usually comes from the region of the shoulder. The upper part is called either *shoulder* or *spare rib*. The lower part of the shoulder is known as *hand and spring*.

The principles of casserole cookery
Trimming and size of meat pieces One thing that's often disappointing with cuts of braising steak (and this is especially true of the packaged meat found in supermarkets) is that they are sliced too thinly. For braising in whole slices, cuts of $\frac{1}{2}$–$\frac{3}{4}$ inch thick (1–2 cm) are alright, but for many casseroles the ideal sized pieces are $1\frac{1}{2}$ inches (4 cm) square and $1\frac{1}{4}$ inches (3 cm) deep. Therefore it is preferable, wherever possible, to buy a quantity in one piece and cut it up yourself. Trim off *excess* fat and gristle before using, but remember that some connective tissue and marbling will add richness to the finished dish.

How much per person? This depends on all sorts of things—how much the meat needs to be trimmed, what extra ingredients go into the casserole, what other dishes you plan to serve at the same meal and so on—but, on average, I find that 8 oz (225 g) of meat per person is needed if someone has a large appetite, like my husband. For a normal appetite 6 oz (175 g) per person is usually adequate.

Browning the meat Most, though not all, meat benefits from being seared in hot fat before the liquid is added. I have found that searing meat at a *high* temperature, as compared with browning it over a *medium* heat results in far less visible loss of juices. Meat fibres contract when heat is applied, squeezing out juices from inside: but if the heat is high enough these juices will be burnt into a crust on the meat instead of being lost in the cooking fat. I would also add that this dark, mahogany-coloured crust on the outside of the pieces of meat gives a richer, better flavour to a casserole.

One important point, if you're browning meat in batches and removing it to a plate, is to make sure that whatever juices do run out are re-incorporated into the casserole and not lost. And one final point: never overcrowd the pan during the browning. If you do, there will be too much steam rushing out and the meat will never brown because it will have become damp. So remember, brown only a few pieces at a time.

Liquid for casseroles The liquid in a casserole, mingling with the meat juices that do escape, provides the finished sauce. *Bone stock* is good for beef casseroles, but failing that plain hot water enriched with a few drops of Worcester sauce and mushroom ketchup makes a handy instant stock. Red or white *wine* will add extra flavour of its own, and its acidity will actually help to tenderise the meat as it cooks. *Beer* (pale or brown ale, or stout) makes a deliciously rich sauce: the long slow cooking transforms it completely, leaving no trace of its original bitterness.
Tomatoes —fresh peeled or tinned Italian plum tomatoes—also give body and flavour to certain casseroles, like *Goulash* (see page 329). A good alternative is hot water enriched with tomato puree. *Cider* is also delicious in casseroles—but it must be dry cider.

Thickening casseroles Some casserole recipes call for the liquid to be thickened, and this can be done in various ways. The most popular way is to add some flour to the casserole after the meat has been browned (so that it can mingle with the juices and fat in the pan) and before the liquid is added. It is exactly the same principle as for the thickening of a white sauce (described in Part One page 147). Another way to thicken a casserole is to toss the meat in seasoned flour before browning it (see recipe for *Braised steak and onions in stout*, page 331). Alternatively, when the casserole has completed cooking, the liquid can be strained off and simmered until slightly reduced and thickened. Or a flour and butter paste can be stirred into the liquid at the end of cooking time.

Vegetables If vegetables are to be included along with the meat in a casserole, the main consideration is not to cut them too small. This is a common mistake and results in the vegetables disintegrating under the strain of the long cooking. This applies particularly to onions, which if sliced too small can collapse altogether. It's far nicer, I think, to be able to discern slices of onion that have retained their shape. Vegetables that cook quite quickly (such as green peppers and mushrooms) are usually added to a casserole half way through or towards the end of cooking time.

Cooking temperatures and times Slowly, slowly is the word that needs to be emphasised here. It is said that the correct simmering temperature is reached when the liquid shows the barest shimmer of movement and an occasional bubble breaks the surface. I have found that, using a heavy flameproof casserole, the ingredients for a beef casserole can be brought slowly up to simmering point on top of the stove, then transferred to the middle or low shelf of a pre-heated oven. Gas mark 1, 275°F (140°C) is gentle enough to produce the very best results. But ovens vary and different types of cooking pots will affect temperatures too so you may have to adjust the oven temperature accordingly.

The time a casserole takes to cook will vary from $2-2\frac{1}{2}$ hours for chuck, blade and thick flank, up to 4 hours for shin, leg and neck. Pork cuts for braising and casseroling normally take $1\frac{1}{2}-2$ hours, and lamb much the same.

Skimming If a fair amount of fat has come out of the meat during the cooking, it will settle on the surface and can be removed by tilting the casserole slightly and spooning off with a large kitchen spoon. And if there's still some left, another tip is to float two or three pieces of absorbent kitchen paper on the surface—this should soak up any fat remaining. Of course, if you've had time to make the casserole ahead of time, the fat on the surface will solidify as it cools and can then just be lifted off. Which brings me to:

Re-heating Many casseroles seem to improve in flavour if kept overnight (cool them quickly and keep them in a refrigerator, by the way, once they're cold). This means it's quite possible to make two casseroles while the oven is in full swing, and keep one for the next day. The re-heating must be done very thoroughly, though, either on top of the stove over a very low heat or in an oven heated to gas mark 3, 325°F, (170°C). Either way, the food must come up to a gentle simmer and maintain that temperature for 30 minutes in order to kill off any harmful bacteria.

Notes on cooking casseroles

Cooking pots and casseroles I've found the most useful type of casserole is the heavy cast-iron kind with enamelled lining. It isn't the cheapest *but* it does conduct the heat evenly and has the advantage of being suitable for cooking on top of the stove and inside the oven. It is also attractive enough to take to the table.

A 4½ pint (2½ litre) capacity casserole is the average family size, but you might also find a smaller size (3 pt or 1¾ litre) useful at times and a larger one (6½–7 pt or 4 litre) for entertaining. What one's aiming for is a pot that contains the ingredients comfortably without leaving masses of empty space. Well-fitting lids are *very* important, because they minimise the loss of liquid by evaporation during the cooking. If you happen to have a lid that doesn't fit too well, then cover the casserole with foil first to make it fit more snugly. And it follows that you should leave it be: too many peeps and stirs will let some of the flavour out as effectively as an ill-fitting lid.

Electric slow cookers These are self-contained cooking pots which are sometimes called crockpots, with their own electric element which is geared to producing the slow continuous heat needed for casseroles. It uses very little electricity, and is useful for those who are out at work all day since it can be left unattended quite safely. On a high setting a casserole will take around 5 hours; on a low one it will take an average of 8 hours, and won't come to any harm if left for 10!

If you're not at home all day, to use one of these effectively you must of course prepare everything before you go and allow 20 minutes or so for the casserole to pre-heat. If you're considering buying one, ask yourself if you are the sort of person who is organised enough to see to all this before you go out.

Pressure cookers Pressure cooking can cut the time needed for casseroles down to about one-third of the normal time. So speed, and the consequent saving on fuel costs, are the self-evident advantages of this method. It has also been pointed out that because everything is locked away from the air, and cooked for a shorter time, losses of vitamins and minerals are reduced to a minimum. Pressure cookers can be transported easily and used on any sort of cooker, so they're ideal to take on self-catering or camping holidays.

Those are the pluses, but there are also disadvantages: (i) as I have explained, the flavour of the cheaper cuts develops with long slow cooking—so a certain amount can be lost with speedier cooking under pressure; (ii) the liquid content in pressure cookers has to be a minimum of ¾ pint (425 ml), and I often find I want to use less than this. Also no thickening can be added till after the pressure cooking, so this has to be a separate process at the end.

In my experience many busy people swear by their pressure cookers and use them whenever possible: others (like myself) use them very rarely. In the end it's a matter of personal preference, so if you are wondering whether or not to invest in one yourself, do get a book on pressure cooking from the library and study the facts for yourself first.

Beef in beer
(serves 6–8 people)

This is an old Flemish recipe often known by its original name *Carbonnades de boeuf à la flamande*. Sometimes large baked croûtons sprinkled with grated cheese are arranged on the top of the cooked beef and the dish is then popped under the grill until the cheese is bubbling. Whether you do this or not, this recipe has a beautiful rich sauce and is one of my firm favourites.

2 lb chuck steak (900 g), cut into 2 inch (5 cm) squares
¾ lb onions, peeled, sliced in quarters then separated into layers (350 g)
1 fat clove of garlic, crushed
1 tablespoon olive oil
1 sprig fresh thyme or ½ teaspoon dried thyme
1 bayleaf
1 well-heaped tablespoon plain flour
½ pint pale ale (275 ml)
Salt and freshly-milled black pepper

Pre-heat the oven to gas mark 1, 275°F (140°C)

Heat the oil in a large flameproof casserole until sizzling hot then sear the meat in it—just a few pieces at a time—till they become a dark mahogany brown all over. As the pieces brown, remove them to a plate then add the onions to the casserole and, with the heat still high, toss them around until brown at the edges. Now return the meat to the casserole together with any juices. Add the flour, turn the heat down, and using a wooden spoon stir it around to soak up all the juices. It will look rather stodgy and unattractive at this stage but that's quite normal.

Next gradually stir in the pale ale and, whilst everything *slowly* comes up to simmering point, add the thyme, bayleaf, crushed garlic, and some salt and freshly-milled black pepper.

As soon as it begins to simmer, stir thoroughly, put on a tight-fitting lid and transfer the casserole to the middle shelf of the oven.

Cook at a gentle simmer for $2\frac{1}{2}$ hours. Don't take the lid off and have a taste half-way through because, early on, the beer hasn't had time to develop into a delicious sauce; the beautiful aroma will make you very hungry, but please leave it alone!

Simple Stroganoff

(serves 4–6 people)

The classic recipe for Stroganoff is made with thin strips of fillet steak, cooked and served very quickly; it needs rather exact timing. This version, however, is made with strips of chuck steak, which costs less, has more flavour, and can be cooked slowly on top of the stove demanding no particular skill.

$1\frac{1}{2}$ lb lean chuck steak (700 g)
1 lb mushrooms, sliced (450 g)
2 large onions
$\frac{1}{2}$ pint dry white wine or dry cider (275 ml)
3 oz butter (75 g)
$\frac{1}{2}$ pint soured cream (275 ml)
Nutmeg
Salt and freshly-milled black pepper

First trim the meat and cut it into thin strips, about $\frac{1}{4}$ inch ($\frac{1}{2}$ cm) wide and no more than $2\frac{1}{2}$ inches (6 cm) long. The onion should be peeled, cut in half, then each half sliced and the layers separated out into thin half-moon shapes.

Now melt the butter in a thick-based saucepan or flameproof casserole and gently soften the onion for 5 minutes or until it has turned pale gold. Then, with a slotted spoon, remove it to a plate.

Next, turn the heat up high, add the pieces of meat to the casserole (a few at a time) and brown them. Then reduce the heat, return the onion and all the meat to the pan, season with salt and pepper and pour in the wine or cider. Bring to simmering point, cover and let it cook very gently on top of the stove for 1½ hours—stirring it just now and then.

When the time is up stir in the mushrooms (which will add a lot of juice in case you think it seems a little dry), put the lid back on and leave to cook for a further 30 minutes or until the meat is tender.

Then taste to check the seasoning, and stir in the soured cream with a good grating of fresh nutmeg. Let the cream heat through (but not boil) and serve the Stroganoff with plain boiled rice.

Hungarian goulash

(serves 4 people)

This makes a fairly economical dinner party dish: it is very easy to prepare and won't mind hanging around if your guests are late. It also goes very well with braised red cabbage (see recipe in Part One, page 206).

1½ lb chuck steak (700 g) trimmed and cut into 1½ inch (4 cm) cubes
2 large onions, roughly chopped
1 clove of garlic, crushed
1 tablespoon olive oil
1 rounded tablespoon plain flour
1 rounded tablespoon Hungarian paprika
1 × 14 oz tin Italian tomatoes (400 g)
1 medium-sized green or red pepper
1 × 5 fl oz carton soured cream (150 ml)
Salt and freshly-milled black pepper

Pre-heat the oven to gas mark 1, 275°F (140°C)

Begin by heating the oil in a flameproof casserole till sizzling hot. Then brown the cubes of beef on all sides, cooking a few at a time and transferring them to a plate as they brown.

Now, with the heat turned to medium, stir in the onions and cook them for about 5 minutes or until they turn a pale golden colour. Then add the crushed garlic and return the meat to the casserole.

Sprinkle in the flour and paprika and stir to soak up the juices. Next, add the contents of the tin of tomatoes, season with salt and pepper and bring everything slowly up to simmering point before covering with a tight-fitting lid and transferring the casserole to the middle shelf of the oven. Cook for 2 hours.

Prepare the pepper by halving it, removing the seeds and cutting the flesh into 2 inch (5 cm) strips. Then, when the 2 hours are up, stir the chopped pepper into the goulash, replace the lid and cook for a further 30 minutes.

Just before serving, stir in the soured cream to give a marbled, creamy effect, then sprinkle a little more paprika over, and serve straight from the casserole, with some rice (or vegetables).

Boeuf Bourguignonne

(serves 6 people)

This is my adaptation of the famous French classic: beef braised in Burgundy, garnished with cubes of bacon, button onions and mushrooms. If you want to cut the cost then try using dry cider, which gives different results but is every bit as good.

2 lb chuck steak (900 g), cut into 2 inch (5 cm) squares
½ lb smoked or green streaky bacon, bought in one piece then cut into cubes (225 g)
¾ lb small onions
1 medium sized onion, sliced
2 cloves of garlic, chopped
2 sprigs fresh thyme or ½ teaspoon dried thyme
1 bayleaf
1 heaped tablespoon plain flour
¾ pint red Burgundy (425 ml)
¼ lb dark flat mushrooms, sliced (110 g)
3 tablespoons olive oil
Salt and freshly-milled black pepper

Pre-heat the oven to gas mark 1, 275°F (140°C)

Heat two tablespoons of oil to sizzling point in a large flameproof casserole and sear the chunks of beef—a few pieces at a time—to a rich, dark brown on all sides. Using a slotted spoon, remove the meat as it browns to a plate. Next add the sliced onion to the casserole and brown that a little too. Now return the meat to the casserole then sprinkle in the flour, stir it around to soak up all the juices, then gradually pour in the Burgundy—stirring all the time. Add the chopped garlic and herbs, season with salt and pepper, put the lid on and cook in the oven for 2 hours.

Then, using a bit more oil, fry the button onions and cubes of bacon in a small frying pan to colour them lightly, and add them to the casserole together with the sliced mushrooms. Put the lid back on and cook for a further hour.

This is nice served with buttered noodles or onion-flavoured rice.

Braised steak and onions in stout

(serves 2 people)

For this recipe you'll need four pieces of braising steak—chuck or blade.

1 lb braising steak, cut into four pieces (450 g)
2 largish onions, halved and sliced
5 fl oz stout (150 ml)
½ teaspoon Worcestershire sauce
Oil
Some seasoned flour
Salt and freshly-milled black pepper

Pre-heat the oven to gas mark 1, 275°F (140°C)

Melt a tablespoon of oil in a flameproof casserole and, when it's sizzling hot, coat the meat in seasoned flour and brown the pieces on both sides till they're a good rich, brown colour. Lift them out of the casserole and reserve on a plate.

Now fry the onions to brown them well at the edges, then arrange the meat on top (plus any juices that are on the plate) and season with salt and pepper. Next pour in the stout and Worcestershire sauce. Then put the lid on and transfer the casserole to the oven. Cook for approximately 2½ hours or until the meat is tender.

Note: if you like you could braise the steak on top of the stove using a very low heat but, because this method seems to cause a bit more evaporation, add one extra fluid ounce (25 ml) of stout.

Stewed shin of beef with mushroom dumplings

(serves 4–6 people)

For years I never bought shin of beef because it looked so unappealing, but I missed out because those sections of connective tissue melt down during the long, slow cooking and provide extra flavour and enrichment to the sauce. Now, if I want an old-fashioned brown stew, I wouldn't use anything else.

2 lb shin of beef, cut in bite-sized cubes (900 g)
¾ lb onions, cut into quarters (350 g)
2 large carrots, scraped and cut into large chunks
1 bayleaf
1 sprig fresh thyme or ½ teaspoon dried thyme
1 heaped tablespoon flour
15 fl oz hot beef bone stock (400 ml)— or hot water enriched with 1 teaspoon Worcester sauce
2 teaspoons mushroom ketchup
Beef dripping
Salt and freshly-milled black pepper

For the dumplings:
4 oz self-raising flour (110 g)
2 oz shredded suet (50 g)
1 onion, finely grated
2 oz mushrooms, very finely chopped
Salt and freshly-milled black pepper

Pre-heat the oven to gas mark 1, 275°F (140°C)

In a flameproof casserole melt about 1 tablespoon of beef dripping and, when its smoking hot, brown the pieces of beef—a few at a time—to a really dark, rich brown colour. As the pieces brown remove them to a plate using a slotted spoon. Next fry the onions and carrots so that they turn dark at the edges. Now spoon off any excess fat, turn the heat down, return everything to the casserole and sprinkle in the flour, stirring it in well to soak up the juices. Next, gradually stir in the hot stock and the mushroom ketchup, add the thyme, bayleaf and seasoning and bring everything slowly up to simmering point. Then put on a very well fitting lid, using foil if you need to. Now transfer the casserole to the lowest shelf of the oven and cook for 3 hours or until the meat is tender.

Towards the end of cooking time make the dumplings. Sift the flour into a mixing bowl, add some pepper and a pinch of salt, then stir in the suet, the chopped mushrooms and the grated onion. Add enough cold water to bring it all together to make a fairly stiff but elastic dough that leaves the bowl cleanly. Divide the dough into 8 pieces and roll each portion into a dumpling shape.

When the stew is ready, using a draining spoon, take out all the meat and vegetables and put them on a large warm serving dish. Cover with foil and keep warm in the bottom of the oven.

Season the liquid to taste then bring it up to a very fast boil. Put the dumplings into the bubbling liquid, cover and cook for 20–25 minutes making sure they don't come off the boil. When the dumplings are ready put them all round the meat and vegetables, pour over some of the gravy and serve the rest in a sauce boat.

Irish stew with parsley dumplings

(serves 4 people)

I don't make any claims about this so far as its Irish authenticity is concerned, but it does taste very good.

2½ lb lean middle neck and scrag-end of mutton or lamb (1 kg)
¾ lb onions, sliced (350 g)
½ lb carrots, sliced (225 g)
2 medium-sized leeks, washed and sliced
1 large potato, peeled and sliced
1 tablespoon pearl barley
2 tablespoons seasoned flour
Hot water
Salt and freshly-milled black pepper

For the dumplings:
4 oz self-raising flour (110 g)
2 oz shredded suet (50 g)
1 tablespoon fresh parsley, chopped (if fresh is not available make plain dumplings)
Salt and freshly-milled black pepper

First wipe the pieces of meat and cut away excess fat, then dip them in the seasoned flour. Now put a layer of meat in the bottom of a large saucepan, followed by some onion, carrot, leek and potato and season with salt and pepper. Then put in some more meat and continue layering the ingredients until everything is in.

Now sprinkle in the pearl barley followed by approximately 2 pints (1·25 litres) hot water and bring to simmering point. Spoon off any scum that rises to the surface then cover the pan with a well-fitting lid and leave to simmer over a low heat for about 2 hours.

About 15 minutes before the end of cooking time, make the dumplings. Mix the flour, salt, pepper and parsley in a bowl. Then mix in the suet—but it mustn't be rubbed in. Add just sufficient cold water to make a fairly stiff but elastic dough that leaves the bowl cleanly. Shape it into 8 dumplings.

When the stew is ready, remove the meat and vegetables with a slotted spoon onto a large warm serving dish. Cover with foil and keep warm.

Season the liquid to taste, then bring to a brisk boil. Put the dumplings in, cover and cook them for 20–25 minutes, making sure that they don't come off the boil.

Serve the meat surrounded by the vegetables and dumplings, with some of the liquid poured over and some in a gravy boat.

Traditional Lancashire hotpot

(serves 4 people)

This has acquired its name from the time when it was baked at home, then wrapped in blankets to keep hot and provide lunch for a day at the races.

4 lambs' kidneys, cored, skinned and chopped
2 lb best end and middle neck of lamb (900 g)
Dripping
1 pint hot water (570 ml) mixed with $\frac{1}{2}$ teaspoon Worcestershire sauce
1 bayleaf
2 sprigs fresh thyme (or $\frac{1}{2}$ teaspoon dried)
2 lb potatoes (900 g), cut into $\frac{3}{4}$ inch (1.5 cm slices)

| ¾ lb onions, roughly chopped (350 g) |
| 1 tablespoon flour |
| A little butter |
| Salt and freshly-milled black pepper |

Pre-heat the oven to gas mark 3,
325°F (170°C)

In a large frying pan heat some dripping until it is smoking hot,
then brown the pieces of meat (2 or 3 pieces at a time) until they
all have a good brown crust. As they cook, remove them to a wide
casserole. Brown the pieces of kidney too, and tuck these in
amongst the meat.

Next fry the onions—add a little butter to the pan if you need any
extra fat—cooking them for about 10 minutes till they turn brown
at the edges. Now stir in the flour to soak up the juices then
gradually add the hot water and Worcestershire sauce, stirring or
whisking until flour and liquid are smoothly blended. Season with
salt and pepper and bring it up to simmering point, then pour it
over the meat in the casserole. Add the bayleaf and thyme, then
arrange the potato slices on top, in an overlapping pattern like
slates on a roof. Season the potatoes and add a few flecks of butter
here and there. Cover with a tight-fitting lid and cook near the top
of the oven for 1½ hours, then remove the lid and cook for a further
50 minutes.

I sometimes finish off the hotpot under the grill. If you brush the
potatoes with a little more butter and place the casserole under a
hot grill they crisp up and brown beautifully. Alternatively, if you
think they're not browning enough during cooking, you can turn
the heat in the oven right up during the last 15 minutes.

Ragoût of lamb
(serves 2–3 people)

Neck of lamb isn't cheap any more but it
is less expensive than many other cuts
and, because of the bones, always gives
the maximum amount of flavour. This, I
think, is an excellent summer casserole.

| 2 lb neck of lamb, either middle neck or scrag end or a mixture of both (900 g) |
| 1 tablespoon oil |
| 2 medium-sized onions, roughly chopped |

1 sprig fresh thyme (or ½ teaspoon dried)
1 bayleaf
2 cloves of garlic, crushed
1 heaped tablespoon flour
1 pint boiling water (570 ml)
¾ lb new potatoes, scraped (350 g)
4 medium-sized tomatoes, peeled
Salt and freshly-milled black pepper

Pre-heat the oven to gas mark 1, 275°F (140°C)

First trim any excess fat from the meat, wipe each piece and season it with salt and freshly-milled pepper. Then heat the oil in a largish flameproof casserole, and brown the meat a few pieces at a time. When they're nicely browned transfer them to a plate, using a draining spoon.

Now gently fry the onions in the fat left in the pan—this will take about 10 minutes or so. Then, when the onions are softened and browned a little bit round the edges, add the garlic. Next stir in the flour, to soak up the juices, and gradually pour in the hot water, stirring to make a sort of gravy.

When simmering point is reached, return the pieces of meat to the casserole and add the thyme, bayleaf and seasoning—it won't look much at this point, but not to worry.

As soon as it comes back to simmering point, put the lid on and transfer the casserole to the oven. Cook it for about 1 hour, then add the scraped potatoes and peeled tomatoes. Put the lid back on and cook for a further 45 minutes, or until the potatoes are cooked.

Normandy pork with cream and apples

(serves 4 people)

This is quite rich and special. It needs a lightly cooked green vegetable or a crisp green side salad to go with it.

4 medium-sized pork spare rib chops or loin chops
2 oz butter (50 g)
1 medium cooking apple
1 large Cox's apple
1 large onion, cut into thin rings

1 clove of garlic, crushed
¾ teaspoon dried thyme
½ pint dry cider (275 ml)
3 tablespoons double cream
Sugar
Salt and freshly-milled black pepper

Pre-heat the oven to gas mark 5,
375°F (190°C)

Begin by melting half the butter in a thick frying pan and frying
the pork chops on both sides to a nice crusty golden colour. Then,
using a draining spoon, transfer them to a suitably sized casserole
and sprinkle with thyme.

Now add the remaining butter to the pan and fry the onion and
garlic for 5 minutes to soften. Meanwhile, core the apples and cut
them into rings, leaving the peel on as this gives extra flavour.
Next transfer the softened onion and garlic to the casserole, then
fry the apple rings in the same fat just for a few seconds on each
side and transfer them to the casserole as well, sprinkling on about
a teaspoon of sugar.

Next, spoon off any fat still left in the pan and then pour in the
cider. Bring it up to simmering point and pour it into the casserole
and season with salt and freshly-milled black pepper. Now put a
lid on and then put the casserole into the oven, and cook for about
30–40 minutes or until the chops are cooked. Then to finish off,
pour in the cream, stir it into the juices and serve immediately.

Pork with apples and cider

(serves 4 people)

This is a hearty winter dish that can be
left on its own for three hours if you plan
to be out. You could also leave some red
cabbage to braise in the oven with it and
return to a complete meal.

4 thick lean belly pork strips or spare rib chops
6 rashers unsmoked streaky bacon
1 large cooking apple, peeled, cored and sliced
2 medium-sized onions, chopped small
¼ pint dry cider (150 ml)

2 cloves of garlic, finely chopped
6 juniper berries, crushed with the back of a spoon
1½ lb potatoes, peeled and thickly sliced (700 g)
Olive oil
A little butter
Salt and freshly-milled black pepper

Pre-heat the oven to gas mark 1, 275°F (140°C)

If the pork is very fatty, trim away the excess. Heat some oil in a frying pan and brown the pork on both sides, then transfer them to a wide shallow casserole. Next, in the same pan, fry the bacon rashers a little until the fat starts to run. Then, using a draining spoon, place the bacon on top of the pork and season, but be careful with the salt as there'll be some in the bacon.

Now sprinkle over the juniper berries and garlic, then spread the slices of apple and onion on top. Add the cider and cover with a layer of overlapping potatoes. Finally, put a few dabs of butter on top, cover the dish first with greaseproof paper or foil, and then with a close-fitting lid. Transfer to the oven and cook for 3 hours.

Toward the end of the cooking time, pre-heat the grill to its highest setting. When the oven time is completed, place it, uncovered, under the grill so that the potatoes become brown and crispy.

Spanish pork with olives

(serves 4–6 people)

This casserole has what I'd call a rich Mediterranean flavour. Nice served with *Saffron rice* (page 351).

2 lb shoulder of pork, trimmed and cut into bite-sized cubes (900 g)
2 tablespoons olive oil
1 rounded tablespoon plain flour
2 medium-sized onions, sliced
2 cloves of garlic, crushed
1 teaspoon dried basil
1 lb tomatoes, peeled and chopped (450 g), or 1 × 14 oz (400 g), tin of tomatoes
6 fl oz red wine (175 ml)
1 green pepper, de-seeded and chopped

| 2 oz Spanish pimento stuffed olives, sliced (50 g) |
| Salt and freshly-milled black pepper |

Pre-heat the oven to gas mark 1, 275°F (140°C)

Begin by heating the oil in a large flameproof casserole, then add the cubes of pork and brown them on all sides. Cook only a few cubes at a time and remove them to a plate as they're done. Then add the onions to the casserole and brown them for a few minutes before returning the meat to the pan and sprinkling in the flour.

Stir everything well and add the chopped tomatoes—pour boiling water over fresh tomatoes first to help get the skins off. Pour in wine, add the garlic, basil and a seasoning of salt and pepper. Stir, bring slowly to simmering point then cover with a tight-fitting lid.

Transfer the casserole to the centre shelf of the oven and cook for 1½ hours. After that add the chopped pepper and sliced olives, cover again, then cook for a further 30 minutes. This is delicious served with rice and a crisp green salad.

Ossobuco

(serves 4 people)

This is a famous Italian casserole: shin of veal cooked in white wine with tomatoes. Try to buy the pieces of shin about 2 inches (5 cm) thick.

| 4 large pieces shin of veal |
| ½ pint dry white wine (275 ml) |
| ¾ lb tomatoes, peeled and chopped (350 g) |
| 1 tablespoon tomato purée |
| 1 large clove of garlic, finely chopped |
| The grated rind of 1 small lemon |
| 2 heaped tablespoons fresh chopped parsley |
| Butter |
| Salt and freshly-milled black pepper |

You'll need a wide, shallow flameproof casserole that can hold the pieces of veal in one layer.

In the casserole melt 1 tablespoon of butter and fry the pieces of veal to brown them lightly on both sides, keeping them arranged upright in the pan. Then pour over the wine, let it bubble and reduce a little before adding the tomatoes, tomato purée and a seasoning of salt and freshly-milled black pepper.

Then cover the casserole and leave it to cook gently on top of the stove for about 1 hour. After that, take off the lid and let it cook for another half an hour or so or until the meat is tender and the sauce reduced. Before serving, mix the chopped garlic, parsley and lemon rind together, then sprinkle this all over the meat. Serve this with rice (preferably *Risotto alla Milanese*, see recipe page 355) — and don't forget to dig out the marrow from the centre of the bone, it's delicious.

Sausages braised in red wine

(serves 3 people)

This is best made with very good quality pork sausages, preferably the spicy, herby sort that some butchers make themselves.

1 lb pork sausages (450 g)
½ lb lean streaky bacon in one piece, then cut into cubes (225 g)
½ lb small button onions (225 g)
½ teaspoon dried thyme
1 bayleaf
1 clove of garlic, crushed
1 heaped teaspoon flour
½ pint red wine (275 ml)
6 oz mushrooms, sliced if large (175 g)
Lard
Olive oil
Salt and freshly-milled black pepper

Take a large flameproof casserole, melt a little lard in it and brown the sausages all round. Then, using a slotted spoon, remove them to a plate whilst you lightly brown the bacon cubes and onions. When they're done, sprinkle in a heaped teaspoon of flour to soak up the juices, then gradually stir in the wine. Now pop the sausages back in, plus the garlic, bayleaf, thyme and a little seasoning. Put the lid on when simmering point is reached, turn the heat as low as possible and simmer very gently for 30 minutes.

Meanwhile brown the mushrooms in a little olive oil in a frying pan. Then, after the sausages have been cooking for the 30 minutes, stir the mushrooms into the casserole and continue to cook for a further 20 minutes—this time with the lid off.

Serve with what else but a pile of creamy mashed potato!

Braised meatballs with peppers and tomatoes

(serves 4–6 people)

This is another economical but really delicious recipe, probably best made in the autumn when there's a glut of tomatoes and green peppers.

1 lb best quality minced beef (450 g)
½ lb good pork sausage meat (225 g)
Half a green pepper, deseeded and finely chopped
1 egg, beaten
1 medium onion, minced or very finely chopped
1 large clove of garlic, crushed
¾ teaspoon dried mixed herbs
1 tablespoon freshly chopped parsley
2 slices bread
1 dessertspoon tomato purée
Flour, for coating the meatballs
Oil, for frying the meatballs
Salt and freshly-milled black pepper

For the sauce:
14 oz tin Italian tomatoes (400 g) or 1 lb ripe tomatoes (450 g)
1 small onion, chopped
1 clove of garlic, crushed
Half a green pepper, deseeded and chopped
1 teaspoon dried basil

Begin by making the meatballs: cut the crusts of the bread, then mash it to crumbs with a fork and, in a large mixing bowl, mix it together with the rest of the meatball ingredients and salt and pepper very thoroughly with your hands.

Now take pieces of the mixture—about a tablespoonful at a time—and roll each into a small round. You should get about

16–18 altogether. Coat each one lightly with flour, then in a large frying pan, brown them in the oil.

Meanwhile pre-heat the oven to gas mark 5, 375°F (190°C). When the meatballs are browned transfer them to a casserole and, in the juices remaining in the frying pan, prepare the sauce by softening the onion and green pepper for 5 minutes before adding the tomatoes, garlic and basil, then simmer for a couple of minutes. Taste and season, then pour the sauce over the meatballs in the casserole and cook, with a lid on, in the oven for 45 minutes. After that take off the lid and cook for a further 15–20 minutes.

This is nice served on a bed of buttered noodles, with a crisp green salad.

Rice and other grains

Including recipes for:

Without cereals (which for our purposes means rice, wheat, oats, maize, rye, barley, buckwheat and millet) man would not have got very far on this planet. Their cultivation goes back at least to the Stone Age, and every great civilisation since then has relied on one or other of them. Even today, rice is still the staple food for half the world's population, and very efficient it is too, being a good source of the proteins and vitamins essential to health—at least in its natural form. For here is a certain irony: for a long time now all our energy and ingenuity has been directed towards transforming our cereals into forms far removed from their natural state— refining and whitening our wheat flour, polishing our rice grains, creating new breakfast cereals. The result of course has been a loss in nutrients, and flavour. I touched on the problem—in so far as it concerned wheat—in the chapter on Bread in Part One but the situation is much the same for most of our grain products, and rice in particular.

As it happens, I think the pendulum is swinging back. The encouragement of 'natural' cereals is one of the main aims of the wholefood movement, and more and more people are now discovering for themselves the versatility of grains and grain products. I hope this section will offer a few ideas on these lines; but first let's look at the most adaptable of all the grains, rice, and see what happens to it in its preparation.

What's in a grain of rice?

If you were able to magnify a rice grain, when it's first harvested and cleaned of mud, leaves and stem, what you would see is something rather like a nut with an outer inedible shell, which has to be removed and discarded. Inside that would be the outer casings (again just like nuts—think of unblanched almonds): these are bran layers, a brown outer layer and a whiter inner one. Beyond these is the starchy centre (endosperm) which also contains the embryo (or germ). It so happens that this starchy kernel is one of the most easily-digested of all available foods, taking about half the time to be digested that most other foods require.

How rice is treated

In poorer countries rice is still pounded by hand, either with pestle and mortar or between grinding stones, to remove the inedible husk. In industrialized countries (like America where much of our rice now comes from) this is done in large, modern rice mills where the grain is not only cleaned and hulled by machine, but also 'polished' to remove the bran layers and germ and to scour the grain down to a translucent white refined, purified endosperm— in other words the end product is depleted of a lot of its original vitamins and minerals.

Grades of rice

Rice is produced, in most major growing countries, in three sizes of grain, each one suitable for different kinds of dish:

Short grain Often simply called pudding rice in Britain, this is a quick-growing rice (which is why it is the cheapest). The grains are fat and almost round, with barely more length than width. They are also rather chalky, which makes them sticky when cooked and are therefore best suited to rice puddings—they cook to a lovely creamy consistency in the milk.

Medium grain A sort of half-way rice, neither as sticky when cooked as short grain nor as cleanly separate as long grain. It isn't widely available in this country, but when it is, it should be used for croquettes, rice moulds or some risottos.

Long grain These grains are four or five times as long as they are wide, with scarcely any chalkiness (which means they are fluffy and separate when cooked). To buy good quality long grain you should look for really fine, needle-pointed ends and, with white rice, a certain translucence.

Then, apart from the shape of the grain, rice also reaches the shops in different degrees of preparation, which affect both the cooking and the taste:

Prepared rice

Brown rice This is the whole natural rice grain, with only the inedible outer husk removed, the bran layers and germ are left intact. It comes in the three sizes mentioned above, and is a rather appealing mixture of green and brown in colour. Personally I think long grain brown rice is the nicest of all rices, and for two reasons: (i) it contains the highest percentage of fibre, natural vitamins and minerals, and (ii) it has most flavour and 'bite' to it after it's cooked. It takes longer to cook than white rice and, paradoxically, it is more expensive to buy (considering it has gone through fewer processes). But it stores well and I try to balance out the cost by buying in bulk.

White (polished) rice This is the refined one that has had all but the starchy endosperm removed. It is pearly white and comes in all three grain sizes, the long grain type being the most commonly available rice in shops and supermarkets.

Easy-cook rice This white rice is so-called because it has been treated by a special steaming process (rather like pressure cooking) *before* milling. It is claimed by the manufacturers that this processing helps the grain to retain much of its nutritional content, and hardens it so it becomes less starchy and remains separate in the cooking—although it needs a little more cooking time than ordinary polished white rice. (However, I tested a batch of easy-cook rice alongside some ordinary long grain white rice, both of them American, and found that using the *perfect rice* method given on page 349, the ordinary long grain was every bit as easy—and 25% cheaper! Still, if you feel safer using easy-cook then just allow ten minutes extra cooking.)

Pre-cooked Rice Sometimes described as pre-digested! This is polished white rice which is cooked or half-cooked after milling, then dried so all it needs is to re-absorb the water it lost in the drying. My own opinion of it is, like my opinion of sliced white bread—blotting paper!

Some regional varieties
Finally, rice is sometimes described by names which refer to the countries or regions where it was grown. Here are some of them:

Patna rice Is a generic term used to describe the long grain rice grown all round the world. The name derives from the days when it was first grown in Patna (an area of north-east India) and exported to Europe. Since most of our long grain rice now comes from America, the Americans are slightly puzzled as to why we should still refer to their rice as 'Patna'!

Basmati This is a very fine quality rice with a superb flavour, and does in fact come from India. Usually only available in Indian provision stores and, in my opinion, the best sort to serve with a curry. I used to find it quite tricky to cook until I used Elizabeth David's method, given in her book *Salts, Spices and Aromatics* and have never had a failure since.

Carolina A general word to describe rice, referring to the region in America where rice was first planted in (1694). In actual fact most rice production in America has now shifted to other states.

Arborio (Italian) rice This is the rice that's grown in northern Italy. It's quality is superb and I think it has the best flavour of all. The grains are rounder and much plumper than long grain, and if you rub a grain of it between your fingers, you can see clearly an outer translucent edge and a white core in the centre. To make a true risotto you need arborio rice—it takes longer and in this case it's not meant to be fluffy and separate, but because it's stirred quite frequently it cooks to a rather creamy consistency (see recipes for *Risotto alla Milanese* and *Risotto with chicken livers and mushrooms*, pages 354 and 355).

There are two types available: one is very white and the grains look chalky. The other is browny-yellow and has a more polished look. This latter kind is treated to make the grains firmer and more separate (presumably because that is what the export market wants rather than the true risotto).

If you can get hold of the so-called 'easy-cook' Italian (one quality supermarket chain now sells it), then as an all-purpose rice it does have a better flavour and texture, I think, than ordinary long-grain white rice—and can be cooked exactly as in the *perfect rice* recipe.

Other rice products

When rice is milled, some of the grains are broken and these are used to make *rice flakes*, which are used for puddings, and *rice flour* which is used for confectionary and cooking, and makes a good thickening agent. Onc tablespoon of rice flour per $\frac{1}{2}$ pint (275 ml) of liquid will thicken a soup or stew beautifully: just whisk it into the liquid and bring to simmering point.

Do not be afraid!

So many people have told me they can't cook rice, and yet (rather like omelette-making) there's nothing intrinsically difficult about it: once it has been explained, you should be well away. So if you're one of those people who live in fear of cooking rice, here is a complete guide to trouble-free rice cookery. The following points apply to long grain white and brown rice but not to Italian rice—for which guidelines are given in the recipe for *Risotto alla Milanese*.

(1) First of all buy good quality long grain rice. My white rice comes from a reliable supermarket chain who market it under their own name. My long grain brown rice comes from a

wholefood shop where I can buy it in 7 or 14 lb (3 or 6 kg) packs, which reduces the price per pound considerably.

(2) Don't wash rice (except Basmati). All other rice is thoroughly cleaned at the milling stage, and washing it later removes some of the nutrients (anyway the high temperature of the cooking will purify it).

(3) Always measure rice and liquid by *volume* and not by weight. Cups and mugs are often recommended, but I find they vary so much it's impossible to gauge whether a certain cup will be enough for such and such a number of people. So I now always measure both rice and cooking liquid in a glass measuring jug. I find that filling the jug with rice up to the 5 fl oz level gives enough for 2 people (up to the 10 fl oz level for 4 people and so on) and this provides fairly generous portions. Then I empty the rice out of the jug and measure into it exactly *twice* that amount of liquid (i.e. up to the 10 fl oz level for 2 people, up to the 20 fl oz level for 4 people and so on).

(4) Please leave rice alone while it's cooking! Lack of confidence in the kitchen always manifests itself in over-handling, and it is the nervous cooks who are forever peeping, prodding and stirring and that, so far as rice is concerned, is a disaster. Why? Because rice grains are delicate and easily broken: if you start to stir them while they're cooking, they break, releasing the starch inside and turning them sticky.

(5) Use a thick-based saucepan or flameproof casserole, and be gentle. Once boiling point has been reached turn the heat down to the barest simmer. Try not to lift the lid: I think rice should be cooked as briefly as possible and each time the lid is lifted, steam and heat escape and the cooking time is unnecessarily prolonged.

(6) Timing *is* important and it remains the same regardless of the quantity of rice you are cooking. For long grain white rice I find 15 minutes is just enough. When the time is up, tip the pan to one side and check there is no liquid left unabsorbed—if there is, give the rice a couple of minutes more.

(7) The way to test rice is to bite a couple of grains: they should be tender but firm. Then tip the rice into a warm serving bowl—if you leave it in the pot it will go on cooking. Then fluff the grains with a skewer (lots of cooks say with a fork, but I find a skewer separates them more efficiently).

(8) It is inadvisable to keep rice warm for long but it will keep for 10 minutes without coming to harm if you put it in a bowl placed over a saucepan of barely simmering water. Cover the bowl with a clean tea towel but don't put a lid on top.

(9) Cooked rice keeps well (even up to a week) in a bowl covered with clingfilm in the refrigerator. To re-heat it, just place it in a thick-based saucepan with a couple of tablespoons of water, cover and warm it gently, shaking the pan from time to time. It will only take a couple of minutes.

(10) All the above information applies also to the cooking of brown rice, except that this takes 40–45 minutes to cook instead of 15 (extra time that's easily warranted by the character and flavour of brown rice).

Liquid for cooking rice
Plain salted water is fine for cooking savoury rice. The liquid should be boiling (to save time I always pour it into the measuring jug straight from a boiling kettle). Stock is an excellent alternative particularly if the rice is to be served with chicken (use chicken stock) or beef (use beef stock). I don't recommend stock cubes, as I find them too strong, masking the delicate flavour of the rice.

Perfect rice
(serves 2 people)

A friend of mine swore she'd *never* be able to cook rice: she had tried—she said—every sort of rice and every kind of method, only to be teased so much by her family that she gave up completely. Now I'm happy to report she has been persuaded to follow the method below and has had perfect rice every time. What is perfect rice? Simply this, that when it's cool enough to handle you can pick up a handful that will run through your hands in a stream of perfectly separate grains. So here goes. You will need:

Long grain white or brown rice measured to the 5 fl oz level in a glass measuring jug

Boiling water or stock, measured to the 10 fl oz level in a glass measuring jug

| 1 dessertspoon of oil, or $\frac{1}{2}$ oz (10 g) butter |
| Salt |

One small, solid based saucepan or flameproof casserole and a shallow serving dish, warmed.

Begin by heating the oil or butter gently, just to the melting stage, then add the rice and, using a wooden spoon, stir the grains to get them all thoroughly coated and glistening with fat.

Now add the boiling stock or water and salt, stir just once as the liquid comes up to simmering point, then put on a tight-fitting lid. Turn the heat down to keep the gentlest simmer—then go away and leave it completely alone. Don't take the lid off and, above all, don't stir it. After exactly 15 minutes, if the rice is white (40 if it's brown), I give you permission to have a look and test a few grains. If they're tender, and, when you tilt the pan almost on its side, you can see no trace of liquid left, the rice is cooked.

Now tip it out into a warmed serving dish, using a rubber spatula to dislodge any grains that refuse to leave the base. Lightly fluff the grains with a skewer. Serve immediately. Or if you need to keep it warm—say for up to 10 minutes (no longer)—cover the bowl with a tea cloth (which will absorb the steam and help to keep the grains separate) and place it over a pan of barely simmering water.

Note: I find a wide, shallow serving dish makes it easier to fluff the grains, as they can be spread out more easily.

This method of cooking rice can be used with all kinds of other flavourings. Here are some suggestions. The quantities given will be sufficient to flavour rice for 4 people.

Onion rice
Cook 1 finely chopped medium-sized onion in the oil or butter for 5 minutes before stirring in the rice. Then proceed as above.

Rice with peppers
Cook half a chopped onion and half a chopped green or red pepper in the oil or butter before stirring in the rice.

Rice with mushrooms
Cook half a chopped onion and $\frac{1}{4}$ lb (110 g) chopped mushrooms in the oil or butter before stirring in the rice.

Rice with herb butter
When the rice is cooked, add a knob of herb butter (see page 163 in
Part One) so it melts into the rice as you fluff it.

Spiced pilau rice

(serves 4 people)

This fluffy yellow rice, fragrant with
spices, is lovely to serve with curries.

Long grain white rice measured up to the 10 fl oz level in a glass measuring jug
Boiling water measured up to the 20 fl oz level in a glass measuring jug
2 oz butter or oil (50 g)
1 small onion, finely chopped
1 inch whole cinnamon stick (2.5 cm)
¾ teaspoon cumin seeds, crushed
1 bayleaf
2 cardomum pods, crushed
1 dessertspoon ground turmeric
Salt

Melt the butter or oil in a thick-based saucepan and soften the
onion in it for about 3 minutes. Then stir in the spices, bayleaf and
salt and allow a minute or two while the heat draws out their
fragrance. Next stir in the measured rice, and when it's well coated
with oil and spices, pour in the boiling water. Stir once, put on a
tight-fitting lid, and simmer gently for 15 minutes or until the rice
is tender. Tip into a serving dish straightaway, fluff with a skewer
and remove cinnamon before serving.

Saffron rice

(serves 4 people)

I buy saffron from a large chain-store
chemist and crush the strands with a
pestle and mortar.

Long grain white rice, measured up to the 10 fl oz level in a measuring jug
Boiling water or chicken stock, measured up to the 20 fl oz level in a measuring jug
1 small onion, finely chopped
1 tablespoon butter
1 tablespoon olive oil
½ teaspoon saffron
Salt

Begin by softening the onion in the oil and butter for 5 minutes, then stir in the powdered saffron and allow 1 minute for the heat to draw out the flavour before adding the rice. Stir to get the rice nicely coated with the oil and butter then add the boiling water or stock. Stir again once and add salt.

Then, when it comes to the boil, cover with a lid and leave it to simmer very gently for 15 minutes or until all the liquid has been absorbed. Don't stir it or peek, but leave it alone until the 15 minutes are up. Then taste a grain without stirring the rice and tilt the pan a little to check that the liquid has been absorbed.

When the rice is cooked tip it onto a warm, shallow serving dish and fluff with a fork before serving.

Brown rice, lentil and mushroom salad

This recipe is enough for four people as a main course or for eight as a side salad.

Brown rice, measured to the 8 fl oz level in a measuring jug

Boiling water, measured to the 16 fl oz level

8 oz whole brown lentils (225 g)

$\frac{1}{2}$ oz butter (10 g)

Some salt

4 oz mushrooms, thinly sliced (110 g)

8 spring onions, thinly sliced—green tops as well

Half a large green pepper, chopped small

1 tablespoon finely chopped walnuts

One 6 inch piece unpeeled cucumber, chopped (15 cm)

For the dressing:

5 dessertspoons oil

1 dessertspoon wine vinegar

1 rounded teaspoon mustard powder

1 clove of garlic, crushed

Salt and freshly-milled black pepper

To garnish:

A few crisp lettuce leaves

2 heaped tablespoons chopped parsley
Sliced tomatoes

Begin by cooking the lentils in plenty of (unsalted) boiling water for about 30–40 minutes or until they're *just* soft but not mushy. Meanwhile, in another saucepan melt the butter, stir in the rice to get it nicely coated, then pour in the boiling water. Stir once, cover and simmer very gently for 40–45 minutes until the rice is tender and has absorbed all the liquid.

Whilst the lentils and rice are cooking, prepare the dressing by mixing together in a bowl the oil, vinegar, mustard, garlic, salt and some freshly-milled pepper.

Then drain the lentils and combine them with the cooked rice in a salad bowl and, while they're still warm pour on the dressing. Mix well and leave to cool. Then stir in the rest of the ingredients and serve on a bed of crisp lettuce leaves. Finally garnish with sliced tomatoes and fresh chopped parsley.

Turkish stuffed peppers

(serves 4 people)

This is one of the nicest recipes for using left-over cooked lamb or beef and making it into something really special.

Long grain white rice, measured to the 8 fl oz level in a measuring jug
Boiling water measured to the 16 fl oz level
4 medium sized green or red peppers
¾ lb (approx) cooked lamb or beef cut up into very small pieces (350 g)
2 medium onions, peeled and chopped
2 cloves of garlic, finely chopped
1 × 14 oz tin Italian tomatoes (400 g)
4 teaspoons tomato purée
2 tablespoons currants
½ teaspoon ground cinnamon
½ teaspoon marjoram
2 dessertspoons pine nuts, if available (most health food shops stock them)
Olive oil
Salt and freshly milled black pepper

Pre-heat the oven to gas mark 5, 375°F (190°C)

Begin by melting some oil in a saucepan, then stir in the rice. When it is well-coated with oil, pour in the boiling water and add a sprinkling of salt. Put a lid on and simmer for approximately 15 minutes, or until all the liquid has been absorbed.

Meanwhile fry the onions and garlic in a little more oil for a couple of minutes, then add the meat together with the currants and pine nuts. Season well with salt and pepper, stir in the cinnamon, marjoram and two of the tomatoes plus a tablespoon of juice from the contents of the tin, then turn the heat very low and leave to simmer very gently.

Now prepare the peppers by slicing off the stalk ends and pulling out the core and the seeds. Run each one under cold water to make sure all the seeds are gone, then sit them upright in a small casserole (just so there's not too much room for them to keel over). When the rice is cooked, add it to the pan containing the meat and stir well to combine everything. Taste to check the seasoning at this point.

Now spoon the mixture into each of the peppers—pack it down well to get as much in as you can—put the rest of it all around the base of the peppers. Finally, put a teaspoon of tomato purée on top of each stuffed pepper and pour the rest of the tin of tomatoes all around the peppers.

Cover the casserole, and cook in the oven for 45–50 minutes or until the peppers are tender when tested with a skewer.

Risotto with chicken livers and mushrooms

(serves 2–3 people)

If you're using frozen chicken livers—the sort that come in 8 oz (225 g) cartons—do make sure they are thoroughly defrosted before you start.

3 oz butter (75 g)
2 medium onions, one thinly sliced, the other chopped
2 oz streaky bacon, chopped (50 g)
Italian rice, measured to the 8 fl oz level in a measuring jug
¼ pint dry white wine (150 ml)
1½ pints boiling chicken stock (875 ml)
½ lb chicken livers cut into lobes (225 g)

½ lb mushrooms, sliced (225 g)
A bayleaf
1 heaped tablespoon tomato purée
1 teaspoon dried basil
1 oz freshly-grated Parmesan cheese (25 g)
Salt and freshly-milled black pepper

The risotto and sauce are made in separate saucepans, but need to be cooked at the same time. For the sauce, put half the butter in a fairly large saucepan and sauté the sliced onion until soft and golden. Add the bacon and cook for a further 2 or 3 minutes.

Now melt the rest of the butter in a bigger saucepan and cook the chopped onion until softened. Stir in the rice and cook until slightly browned. Next add the wine and continue to cook, uncovered, over low heat until it has all but evaporated. Then add a generous half pint (275 ml) of the boiling chicken stock. Cover and cook over a gentle heat for approximately 20 minutes. Then add a ladleful of stock and when that is absorbed continue to add a ladleful at a time, as and when the rice requires it—it will probably take 1¼ pints (725 ml) in all.

While the rice is cooking you can go back to the sauce: turn the heat up high under the pan and add the chicken livers and, when they've turned a rich brown, stir in the mushrooms. Let them cook for 2 or 3 minutes before adding ¼ pint (150 ml) chicken stock, the bayleaf, tomato purée and basil. Season and cook gently for 10 minutes until the mixture is reduced to a good sauce consistency. Keep the sauce warm and, when the rice is ready, serve the risotto with the sauce spooned on top and sprinkled with freshly-grated Parmesan cheese.

Risotto alla Milanese

(serves 4 people as a main course)

This recipe is only suitable for Italian rice, which needs quite different treatment from long grain rice. A high proportion of liquid is used, the rice is cooked in an uncovered pan and a good deal of stirring is necessary — particularly towards the end of cooking. It's a relatively simple dish but absolutely beautiful if made properly. You can either serve it on its own as a

first course or it's very good served as an
accompaniment to *Ossobuco* (page 339).

½ teaspoon powdered saffron
4 tablespoons butter
1 medium-sized onion, chopped
2 tablespoons bone marrow (from an obliging butcher)
Italian rice, measured to the 12 fl oz level in a measuring jug
5 tablespoons dry white wine
Approximately 2 pints boiling chicken stock (1·25 litres)
4 tablespoons of, if possible, freshly-grated Parmesan cheese
Salt and freshly-milled black pepper

Begin by melting 2 tablespoons of butter in a heavy-based
saucepan, add the saffron and allow 1 minute for the heat to draw
out the flavour. Then add the chopped onion and bone marrow
and cook, over a low heat, for about 10 minutes until softened.

Stir in the rice and cook for a minute or two before adding the wine
and some salt. Stir gently once, then simmer over a low heat,
without a lid, until the liquid has been absorbed (about 10–15
minutes). Now put in a ladleful of the boiling stock and again let it
simmer until the stock has nearly all been absorbed but the rice is
still moist. Continue adding the boiling stock a ladleful at a time
until the rice is tender but still firm and creamy rather than
mushy. Stir as necessary to prevent the rice from sticking to the
bottom of the pan—particularly towards the end.

When the rice is cooked, remove the pan from the heat, stir in the
remaining butter and Parmesan cheese. Cover and leave to stand,
off the heat, for 5 minutes before serving. Season to taste then serve
with lots more freshly-grated Parmesan cheese on the table.

A risotto for spring

(serves 4–6 people)

This sounds almost like a musical
composition but is a good description, I
think, for this dish of brown rice, cheese
and lightly sautéed green vegetables.

Long grain brown rice, measured up to the 15 fl oz level in a measuring jug

1½ pints boiling water (850 ml)
1 small onion, chopped
3½ tablespoons olive oil
2 leeks, cleaned and chopped into ½ inch (1 cm) pieces
1 small cauliflower, divided up into thumbnail-sized florettes
1 lb broccoli (pick off and use the heads only) (450 g)
½ lb fresh spinach, washed, dried and shredded (225 g)
4 oz strong Cheddar cheese, grated (110 g)
2 tablespoons freshly-grated Parmesan cheese
1 tablespoon butter
Salt, cayenne and freshly-milled black pepper

For the garnish:

4 spring onions, very finely chopped, including the green parts

Begin by heating 1½ tablespoons of the olive oil in a medium-sized, thick-based saucepan and frying the onion for 5 minutes. Next, add the rice and stir it around so that the grains are well coated with oil. Now add the boiling water and some salt, stir once, then bring to simmering point. Cover and let the rice simmer very gently for 40 minutes or until the grains are tender.

About half-way through the cooking time, melt the 2 remaining tablespoons of oil with the butter in a very large frying pan (or divide between two medium-sized pans), add the cauliflower, broccoli, leeks and some seasoning. Then, over a medium heat, move the vegetables around until they have browned a little but still retain their crispness—say for about 8 minutes. Now add the spinach; it will appear somewhat bulky to begin with but will soon collapse. Cook, stirring occasionally, for about 5 minutes. Meanwhile turn the grill on to high.

When the rice is cooked put it into a shallow heatproof serving dish and fluff it. Add half the Cheddar cheese and half the Parmesan and stir them in. Add the vegetables and stir again. Then sprinkle the remaining Cheddar and Parmesan cheese on top, together with a pinch or two of cayenne.

Now place the dish under the heated grill and let the cheese topping melt and brown. Before serving, garnish with the chopped spring onions.

Buttery kedgeree

(serves 4 people)

This was a typical breakfast dish in the days when grand Victorian breakfast dishes were spread out on handsome Victorian sideboards. Nowadays it is a very good lunch or late supper dish.

1½ lb thick smoked haddock fillets (700 g)
3 oz butter (75 g)
1 onion, chopped
Long grain white rice measured up to the 8 fl oz level in a measuring jug
16 fl oz of boiling liquid (see recipe method)
¾ teaspoon hot curry powder (Madras)
3 hard-boiled eggs, chopped
3 heaped tablespoons fresh parsley, chopped
1 tablespoon lemon juice
Salt and freshly-milled black pepper

First place the haddock fillets in a saucepan and cover them with 1 pint (570 ml) cold water. Bring to the boil, put on a lid, and simmer gently for about 8 minutes. Then drain off the water into a measuring jug. Transfer the haddock to a dish, cover with foil and keep it warm.

Now, using the same saucepan, melt 2 oz (50 g) butter and soften the onion in it for 5 minutes. Next stir in the curry powder, cook for half a minute then stir in the measured rice and add 16 fl oz (450 ml) of the haddock cooking water. Stir once then, when it comes up to simmering point, cover with a tight-fitting lid and cook, very gently, for 15 minutes or until the rice grains are tender.

When the rice has been cooking for 10 minutes, remove the skins from the fish and flake it. Then, when the rice is ready, remove it from the heat and fork in the flaked fish, hard-boiled eggs, parsley and lemon juice and the remaining 1 oz (25 g) of butter.

Now cover the pan with a folded tea towel and replace it on very gentle heat for five minutes. Then tip the kedgeree quickly onto a hot serving dish, season to taste and serve.

Brown rice pudding with prunes and apricots

(serves 4–6 people)

This is a pudding for wholefood-minded people, deliciously different from the traditional rice pudding.

Brown rice, measured to the 10 fl oz level in a measuring jug
Milk, measured to the 20 fl oz level
4 tablespoons dark brown sugar
1 egg, beaten
½ teaspoon ground cinnamon
Quarter of a nutmeg, grated
4 oz dried apricots (110 g) and 6 oz prunes (175 g) both soaked overnight then drained and chopped
5 fl oz yoghurt (150 ml)

In a thick-based saucepan bring the milk to the boil and sprinkle in the rice. Stir, then cover and cook over a very low heat for about 50 minutes or until the rice is tender. Keep an eye on it or the milk may boil over and, towards the end of the cooking time, have a peep as you might need to add a drop more milk. Then take it off the heat and stir in 3 tablespoons of the sugar, the beaten egg, cinnamon and nutmeg.

Next, butter a 4 pint (2 litre) casserole, spread half the rice mixture in it and top this with half the fruit. Spread the rest of the rice on top and cover this with the remaining fruit. Cover the casserole with a lid and bake in a pre-heated oven for 30 minutes at gas mark 4, 350°F (180°C).

At the end of the cooking time, remove the pudding from the oven, spread the yoghurt over the top and sprinkle with the remaining tablespoon of sugar.

Note: this is just as delicious served cold, if you have any left over.

Other cereal grains

A couple of years ago I attended a lecture by Prof. Mellanby on the question 'Can Britain feed herself?'. I am happy to report that if Britain were to *decide* to feed herself—or had to under siege conditions—we could all live quite happily on a perfectly balanced diet. Of course we couldn't rely on as much meat as we used to, and the proposition assumed that we would have to increase our cereal production and consumption quite considerably.

That wouldn't be a bad thing in any event. Meat *is* becoming less affordable, and perhaps that's nature's way of enticing us away from excessive consumption of animal fat and towards an increased awareness of the nutritional advantages of natural cereals? But first, there is a distinction to be made. There are two kinds of cereal available: one whole natural cereals, the other refined cereals.

Although we eat far more of the latter—because millions of pounds of advertising has persuaded us to do so—we might do better to choose for ourselves. Examine the packets: among the details of free tea-towels and cut-out speed boats you will find that many cereals have been re-fortified, even 'enriched', with the vitamins lost in the refining process. What is rarely replaced is the fibre that was contained in the bran and germ. However there are breakfast cereals which are made from 100% wholewheat, and say so on the packet. My advice is to choose these: they contain the whole grain, fibre and all, and have no need of added vitamins.

Whole grain cereals
Packaged breakfast foods are by no means the only way to consume cereals. A whole variety of grains come to us (as rice does) in several guises. The uses of some may be unfamiliar; but if they are natural whole grains as opposed to refined ones, what they all have in common is real nutrition and flavour.

To be sure that the grains you buy are whole grains, it makes sense to go to a wholefood shop—because the grains sold in grocers and supermarkets are often refined.

Barley A great deal of our barley, of course, finds its way into beer, but the grain is also sold—most often as *pearl barley* which is the refined variety or as *pot barley*, which is the whole grain with only the inedible husk removed, and is found in healthfood shops. Both these are good additions to stews or soups (see the recipes for *Irish stew*, page 333, and for *Scots broth*, page 308). *Barley flakes* are the grains mechanically rolled into flakes, and an excellent use for these is in *Muesli* (see page 362).

Rye is most commonly milled into various grades of flour for bread-making—*coarsely-milled rye*, for instance, is used in the production of Pumpernickel bread: and *rye flour* (because of its quick fermentation) is often added to wheat flour to give bread a slightly 'sour' flavour. As with other grains, *flaked rye* can be bought in healthfood shops.

Wheat We've already examined the varieties of wheat flour in the section on Bread (Part One, page 44), but the grain itself—or parts of it—has many other applications. *Wholewheat grains* can be soaked for a few hours, then cooked in the same way as rice (but it takes longer): the result is chewier, and some people prefer to combine the wholewheat grains with some rice or beans. *Wholewheat flakes* are good in muesli (see page 362). *Cracked wheat* (which is simply the whole grain lightly crushed) is sometimes sprinkled on bread before baking or included, as in Granary loaves, in the dough itself. *Wheatgerm* is the embryo of the grain, and contains a very high proportion of vitamins, minerals and oils: it is sold separately and a few teaspoonfuls sprinkled on your yoghurt, porridge or fruit salad is a good way of upping your vitamin intake for the day! *Wheat bran* is the layer that lies just below the inedible outer husk of the wheat grain. If you're living on a diet that contains about five slices of wholewheat bread a day plus fresh fruit and other wholefoods, you'll probably be getting enough dietary fibre. On the other hand if you prefer white bread and other refined foods, it might be a good idea to incorporate some wheat bran into your diet. The best way to do this, I think, is to sprinkle it onto ordinary breakfast cereals and pour on some milk so that it slips down almost unnoticed. *Semolina* is also made from wheat grain: basically it's the starchy part of hard wheat in granular form, before it has been finely milled.

Oats Much used in biscuit-making—see the chapter beginning on page 279 for the different grades of *oatmeal* (milled oats) and varieties of *oat flakes*. In F. Marian MacNeill's charming book *The Scots Kitchen*, oats are referred to as 'the flower of the Scottish soil', so it's not surprising that some of the best recipes for using oats come from Scotland, and the pride of them all is *Porridge* (see recipe, page 363).

Buckwheat This is strictly speaking not a grain, but its use and preparation are much the same. *Buckwheat flour* is traditionally used for the Russian type of pancakes known as blinis, and for the Breton version known as galettes (see chapter on pancakes, beginning page 365). The *whole buckwheat* seeds can be bought roasted—in which case they're sometimes called *kasha*—or in their natural state. They have a delicious and distinctive grainy flavour, cook very much like rice, and combine beautifully with vegetables for a savoury dish like the one on page 364.

Home-made muesli

If you've not yet made its acquaintance, this is a mixture of whole cereal grains with the addition of fruit, nuts and other things ad lib. Its ancestor was a Swiss peasant dish, but it became world famous after it had been adapted as part of a health diet at the Bircher-Benner Clinic in Switzerland. Very soon the cornflake brigade cashed in and now any number of versions appear in the supermarkets. My quarrel with the branded mueslis is that they usually contain rather a lot of dried milk powder (which is not really something I want to eat in spoonfuls) plus the inevitable sugar, making most of them too sweet. If you have a wholefood shop within easy distance you can probably buy an unsweetened muesli base, or you can do what I do: buy the grains and other ingredients and make it at home.

½ lb wholewheat flakes (225 g)
½ lb rye flakes (225 g)
½ lb whole oat flakes (225 g)
½ lb barley flakes (225 g)
¾ lb roasted peanuts (350 g) (you can roast these yourself under a medium grill), chopped
1 lb sultanas (450 g)
½ lb raisins (225 g)

This is a basic mixture, but there are 101 variations—the nuts for instance could be roasted hazelnuts, brazils, walnuts or if you're feeling rich, slivered roast almonds with the skins left on. The fruit too can be varied: chopped dates, dried apricots or figs, or chopped dried apple rings. Personally I think the proportions of fruit here make the addition of sugar unnecessary, but if it isn't sweet enough for you, add some more dried fruit. When serving muesli you can sprinkle in some bran, which will slip down unnoticed among all the other good things. Wheatgerm too (see page 361) can be added and fresh fruits in season. Milk is always poured over and, if you're trying to cut down on fats, skimmed milk is fine.

Traditional oatmeal porridge

(serves 2 people)

Traditions surrounding porridge-making are legion: formerly a cast-iron pot was used, with fresh spring water brought to the boil, and a long wooden stick (called a spurtle) used to stir 'sunwise' with one hand, while the oats trickled into the water in a steady stream through the other. Sometimes the oats were added in batches, some at the beginning, some halfway through, and some at the end—the undercooked ones giving a contrast in texture and a nuttier flavour. Salt wasn't added till halfway through, in case it should toughen the grains before they cooked: today the Scots still like their porridge well salted.

The best porridge I ever ate was at Houston House near Edinburgh, where they tend to frown a bit on sugar, but provide a separate bowl of cream with every serving of porridge: the idea is to take a spoonful of hot porridge, lower it into the cream so it cools and absorbs some cream, then eat!

1 pint water (570 ml)
2½ oz medium oatmeal (60 g)
1 teaspoon salt
To serve: ¼ pint single cream (150 ml)

In a medium-sized saucepan, bring the water up to a fast boil, then sprinkle in the oatmeal slowly whisking it in with a balloon whisk. Carry on whisking until the mixture returns to the boil, then reduce the heat, cover the pan and let the porridge cook very gently for 10 minutes. After that add the salt, whisk it in, cover again and cook gently for a further 15 minutes or so.

As I explained above, the traditional way to eat porridge would be without sugar, and with an individual bowl of cream each. But if you have a sweet tooth, sprinkle dark brown sugar over the porridge, let it melt a little, then pour in the cream so that it mingles with the sugar and marbles the surface.

Buckwheat and vegetable pie

(serves 3–4 people)

Buckwheat has a distinctive flavour of its own, and baked in the oven with vegetables it makes an excellent vegetarian main course.

8 oz roasted buckwheat (225 g)
1 oz butter (25 g)
1 pint boiling water (570 ml)
1 tablespoon tomato purée
1 large onion, chopped
1 green or red pepper, de-seeded and chopped
8 oz mushrooms, sliced if large (225 g)
1 × 14 oz tin tomatoes (400 g)
1 clove of garlic, crushed
1 rounded teaspoon dried oregano
1½ oz grated cheese, any sort will do (40 g)
1 oz wholemeal breadcrumbs (25 g)
2 tablespoons oil
Cayenne pepper
Salt and freshly-milled black pepper

Pre-heat the oven to gas mark 5, 375°F (190°C).

First combine the boiling water with the tomato purée; next melt the butter in a saucepan. Add the buckwheat and stir until it is thoroughly coated with fat. Then pour in the liquid, bring up to simmering point, stir once and add some salt, then put the lid on and cook gently for about 10 minutes.

Meanwhile, heat 2 tablespoons of oil in a frying pan and cook the onion and pepper in it for 5 minutes to soften but not to colour them. Add the mushrooms and cook gently for a further 5 minutes. Then stir in the garlic and oregano, season with salt and pepper and add the contents of the tin of tomatoes. Stir well then leave to simmer gently without a lid so that the liquid reduces slightly.

Stir the cooked buckwheat into the vegetable mixture then transfer the contents of the pan to a lightly buttered 2½ pint (1·5 litre) pie dish. Scatter the grated cheese and breadcrumbs over the surface, and a sprinkling of cayenne if you like. Place the dish in the centre of the oven and bake for 20–30 minutes or until the topping is golden and bubbling.

Pasta and pancakes

Including recipes for:
Fresh tomato sauce
Ragù Bolognese
Spaghetti alla carbonara
Spaghetti with anchovies, mushrooms and olives
Lasagne al forno
Baked meat and macaroni pie
Macaroni with leeks and bacon
Wholewheat macaroni cheese
Basic pancakes
Crêpes Suzette
Pancake canelloni
Spinach-stuffed pancakes
Cheese soufflé pancakes
Apple and cinnamon crêpes

Pasta

If I were asked to choose between a meal in a multi-starred French restaurant or with an Italian family at home, without hesitation I'd choose the latter. Marcella Hazan, in one of my favourite Italian cookbooks, describes the experience beautifully. The whole country, she says, shuts down at midday for this two-hour event and 'there probably has been no influence, not even religion, so effective in creating a rich family life, in maintaining a civilised link between the generations, as this daily sharing of a common joy'.

She says so much more, and so could I, about the Italian way of eating. But let me just commend its simplicity: it is never lavish, vulgar or pretentious. The Italians are not a nation who rely heavily on freezers or canned foods, but manage on very little meat and plenty of seasonal vegetables and fruit. Butter is something of a luxury—in my experience served with bread only at breakfast —and in passing it's interesting to note that, despite their rather obese image, the Italians have one of the lowest incidence of heart disease in the world: so perhaps their use of olive oil in place of butter and their enthusiasm for lots of fresh fruit and salads shows that 'preventative' eating need not be as dull as is sometimes suggested.

However this part of the chapter is concerned with just one item that the Italians have made famous, namely pasta, which is one thing that I think should be a permanent resident in any larder or storecupboard. The marvellous thing about pasta is that, with a little imagination, this one basic ingredient can be made into a whole range of different dishes.

What is pasta?

When I was a child, just after the war, spaghetti was something that came out of a tin, in a bright orange sauce and was usually served on toast, sometimes with a poached egg on top! Later on it began to appear in the shops in its natural state, though in quite unmanageable packets, as I recall, at least a yard long. In those days it was dismissed, at any rate by the elderly, as 'foreign' but nowadays foreign holidays and a steady flow of cookbooks have helped to establish it on supermarket shelves, in quite a number of its infinite varieties.

Pasta is simply the Italian word for dough, and in particular a dough made from durum (or hard) wheat. When hard wheat is first ground it produces not flour, but semolina and this is used—with hard wheat flour and water—to produce pasta. The dough is then moulded or stamped into the appropriate shape by machine and (unless it is to be sold immediately as fresh pasta) it is then dried. Once it was dried in the back gardens of Naples by the Mediterranean breezes, but now technology has reproduced this wonder of nature.

Egg pasta Most commercial pastas are purely wheat-and-water but sometimes you come across egg pastas, in which eggs have been added to the basic dough (as they are in home-made pasta). Egg pasta is richer, more filling and quite delicious—and if the packet is printed in Italian it will be described as 'pasta all'uovo'.

Green pasta (pasta verde) is just pasta into which spinach has been worked at the dough-making stage. This is done, I suspect, more for the sake of colour than for flavour, but it does look most attractive in dishes like lasagne.

Wholewheat pasta It's hard to imagine that we, the British, actually export pasta to Italy, but we do! The Italians are now buying wholewheat pasta that's made here. I was a bit hesitant about it at first, but I was wrong to think that because of its pale brown colour it would taste very different to ordinary pasta. It doesn't and now I use it quite often.

Home-made pasta If you're within easy reach of London's Soho, or anywhere else where there is an Italian community, you might be lucky enough to buy home-made fresh pasta. It's certainly worth seeking out as it is nicer than the dried sort. Failing that, you could make it at home yourself, but be warned—it is very hard work kneading pasta and then you are faced with a lump of very resilient, elastic dough which needs to be rolled and stretched out to a transparent thinness! It can be difficult, too, to obtain the correct ingredients, (although a strong flour will do). If you want to get really serious about home-made pasta you could, of course, invest in a pasta machine which costs upwards of £30. It's a sort of mangle which can be adjusted for different pasta shapes, and it squeezes and presses the pasta out thinly, which does eliminate a lot of the hard work. However if, like me, you're not an absolute perfectionist, a good quality packaged pasta will probably suit you well enough.

Pasta shapes
There are literally hundreds of different pasta shapes, which may seem a bit daunting. But it needn't be: for one thing, there is no

definitive list—manufacturers can and do add further shapes from time to time. And in fact there are only five basic types:

(1) First there are the tiny decorative shapes that go into soups (pasta in brodo) and sometimes into puddings: they can be stars, flowers, letters of the alphabet, little animals . . . the list is endless.

(2) Then there are the sold spaghetti-type pastas, long and thin. Spaghetti itself is cylindrical and usually about 10 inches (25·5 cm) long; it has a thinner cousin, called spaghettini. In this group I would also include the long, noodle varieties—tagliatelle which is flat rather than cylindrical, enriched with eggs, and dried in bunches rather than lengths. It too has a thinner cousin, linguine.

(3) Next are what I'd call the macaroni group or tubular pastas. Some are cut short or curled slightly: some have pointed ends (penne), some are ribbed (rigatoni).

(4) The fancy shapes—bows, shells, twists, wheels, frills and the rest of them—are intriguing to look at but all taste the same in the end. Like the pastas in groups (2) and (3) above, these are usually served with a sauce.

(5) Finally there are the pastas which are stuffed or can be bought ready-stuffed. The very large sheet of lasagne, and big tubular cannelloni, are both meant to be stuffed and baked. Ready-stuffed pasta are usually only available at Italian shops—ravioli are little square packages with a stuffing inside: tortellini are similar but curled in shape.

This list is strictly a basic grouping of variations. My own larder collection consists of spaghetti, tagliatelle, a short-cut macaroni for soups, and a standard macaroni. I find I sometimes buy odd shapes but I can't see any particular advantage in them. On the contrary, the cooking time can be rather uncertain if the shape is thick—and beware of pasta 'shells' in which the boiling water can become trapped, only to escape at the table when it's too late!

Cooking pasta
First let's discuss what pasta *should* be like when cooked. The now-familiar Italian words 'al dente' appear frequently on packets and in many recipes to describe the approved texture of cooked pasta. Translated literally they mean 'to the teeth' which clearly suggests that pasta must have some bite to it.

If it's over-cooked all the guts will have gone out of it, and you'll only have a soggy, sticky mass. As an experienced pasta consumer I have found that, over the years, I have come to cook pasta in less and less time, and I now give ordinary supermarket spaghetti only 8 minutes boiling. In the end there's only one way for you to tell, and that's to bite a bit and see if it's to your liking. I find that macaroni, spaghetti and lasagne take from 8–10 minutes to cook, but if you're using a thick variety it might need a couple of minutes more. These suggested timings are for dried (packet) pasta. Fresh or home-made pasta is quicker to cook.

How much pasta?
Pasta isn't quite as fattening as some people imagine. Of course if it is baked with a rich ragù and covered in a melted cheese sauce, then it can be extremely high in calories; but served with a fresh tomato sauce (or with any sauce which only calls for 2 tablespoons of olive oil for four people) it can be much lower in calories than many meat dishes.

If you are serving a layered pasta dish or pasta that is stuffed and baked, you'll only need quite a small quantity of pasta. If you are serving spaghetti or any other type of pasta just with a sauce, then you'll need more, and I recommend 8–10 oz (225–275 g) of pasta—dry weight—between two people for a main course, or 4–6 oz (110–175 g) as a starter. Mind you, it all depends on your appetites: I have to confess we often get through 12 oz (350 g) between two in our house when we're really hungry!

Notes on ingredients
One of the best reasons for eating pasta is that, in 15 minutes from start to finish, you can provide yourself with a complete meal— and all from a collection of ingredients that are common to most kitchen cupboards. The following are what I'd consider essential items to keep handy.

Olive oil For pasta I *do* think this is essential. Whereas for other types of cooking I might substitute groundnut oil, with pasta olive oil seems a must and well worth the slight extra expense. If I can I buy pure olive oil in 5-litre drums (from Italian shops), which works out very much cheaper than buying several small bottles. Alternatively, the 5-litre containers of blended olive oil sold by a well-known chain of chemists is also very good value.

Basil Tomatoes are one of the principal ingredients of pasta dishes in Italy, and basil has a strong affinity with tomatoes. Even in its dried form it is very useful for cooked tomato (and other) sauces, and it's the one herb I always make sure to have in stock.

Parmesan cheese Grated and sprinkled over soups and pastas, this cheese is used almost like seasoning in Italy. It is a hard cheese, said to need 2–3 years ageing to reach maturity (and some of the more expensive ones have had 5 or more years). The preservative used in the packaged, ready-grated Parmesan gives the cheese an alien taste, I think, and I go out of my way to buy whole pieces of the cheese in delicatessens or Italian shops. It keeps beautifully in a sealed polythene bag in the lowest part of the refrigerator, and this way you can grate it as and when you need it.

Tomatoes So far as tinned tomatoes are concerned, I always buy Italian. They really are the best and very useful indeed for all sorts of cooking purposes when fresh tomatoes are out of season. Tomato purée (or tomato paste as it is sometimes called) is very concentrated in flavour. Useful though it would be to make it oneself when there is a glut of tomatoes in the garden, so far as I am aware it is impossible to make it at home.

How to boil pasta

The number one rule is always to have plenty of boiling water. If too little water is used, the pasta clogs together in a mass and some of it may not cook at all. So allow 4 pints (2¼ litres) of water for each 8 oz (225 g) of pasta.

Always add some salt to the water—about 2 teaspoons for 4 pints (2¼ litres) plus a few drops of olive oil, which will help to keep the strands separate. Have the water boiling rapidly and keep the heat high while you add the pasta (if it's spaghetti, you'll need to push it down gradually into the pan and the water will soften it as it goes down). The water should, if the heat is high enough, come to the boil again very quickly, then give the pasta one really good stir, turn the heat down and let it simmer gently for the required time. *Don't* put a lid on—there's no need to and, if you do, you risk having the water boil over.

When the pasta is cooked to your liking, pour it into a colander sitting in the sink and allow most of the water to drain off. If the sauce is to be served separately, then place the colander over the saucepan in which you cooked the pasta (the heat of the pan will help to keep the pasta hot while you serve) and dish up directly in the kitchen. Serve each helping onto a plate that has been nicely warmed—large soup plates would be ideal because that little bit of depth helps to conserve the heat. Speed is now the important factor (presto pronto! as the Italians say), because there is nothing worse than eating pasta that is the wrong side of tepid.

To serve spaghetti Use two instruments (a large spoon and a fork) to extract a quantity of spaghetti, lifting it as high as possible above the colander and it will separate from the rest with perfect ease.

To eat spaghetti The big mistake here is trying to wind too much onto the fork at once. Select just two or three strands with your fork and coax them over to the rim of the plate. Then, holding the fork at a right angle to the plate, simply wind the fork round and round, so that those few strands extricate themselves from the rest and are twisted round the fork in a little bite-sized bundle. Easier said than done, you're thinking? But remember two things—practice makes perfect and the Italians themselves always wear little napkins tucked neatly under their chins!

Fresh tomato sauce
(serves 2 people)

This sauce is good to serve with almost any kind of pasta—and it's also useful for using up those slightly over-ripe tomatoes at the end of the season.

1 lb ripe tomatoes, skinned and chopped (450 g)
1 small onion, finely chopped
1 clove of garlic, crushed
1 teaspoon tomato purée
1 dessertspoon fresh chopped basil (or ½ dessertspoon dried)
Olive oil
Salt and freshly-milled black pepper

To peel the tomatoes pour some boiling water over them, let them stand for a minute or two, then you'll find the skins slip off very easily. Chop up the flesh quite small.

Heat 1 tablespoon of olive oil in a saucepan, and soften the onion and garlic in it for 5 minutes without letting them brown, then add the tomatoes, tomato purée, basil and a seasoning of salt and pepper. Give everything a good stir, then cover the pan and simmer gently for 15 minutes. After that uncover the pan and simmer for a further 10–15 minutes for the sauce to reduce slightly. It can either be served as it is, or liquidised a little first.

Ragù Bolognese

This is really the all-purpose Italian pasta sauce: it can form the basis of *Lasagne* or *Baked meat and macaroni pie* (see recipes), or served with spaghetti it is enough for 4 people.

6 oz lean minced beef (175 g)
3 oz chicken livers, chopped small (75 g)
2 rashers unsmoked streaky bacon, finely chopped
1 teaspoon dried basil
1 small onion, very finely chopped
1 fat clove of garlic, crushed
1 × 8 oz tin Italian tomatoes (225 g)
4 tablespoons red wine
2 heaped tablespoons tomato purée
1½ tablespoons olive oil
Salt and freshly-milled black pepper

Heat the oil in a thick-based saucepan, then gently soften the onion, bacon and garlic in it for 5 minutes. Now turn the heat up, add the chicken livers and minced beef, and brown them, keeping the ingredients on the move with a wooden spoon. When the meat has browned, pour in the contents of the tin of tomatoes, plus the tomato purée, wine, basil and some seasoning. Put a lid on and simmer gently for 20 minutes, then take the lid off and continue to simmer gently for a further 20–25 minutes to get a nice thick concentrated sauce.

Spaghetti alla carbonara

(serves 2 people)

This doesn't have to be spaghetti—you can use tagliatelle or macaroni. It's a very simple dish of pasta with a bacon and egg sauce which I must admit tastes far nicer than it sounds.

½ lb spaghetti (225 g)
4 oz streaky bacon, de-rinded and chopped (110 g)

2 large eggs
1½ tablespoons olive oil
1 tablespoon Parmesan cheese, grated
Salt and freshly-milled black pepper
Extra Parmesan cheese for serving

To cook the pasta, place it in a very large saucepan of boiling salted water to which ½ tablespoon of olive oil has been added to prevent the spaghetti sticking together. It will need 8–10 minutes from the time it comes to the boil. Meantime, heat 1 tablespoon of olive oil in a small saucepan and fry the chopped bacon till the fat starts to run.

While all this is happening, whisk the eggs in a bowl, adding some freshly-milled black pepper and a tablespoon of grated Parmesan cheese.

As soon as the pasta is cooked, drain it in a colander then return it to the hot saucepan—away from the heat though. Now, quickly and deftly, stir in the beaten eggs and the bacon (plus the oil it was cooked in) and keep stirring to coat the pasta with liquid egg, which will soon cook from the heat of the saucepan and turn slightly granular. Serve on really hot plates with lots of Parmesan cheese to sprinkle over.

Note: if you would like to vary the above recipe slightly, you could add a chopped onion or a crushed clove of garlic to cook with the bacon. Another nice addition is to beat 2 tablespoons of double cream into the eggs, which gives a lovely cream finish to the sauce.

Spaghetti with anchovies, mushrooms and olives

(serves 2 people)

If you like lots of 'gutsy' flavour in food, you'll like this recipe which is absolutely delicious.

½ lb spaghetti (225 g)
3 tablespoons plus 1 teaspoon olive oil
8 oz fresh mushrooms, thinly sliced (225 g)
2 onions, thinly sliced
2 cloves of garlic, crushed
5 anchovy fillets, snipped in half
3 rashers lean bacon, de-rinded and roughly chopped
6 Spanish stuffed olives, sliced

2 tablespoons chopped parsley
2 tablespoons Parmesan cheese
Salt and freshly-milled black pepper

In a heavy-based frying-pan heat the 3 tablespoons of oil then gently cook the mushrooms, onion, and bacon for about 10 minutes, stirring them around occasionally. Then add the garlic, anchovy fillets, parsley and olives and let them heat through. Season to taste.

In the meantime, cook the spaghetti for 8–10 minutes in boiling salted water to which 1 teaspoon of oil has been added. When cooked, drain in a colander, pile it onto a warmed serving dish, pour the savoury mixture on top and sprinkle on the Parmesan cheese.

Lasagne al forno
(serves 6 people)

For me, this is the supreme pasta dish—wafer-thin leaves of green pasta, layered together with a filling of thick ragù bolognese and surrounded by a nutmeg-flavoured cream sauce, hot and bubbling. It isn't something you can dash off in a hurry but it's a superb dinner-party dish, and once made it's very easy just to pop in the oven and serve without any last-minute fuss.

1 quantity of ragù Bolognese (see page 372)
½ lb lasagne verdi (green spinach lasagne) (225 g)
Freshly-grated Parmesan, to finish

For the cream sauce:
3 oz butter (75 g)
2 oz plain flour (50 g)
1½ pints milk (850 ml)
¼ pint single cream (150 ml)
Salt and freshly-milled black pepper
Freshly-grated nutmeg

A roasting tin, measuring about 7 × 9½ inches (18 × 24 cm), well-buttered.

First make up the cream sauce by placing the milk, butter and flour in a thick-based saucepan. Put it over a gentle heat and whisk continuously with a balloon whisk until the sauce comes to simmering point and thickens. Now, with the heat as low as possible, continue to cook the sauce for 10 minutes.

To cook the lasagne ($\frac{1}{2}$ lb will be about 16 sheets, each measuring 7 × 3 inches or 18 by 7·5 cm), have ready a large saucepan of salted, boiling water to which a little oil has been added. Drop in 8 sheets, one at a time. If it is fresh pasta cook them for 3 minutes or until they float to the top: if they're dried cook them for about 8 minutes—but make sure you don't over-cook, or they will be soggy. When cooked transfer them immediately, using a fish slice, to a bowl of cold water (which will prevent them sticking together). Repeat this process with the remaining sheets.

Next sieve the white sauce into a bowl, beat in the cream, season with salt and pepper and grate in about a quarter of a whole nutmeg. Now spread about a quarter of the ragù over the base of the prepared roasting tin. Cover this with approximately a quarter of the sauce, then arrange a single layer of the drained and dried lasagne over the top. Repeat this process, finishing off with a final layer of cream sauce. Cover the top with a good sprinkling of grated Parmesan cheese—and the lasagne is ready for the oven. All this preparation can be done well in advance. When required, bake in a pre-heated oven, gas mark 4, 350°F (180°C) for 30–35 minutes.

Baked meat and macaroni pie

(serves 4 people)

The large, ribbed type of macaroni, sometimes called rigatoni, or the un-ribbed penne are best for this dish. But ordinary macaroni will do.

1 quantity of ragù Bolognese (see page 372)
$\frac{3}{4}$ lb macaroni (350 g)
Olive oil
1 clove of garlic, crushed
2 oz grated Cheddar cheese (50 g)

For the sauce:
$1\frac{1}{2}$ oz butter (40 g)
1 oz plain flour (25 g)

¾ pt cold milk (425 ml)
Nutmeg
Salt and freshly-milled black pepper

Pre-heat the oven to gas mark 4,
350°F (180°C)

First make up the white sauce by placing the butter, flour and
milk together in a pan over a medium heat and whisking until the
sauce starts to bubble and thicken. Stir with a wooden spoon to get
right into the corners of the pan, then whisk again thoroughly.
Turn the heat down as low as you can and cook the sauce gently
for 6 minutes, then grate in a quarter of a whole nutmeg.

Meanwhile cook the macaroni in plenty of boiling salted water
(with a few drops of oil added) for 8–10 minutes—make sure you
don't over-cook it. When cooked, drain it well in a colander, then
in the dry saucepan heat one tablespoon of oil, add the crushed
garlic, return the macaroni to the pan and toss it around well.

Next butter a baking dish or casserole, add the macaroni to it, then
pour in first the ragù Bolognese followed by the white sauce. Stir
everything thoroughly so the macaroni gets properly coated with
both sauces. Finally sprinkle the grated Cheddar cheese over the
top, then bake in the oven for 30–40 minutes.

Macaroni with leeks and bacon

(serves 4 people)

Again, I think this is nicest made with
the larger type of pasta called penne
but supermarket macaroni is almost as
good.

¾ lb macaroni (350 g)
3 small leeks, cleaned and chopped
6 oz streaky bacon, de-rinded and chopped (175 g)
2 oz butter (50 g)
Olive oil

For the sauce:
2 oz butter (50 g)
1½ oz plain flour (40 g)
1 pint milk (570 ml)
6 oz Cheddar cheese, grated (175 g)

3 fl oz double cream (75 ml)
Salt, freshly-milled pepper and freshly-grated nutmeg

For the topping:
2 tablespoons Parmesan cheese
1 tablespoon breadcrumbs
2 pinches cayenne pepper

A 2½ pint (1·5 litre) pie-dish, well buttered.

Start by bringing a large saucepan of water to simmering point, add some salt and a few drops of olive oil, then bring the pasta back to the boil and cook for 10 minutes exactly. Then turn it into a colander and, to prevent it cooking any further, rinse it under the cold tap.

Whilst the pasta's cooking, melt 2 oz butter (50 g) in a pan and soften the leeks and bacon over a gentle heat and, in another pan, make the white sauce with the butter, flour and milk and leave it to simmer very gently.

Now turn the pasta, leeks and bacon into the prepared pie dish and mix them well together. Next stir the grated cheese into the sauce, season to taste with salt, pepper and nutmeg and, finally, add the cream. Then pour the sauce over the ingredients in the pie dish, sprinkle the top with the Parmesan, breadcrumbs and cayenne pepper.

This is a dish which can be prepared well beforehand then, when it's needed, put into an oven pre-heated to gas mark 4, 350°F (180°C) for 30–40 minutes till the top is nicely browned and the sauce bubbling.

Wholewheat macaroni cheese

(serves 2 people)

This is a basic macaroni cheese with a few other goodies added for extra texture and flavour.

4 oz wholewheat macaroni (or any macaroni will do) (110 g)
2 pints water (1·25 litres)
2 oz butter (50 g)
1½ oz plain flour (40 g)

1 teaspoon dried mustard
¾ pint milk (425 ml)
6 oz Cheddar cheese, grated (175 g)
4 rashers streaky bacon, de-rinded and chopped
2 oz mushrooms, sliced (50 g)
1 medium onion, chopped
A little extra butter
Salt, freshly-milled black pepper and freshly-grated nutmeg
2 tomatoes, cut into small pieces

A 2 pint (1·25 litre) baking dish, buttered

In a large saucepan put 2 pints (1·25 litres) of water and 1 teaspoon salt, bring to the boil, add the macaroni and boil, uncovered, for 8–10 minutes. Meanwhile melt 2 oz (50 g) of butter in another saucepan then blend in the flour and mustard, add the milk a little at a time to make a white sauce and cook for about 6 minutes. Then stir in half of the grated Cheddar cheese and let it melt gently into the sauce, adding a seasoning of salt and pepper and a grating of nutmeg.

Now melt a little butter in a small frying-pan and gently fry the onion, bacon and mushrooms together for about 6 minutes or until soft. Next drain the macaroni in a colander, combine it with the sauce and the onion, bacon and mushroom mixture and turn it all into the prepared baking dish. Sprinkle the remainder of the cheese on top together with the pieces of tomato. Finally, place the dish under a pre-heated hot grill until golden brown and bubbling.

Note: this is a dish which can be made well in advance as it can be re-heated in an oven pre-heated to gas mark 6, 400°F (200°C) in about 15–20 minutes.

Pancakes
Pancakes turn up all over the world in various forms. Here in England we have our annual ritual of tossing them out of frying-pans for one reason or another. In Russia they turn up as blinis, made with yeast and served topped with soured cream and caviare. The Jews have blinzes, the nicest of which are those stuffed with cream cheese and cinnamon, folded into parcels, then

crisply fried. The Chinese make theirs into little parcels too, crunchy rolls stuffed with vegetables. In Brittany almost every other eating-place is a crêperie, or pancake-shop, where their galettes and crêpes can accommodate an apparently limitless selection of ingredients, both sweet and savoury.

To make a pancake is not difficult, but to make a good *thin* pancake takes a bit of practice. A beginner using the recipe below will probably end up with 12 pancakes, but in no time at all they'll be able to get 14 or even 16 out of the same mixture.

Choosing the right pan

To make perfect pancakes, you need a good heavy frying pan not more than 7 inches (18 cm) in diameter—that's the inside base measurement. A larger pan would make the batter difficult to spread out and you'd end up with pancakes with ragged edges. The pan needs to be hot and lightly greased. The idea is simply to lubricate the pan enough to prevent the pancake from sticking. Too much fat will make the pancake fry—which is all wrong. I think that using butter is best—and remember you will need to re-grease and re-heat the pan between each pancake.

Keeping pancakes hot and re-heating them

Pancakes are best eaten as soon as cooked but they can be made well ahead, laid flat, wrapped and refrigerated then re-heated next day. Re-heat them by stacking them onto a warm plate, cover the stack with foil and set the plate in a warm oven. Alternatively (and this is the usual way to keep freshly-cooked pancakes warm while you make the rest of the batch) set the foil-covered plate on top of a pan of simmering water.

Basic pancakes

(makes 12–14)

This basic batter is one I have arrived at after many experiments: I think it's light, it does *not* need to stand, and (dare I say it?) it is pretty foolproof.

4 oz plain flour (110 g)
A pinch of salt
2 large eggs
7 fl oz milk (200 ml) mixed together with 3 fl oz water (75 ml)
2 tablespoons melted butter
A little extra butter for cooking the pancakes

First sieve the flour and salt into a large mixing bowl, holding the sieve up high to give the flour an airing. Then make a well in the centre of the flour and break the two eggs into it. Now start to whisk the eggs (with an electric or any sort of whisk, or even a fork), beginning to incorporate bits of flour from around the edges as you do so. Then start to add small quantities of the milk-and-water mixture gradually—and ignore any lumps because they'll eventually disappear as the whisk gets to them. When all the milk-and-water has been added, slide a rubber spatula around the edge of the bowl to bring any elusive bits of flour into the centre of things. Then whisk once more till the batter is smooth and the consistency of thin cream.

When you're ready to cook the pancakes, add the 2 tablespoons of melted butter to the batter and stir it in. Then melt about a teaspoon of butter in the pan then swirl it all round to get the whole of the pan thoroughly lubricated. Now tip the excess butter onto a saucer (remember that the pan needs to be coated with butter but the pancakes should not be cooked in fat). Next get the pan really hot, then turn the heat down to medium, and to start with do a test pancake to determine whether or not you're using the correct amount of batter. I find 2 tablespoons about right.

As soon as the batter hits the hot pan, tip it around from side to side to get the base evenly coated with batter. It should take only half a minute or so to cook: you can lift the edge with a palette knife to see if it's tinged gold as it should be. If the pancake is thin enough there is no need to turn it over—it will be cooked through (and when it's rolled up with sugar and lemon, or a stuffing, the paler coloured inside will not be visible). Just slide each pancake, when it is cooked, out of the pan onto a warm plate. Cover it with foil and put the plate over a pan of simmering water to keep the pancake warm while you cook the next.

Lemon pancakes
Sprinkle each pancake with freshly squeezed lemon juice and caster sugar, fold in half, then in half again to form triangles. Serve sprinkled with a little more juice and extra sections of lemon.

Strawberry jam pancakes
Have some warmed strawberry jam ready, put a dessertspoonful in the centre of each pancake, then roll it up, folding the ends inwards like a parcel. Serve with pouring cream.

Honey or syrup pancakes
Warm some maple syrup or runny honey. Brush each pancake with it, then fold into triangles (as *Lemon pancakes*), and have more syrup or honey in a jug on the table.

Buckwheat pancakes
Buckwheat flour is available from healthfood shops, and is used to make several varieties of pancake, most famous of them the Breton crêpes. I think the best results of all are obtained by using half buckwheat flour and half plain (as all buckwheat tends to give them a slightly rubbery texture).

Crêpes Suzette
(serves 4–6 people)

In restaurants, these tend to be produced like a cabaret act, which put me off them for a time. However, I was asked for a recipe, so I made some and discovered how delicious they are.

For the crêpes:

Make up the basic batter (as given on page 379), adding to it the grated zest of 1 medium-sized orange and 1 tablespoon of caster sugar.

For the sauce:

The juice of 3–4 medium-sized oranges —you need 5 fl oz (150 ml) altogether

The grated rind of 1 medium-sized orange

The grated rind and juice of 1 small lemon

1 tablespoon caster sugar

3 tablespoons Grand Marnier, Cointreau or brandy

2 oz unsalted butter (50 g)

Make the pancakes (crêpes) stacking them as described on page 379. Ideally, they should be thinner than those in the basic recipe, so use only $1\frac{3}{4}$ tablespoons of batter for each crêpe. This should give you at least 16.

When you have cooked and stacked the crêpes, mix together all the sauce ingredients (except the butter) in a bowl, and warm the plates on which the crêpes are to be served. Take a large frying pan—preferably 10 inch (25·5 cm)—and melt the butter in it, add the sauce ingredients and allow them to heat very gently.

Place the first crêpe in the pan, give it time to warm through, then fold it in half and half again, to make a triangle shape. Slide it to the very edge of the pan. Tilt the pan slightly so that the sauce runs back into the centre, then add the next crêpe, and continue in this way until they are all re-heated, folded and soaked with the sauce.

If you want to be dramatic, you might at this point, heat a tablespoon by holding it over a gas flame or resting it on the edge of a hotplate. Then, away from the heat, pour a little liqueur or brandy into the spoon, return it to the heat to warm the spirit, then set light to it. Carry the tablespoon of flames to the table along with the pan, and pour the flames over the crêpes before serving.

Pancake canelloni

(serves 4 people)

This is one of my own favourites. In Italy they make large round tubular pasta called canelloni, which can be stuffed with a filling or they roll up sheets of pasta round a filling. I've adapted this to suit pancakes, which are then baked in a creamy sauce and topped with cheese. Lovely!

1 quantity of basic pancakes (see page 379) (approximately 12)

1 quantity of ragù Bolognese (see page 372)

For the sauce:
1½ oz butter (40 g)
1 oz plain flour (25 g)
¾ pint cold milk (425 ml)
Freshly-grated nutmeg
Salt and freshly-milled pepper

For the topping:
2 heaped tablespoons Parmesan cheese
A few drops olive oil

Pre-heat the oven to gas mark 6, 400°F (200°C)

A shallow gratin dish or baking tin, well-buttered.

To make the sauce place the cold milk, flour and butter together in a saucepan and whisk over a medium heat until the sauce begins to bubble and thicken. Then reduce the heat as low as possible and allow the sauce to cook gently for 6 minutes. Season with salt and freshly-milled pepper and a good grating of whole nutmeg.

Now spread the pancakes out, place an equal quantity of ragù Bolognese on each one, roll them up tightly and fold in the ends. Then tuck them side by side into the prepared gratin dish, pour the sauce over, sprinkle with the Parmesan cheese and drizzle about one teaspoonful of olive oil over the surface. Bake on a high shelf for 30 minutes.

Spinach stuffed pancakes with cheese sauce

(serves 4 people)

In the summer months, instead of using frozen spinach these can be made with 2 lb (900 g) of fresh spinach cooked with butter and salt (no water), in its own steam in a lidded saucepan, for about 5–7 minutes.

1 quantity of pancake batter (page 379), made with half wholewheat flour and half plain flour

2 × 8 oz packets frozen spinach (2 × 225 g)

2 oz butter (50 g)

⅛ pint double cream (about 75 ml)

1½ oz strong Cheddar cheese, grated (40 g)

1 oz Parmesan cheese, grated (25 g)

For the sauce:

2 oz butter (50 g)

1½ oz plain flour (40 g)

¾ pint milk (425 ml)

⅛ pint double cream (about 75 ml)

1½ oz strong Cheddar cheese, grated (40 g)

Salt, freshly-milled black pepper and freshly-grated nutmeg

Pre-heat the oven to gas mark 6, 400°F (200°C)

A shallow baking dish or tin, well-buttered.

Allow the spinach to defrost in a colander placed over a plate, so that the excess liquid drains out of it.

Make up 12 pancakes according to the basic recipe and stack them on a plate (there's no need to keep them warm).

Then make up an all-in-one cheese sauce: place the butter, flour and milk in a saucepan and whisk over a medium heat till thickened. Stir in the cheese, the cream, and season with salt, pepper and nutmeg.

Next, press all the excess liquid out of the spinach, melt 2 oz butter (50 g) in a saucepan, stir in the spinach followed by the cream. Continue to stir, preferably with a wooden fork, to break up the spinach. Cook gently until the spinach has absorbed the cream and is a nice soft consistency. Now taste it and season with salt, pepper and a little grated nutmeg.

Next, place about a tablespoonful of the spinach mixture on each pancake and roll each up, folding in the ends. Now pack them side by side in the baking dish or tin. Then pour over the prepared sauce, sprinkle with the Cheddar and Parmesan cheeses and bake on a high shelf for 25 minutes or until it's browned and bubbling.

Note: this dish can be prepared well in advance and just popped into the oven to re-heat 30 minutes before you need it.

Cheese soufflé pancakes

(serves 4 people)

I first ate these in Italy where they were called *Crespollini Amalfitan* and this version is, I think, exactly the same.

12 thin pancakes (made as on page 379)
2 oz butter (50 g)
2 oz plain flour, sifted (50 g)
4 tablespoons milk (warmed and infused with a bayleaf, a slice of onion and a few peppercorns for 30 minutes)
2 oz strong Cheddar cheese, grated (50 g)
½ teaspoon mustard powder
2 pinches cayenne pepper
3 large eggs, separated
1½ tablespoons grated Parmesan cheese
Extra butter
Salt and freshly-milled black pepper

Pre-heat the oven to gas mark 6,
400°F (200°C)

A shallow baking-dish or tin, buttered.

First melt the butter in a saucepan, add the flour and mix to a
smooth paste. Then blend in, a little at a time, the flavoured and
strained milk and cook over very gentle heat for 5 minutes. Next
stir in the grated Cheddar cheese, the mustard powder, cayenne
pepper and add salt and freshly-milled pepper to taste.

Now turn the mixture into a bowl, beat the egg yolks, and very
carefully incorporate them with the mixture. In another bowl
whisk the egg whites to the soft peak stage, stir 1 tablespoonful into
the cheese sauce then gently fold in the rest, using a metal spoon.

Now spoon a generous portion of the mixture onto one half of each
pancake and fold the other half over like a Cornish pasty. Place
them side by side in the buttered baking dish, sprinkle with
Parmesan cheese, put a few dabs of butter on top, and bake in the
centre of the oven for approximately 10–15 minutes.

Apple and cinnamon crêpes

(serves 2–3 people)

These are the French type of pancakes,
served flat and made with buckwheat
flour, which is available from wholefood
shops; if you can't get any, use
wholewheat flour instead.

2 oz plain flour, sifted (50 g)
1 oz buckwheat flour (25 g)
1 large egg
4 fl oz milk (110 ml) mixed with 2 fl oz water (55 ml)
¼ teaspoon vanilla essence
¼ teaspoon ground cinnamon
2 small Cox's apples, peeled and cored
3 tablespoons dry cider
Butter
Caster sugar
Chilled pouring cream

Begin by mixing the flours together in a bowl, then make a hollow
in the centre and break the egg into it and whisk it into the flour
together with the milk and water mixture, added a little at a time.

Beat until you have a perfectly smooth batter then add the cinnamon and vanilla essence. Next grate the peeled and cored apples straight into the batter.

At this stage put some plates in the oven to warm and also put the cider in a small saucepan to heat.

Now melt a generous piece of butter in a 7 or 8 inch (18 or 20 cm) frying pan and, when hot, rotate the pan so that the sides as well as the base are well-coated with the butter and pour off any excess into the batter.

Now drop 2 tablespoons of batter into the hot buttery frying-pan and shake and ease the mixture to spread all over the pan base—using a palette knife if necessary.

Cook until the crêpe becomes crisp at the edges and is a lovely golden colour underneath then, using a fish slice, knife or spatula, toss or turn the crêpe over and cook the other side until crisp and golden too. Serve the crêpes flat on warmed plates, sprinkled with a little of the hot cider, some caster sugar and some chilled pouring cream.

Note: this quantity of batter should make 7 crêpes. If you want to keep them warm between cooking and serving, lay them flat on top of each other between two warmed plates either in a warm oven or on top of a saucepan of simmering water.

Poultry

Including recipes for:
Traditional roast chicken
Creamed chicken with avocado
Coq au vin
Chicken in the pot
Fried mustard-and-
  herb-coated chicken
Chicken with lemon sauce
Chicken in barbecue sauce
Chicken with whole spices
Cold chicken pie
Chicken with grape stuffing

Roast duck with cherry sauce
Bitter orange sauce
Turkey giblet stock
Traditional roast turkey
Pork, sage and onion stuffing
Chestnut and apple stuffing
Roast stuffed goose with
  prune and apple sauce

Chicken

Once upon a time chicken was a luxury, an expensive family treat
for a special occasion. Now we have moved to the other extreme:
chickens are available absolutely everywhere. They are threaded
onto rotisseries in shop windows in every high street, there are
chains of take-away chicken shops, freezer centres are full of them.
Any part or portion of a chicken can be bought separately. It is a
credit to our farmers that they have put chicken within the reach of
everyone at what, in these days, is a very reasonable price.

At the same time a question remains, one which in our passion
for progress I hope we won't overlook. The question of flavour—a
word which I fear is too rarely mentioned in our modern chicken
production industry. Loss of flavour is the price we seem to have
paid for our abundance of chickens. So what's happened, and
where has the flavour gone? Let's consider our chickens' progress
to the table from scratch, as it were.

Rearing To produce today's enormous quantity of chicken, speed is
the one thing that's necessary. And what farmers have done is to
speed up growth and development so that the ubiquitous broiler of
$1\frac{1}{2}$–3 lb (700 g–1·35 kg) in weight is ready for cooking in eight
weeks or so. Such a chicken is already at a disadvantage, as lack of
maturity also means lack of flavour. To speed up growth
sufficiently, first-class protein of animal and vegetable origin has
to be used for part of the feeding. In some cases where this type of
feed is not correctly controlled it is sometimes possible for the
chicken's flesh to be impregnated with a foreign flavour! (I should
also add that a code of practice for the poultry industry has been
established since 1969 and, although there may be exceptions—as
in any industry—it is generally followed. And one popular
misconception that needs to be cleared up is the belief that
chickens produced for the table are reared in battery cages.
They're not, they are actually reared in deep litter (soft shavings)
in well-ventilated houses and should—according to the
code—have plenty of room to move about.)

Production When a chicken is killed in a factory it is immediately
eviscerated and very quickly moves on to the next stage, the
cooling. Now the fastest cooling process is by water, which is fine
for quick turnover but, from the point of view of the consumer,
means that the cooling chickens can—and do—absorb quite a bit
of water. Up to 7·4 per cent of its weight is the permitted level, but
in some chickens it is even more. In some instances the birds are

Right: Roman gnocchi, page 471; Spaghetti alla carbonara, page 372.

injected with a chemical called polyphosphate, which encourages water absorption. Producers claim this makes the flesh moist: I would claim it makes it watery. (You do have a choice here—polyphosphate-injected chickens have to be labelled as such). Our water-logged chickens then move along in sub-zero temperatures to be deep-frozen (water and all).

What's wrong with freezing? Not a lot, provided (a) the chicken has not absorbed nearly 10% of its weight in water, (b) the process of rigor mortis has been completed, and (c) some maturation has been allowed to take place before freezing so that flavour has a chance to develop (as it would naturally if a bird is hung). The trouble with the freezing of most chickens is that none of the above happens and—quite apart from flavour—if a bird is frozen within 6 or 8 hours of killing and rigor mortis is not complete, the flesh becomes tough and chewy. Equally, when the birds are frozen the process must be done quickly or else large ice crystals can form which penetrate the flesh and cause the texture to be stringy.

Alternative chicken
Free-range is one alternative to frozen chicken, but it's only fair to point out here that the free farmyard type of chicken is not necessarily always better: hens scratch about and can eat all sorts of undesirable things which could taint the flesh. Also it is simply unrealistic to supply our size of population with free-range chickens. However it's not all gloom:

Chill-fresh One quality chain store with branches throughout the country has pioneered a method of chicken production which, although the cost is higher, now supplies the country with some half a million fresh chickens each week, not just production-line broilers but mature chickens. (In fact they handle the largest number of 4–5 lb, 1·8–2·25 kg birds in Britain). These are reared on some 450 selected farms spread over the country, where the chickens can feed and take water ad lib and stress and crowding are avoided (a good-tasting chicken, it seems, has to be contented!). After they're killed these birds are cooled by air; rigor mortis occurs naturally and, by enzyme action, there is a certain amount of maturation and flavour development under correct temperature control.

New York dressed This is the name given to fresh chicken which is hung, so that flavour matures. In this case the bird is eviscerated only at the point of purchase.

Left: Crêpes Suzette, page 381.

The choice for us We can choose the quality of chicken we want to eat. First, from a reliable poulterer, who knows his source of supply is of high quality and whose poultry is eviscerated only at the point of purchase. Secondly we can choose a fresh, chilled chicken that has not been subjected to water-cooling (water-cooled chicken looks very pale and white, air-cooled chicken has a healthy, pinkish tone). Or we can choose frozen chicken from a good supplier. I have outlined the hazards of freezing broilers above, but with correct and careful freezing quality *can* be achieved. My suggestion is to use frozen chickens for casserole cooking (because the water content can cause them to steam rather than roast).

Choosing the right chicken

Chickens are sold in various categories of size and weight and, obviously, you need to select the right chicken for the right recipe. There are four principal ways of cooking chicken, (i) roasting (ii) pot-roasting and casseroling (iii) shallow and deep-frying (iv) grilling and barbecuing. Here is the range of chickens, and notes as to what each is suitable for:

Poussins and double poussins These are baby chickens weighing up to 2 lb (about 1 kg) each, with not a lot of flavour to them. But split in half and marinaded overnight they make very good barbecue food.

Broilers are the uniform immature birds which weigh in at $2\frac{1}{2}$–$3\frac{1}{2}$ lb (1·125–1·675 kg). If good quality, what they lack in flavour is made up for in tenderness. So, jointed, they're suitable for any recipe that calls for chicken to be grilled or fried.

Roasting chickens These are the 4–5 lb birds (1·8–2·25 kg). Their extra age and development means more chicken flavour, and they can take the longer cooking time needed for roasting. I also think these are the best for casseroles too.

Boiling fowl It is said that chickens (as opposed to capons) weighing from 6–8lb (2·7–3·15 kg) are only suitable for slow casserole cooking or stock-making, yet I have given an $8\frac{1}{2}$ lb (3·375 kg) bird exactly the same type of cooking as turkey (see page 415) and found it superbly rich in flavour. If you plan to roast a boiling fowl, however, you must be sure of your supplier.

Capons I'm not at all keen on chickens being injected in the neck with hormone capsules which de-sex (caponise) them. True, they will have an enlarged breast, but an abnormal one. Capons are usually sold at Christmas and claim only 1–2% of the market.

Storing fresh chicken

If you buy a fresh chicken, try to get it home as soon as possible. Then remove the wrapping and, most important, the giblets if they are tucked inside. Place it on a plate, cover loosely and put it in the lowest part of the fridge, where it will keep for three days.

Storing and thawing frozen chicken

If you're tackling a frozen chicken, the most important rule is that the bird must be completely and thoroughly de-frosted before it is cooked. Food poisoning can occur if you begin to cook the bird while it is still partly frozen, because this creates the semi-warm conditions in which food bugs thrive and multiply. The thawing times below are produced by the Poultry Information Service.

Size of bird	2 lb (900 g)	3 lb (1·35 kg)	4 lb (1·8 kg)	5 lb (2·25 kg)	6 lb (2·7 kg)	7 lb (3·15 kg)
Thawed at room temperature 65°F (16°C)	8 hrs	9 hrs	10 hrs	12 hrs	14 hrs	16 hrs
Thawed in a refrigerator 40°F (4°C)	28 hrs	32 hrs	38 hrs	44 hrs	50 hrs	56 hrs

Frozen chicken can be stored in the freezer for up to nine months, or up to 1 month in the frozen food compartment of a refrigerator (depending on the star rating of your model), but once thawed should not be re-frozen.

Boning chickens

I'm afraid this is something that goes against the grain with me. I was brought up to believe that bones in the meat during cooking enhance flavour (you can test this yourself: eat that little piece of chicken that adheres to the wing bone, and you can really taste the concentrated chicken). Boning a chicken may indeed make it easier to carve—but what about the trouble of boning it in the first place! I can't help thinking that sheer theatrical effect is the reason for some people producing something resembling a stuffed rugby ball in the name of chicken.

Jointing chickens

This is nothing to be afraid of. First of all, if you're buying chicken from a butcher or poulterer, you can ask him to joint it for you

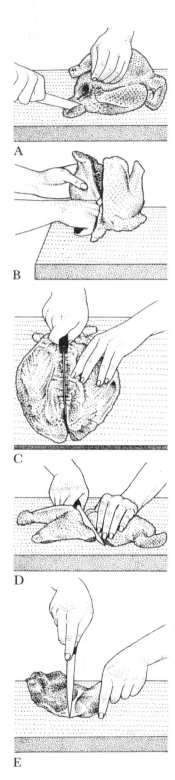

A

B

C

D

E

(everything costs so much these days, we should get all the value we can). If you need to do it yourself at home, there are really only two requirements: a really sharp knife and perhaps a pair of good kitchen scissors (or poultry shears). Follow the diagram and instructions, and don't worry too much if the joints aren't perfectly neat. Once the chicken is cooked no-one will know.

First, cut through the parson's nose, (A), then stand the chicken in a vertical position (neck end down). Insert the knife into the cut you've already made, and cut straight down the back of the chicken (B). Place it skin-side down, open it out flat, and cut right through the breastbone (C). Now turn the two halves of the chicken skin-side up, stretch out the leg as far as you can, then cut through the natural line dividing the leg from the breast (D). For six portions: turn the legs over, find the thin white line at the centre of the joint, and cut through it (E).

Stuffing for chickens

Stuffing was invented for a very good reason. In the case of roasting chicken, where the flesh is very lean and could easily dry out if the fire was fierce, the stuffing provided lubrication—a sort of internal basting to give extra juiciness, particularly to a large bird needing long cooking. A chicken stuffing should have a fair amount of juicy ingredients, like minced pork, sausage meat or a generous quantity of butter.

Trussing chicken

I am happy to say we can all abandon our needles and thread. In all the

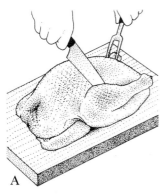

A

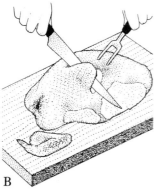

B

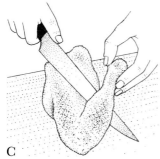

C

research I've done over the years I can find no reason for trussing other than the neat appearance it gives a bird, and the supposed ease of carving. A well-cooked bird which has not been trussed is, in fact, quite simple to carve, and neat appearances don't really matter if you are going to carve in the kitchen —which is always the most suitable place to carve in any case.

Carving chicken

As always, the cardinal requirement is a sharp knife, then it's easy (see the illustrations). And the same rule applies to chicken as to other roast meats and poultry, and that's to allow a good 10–15 minutes between completion of cooking and carving. This lets the juices which have welled up to the surface during cooking seep back into the flesh to keep it succulent. It also makes carving neat slices much easier.

Secure the chicken with a fork, insert knife between leg and body and remove thigh and drumstick in one piece (A). Remove the wing on the same side, then slice the breast (B). Repeat this on the other side of the bird. Lastly, divide the thigh and drumstick cutting through the joint to obtain two leg portions (C).

Traditional roast chicken

As you've probably gathered, I'm a traditionalist and one of the pleasures of the table for me is the aroma of a carefully roasted chicken with crisp brown skin and sizzling juices underneath. Perfect accompaniments would be a stuffing of pork flavoured with sage and onion, a few crisp pieces of bacon (which protected the breast during roasting), a jug of creamy bread sauce, and a gravy made with chicken juices and stock. In this age of fast, convenience living it can be a real therapy to lavish care and thought on cooking something simple really well.

1 × 4½–5 lb roasting chicken, including neck and giblets (2–2·25 kg)
3 oz butter (75 g)
6 rashers fat, streaky bacon
Salt and freshly-milled black pepper

For the stuffing:
½ lb minced pork or good quality pork sausage meat (225 g)
2 oz fresh breadcrumbs (50 g)
1 smallish onion, very finely chopped or grated
1 dessertspoon dried sage
Salt and freshly-milled black pepper

Pre-heat the oven to gas mark 5, 375°F (190°C)

In advance make up a strong, reduced giblet stock according to the instructions on page 300. Then to prepare the chicken for the oven you first need to make the stuffing.

Stuffing Here I part company with many other cooks and follow my mother's advice, which is to place some stuffing inside the body cavity as well as the breast (which provides moisture and flavour to permeate the inside of the whole bird during cooking). It also means there's some stuffing left over to go with the cold chicken next day! You can of course make a smaller quantity of stuffing and just use it for the breast if you prefer.

The stuffing is made simply by combining all the ingredients thoroughly in a bowl, and seasoning well. To stuff the breast: at the neck end you'll find a flap of loose skin, and if you gently loosen this you'll eventually be able to make a triangular pocket between the breast and the skin. Pack about one-third of the stuffing in as far as you can, but not too tightly (or it might swell and burst during cooking) then pat it down to make a nice rounded shape. Now tuck the neck flap under the bird's back and secure it in place with a small skewer. Then place the rest of the stuffing inside the body cavity.

The chicken Next smear the butter generously all over the bird (if the skin was at all damp, dry it first) and tuck an extra lump of butter at the points where the thighs join the body. Season with salt and pepper, then place the bacon strips in a row—slightly overlapping each other—all along the breast.

Lay the chicken on its back in a roasting tin on a highish shelf in the oven, then calculate the cooking time which will be 20 minutes to the pound and *sometimes* 20 minutes over. It is this final 20 minutes that has to be flexible because larger.birds don't take as long as might be expected, and also because ovens vary.

Every 20 minutes or so during roasting baste the bird thoroughly with the buttery juices to keep it moist, and after 1 hour remove the now-crisp bacon slices and reserve them in a warm place for serving. 20 minutes before the end of the cooking time increase the heat to gas mark 7, 425°F (220°C) just to give the skin a final crisping.

Is it cooked? The all-important question. There are three tests I use. (1) If you pierce the thickest part of the thigh with a thin skewer, the juices running out should be golden and clear. If they're pink it is not ready. (2) If the juices were golden and clear, then test the leg by tugging it gently away from the body. If you feel it give, it is ready. (3) (This is if a chicken is not stuffed) Tip the chicken up and examine the juices running out of the body cavity—they should be golden and clear, and not at all pink.

When it's cooked, set the chicken on a hot dish in a warm place and leave it to 'relax' for 10–15 minutes. Meanwhile spoon or pour off any excess fat from the corner of the tin, stir a little flour into the juices and make a gravy with the giblet stock, simmering to reduce and concentrate the flavour. Carve the chicken, and serve with the stuffing, bacon pieces, gravy and creamy bread sauce. (You can find my recipe for *Bread sauce* in Part One, page 155).

Creamed chicken with avocado

(serves 4 people)

This recipe is a delicious way to use left-over cooked chicken or, if you have to work all day and prepare supper when you get home, it's a quick and easy way to jazz up some ready-cooked chicken from a quality chain store.

1 lb cold cooked chicken meat cut into small strips (450 g)
2 oz butter (50 g)
2 oz plain flour (50 g)
½ pint milk (275 ml)
¼ pint chicken stock (150 ml)
¼ pint single cream (150 ml)
1 tablespoon dry sherry
Some lemon juice
2 ripe avocados
1 oz mild cheese, grated (25 g)
Salt and freshly-milled pepper

Pre-heat the oven to gas mark 6, 400°F (200°C)

Begin by melting the butter in a medium-sized saucepan, add the flour and blend to a smooth paste. Cook for 2 minutes then gradually stir in the milk, stock and cream and, stirring all the time, bring to simmering point and cook very gently for 2 or 3 minutes. Then remove the pan from the heat and add the chicken pieces, sherry, salt, pepper and lemon juice to taste.

Now halve and quarter the avocados and, having removed the stone and skins, slice the flesh thinly and cover the base of a casserole with the slices. Sprinkle over a little lemon juice, spoon the chicken mixture on top and, finally, add the grated cheese. Transfer to the pre-heated oven and bake for 20–25 minutes or until the sides start to bubble. A crisp, green salad is a nice accompaniment.

Coq au vin

(serves 6 people)

A truly authentic *Coq au vin* is made, obviously, with a cock bird, and some of the blood goes into the sauce, which by the time it reaches the table, is a rich, almost black colour. In Britain we make

a less authentic adaptation, but it makes
a splendid dinner party dish.

A large 4–5 lb chicken, cut into 6 joints (1·8–2·25 kg)
½ lb unsmoked streaky bacon, in one piece (225 g)
16 button onions
½ lb dark-gilled mushrooms (225 g)
2 cloves of garlic, crushed
2 bayleaves
2 sprigs of fresh thyme
1¼ pints of red wine (725 ml)
1 tablespoon butter
1 tablespoon oil
A butter and flour paste made with 1 rounded tablespoon softened butter and 1 tablespoon plain flour
Salt and freshly-milled black pepper

A large flameproof pot, wide and
shallow to take the joints in one layer.

Melt a little butter and oil in a frying pan, and fry the chicken
joints, skin side down, until they are nicely golden; then turn them
and colour the other side. You may have to do this in three or four
batches—don't overcrowd the pan. Remove the joints from the
pan with a draining spoon, and place them in a large cooking pot.
The pot should be large enough for the joints to be arranged in one
layer yet deep enough so that they can be completely covered with
liquid later. The pot must also be flameproof.

Now de-rind and cut the bacon into fairly small cubes, brown
them also in the frying pan and add them to the chicken, then
finally brown the onions a little and add them too. Next place the
crushed cloves of garlic and the sprigs of thyme among the chicken
pieces, season with freshly-milled pepper and just a little salt, and
pop in a couple of bayleaves.

Pour in the wine, put a lid on the pot and simmer gently for 45
minutes to 1 hour or until the chicken is tender. During the last 15
minutes of the cooking, add the mushrooms and stir them into the
liquid.

Remove the chicken, bacon, onions and mushrooms and place

them on a warmed serving dish and keep warm. (Discard the bay leaves and thyme at this stage.)

Now bring the liquid to a fast boil and reduce it by about one third. Next, add the butter and flour paste to the liquid. Bring it to the boil, whisking all the time until the sauce has thickened, then serve the chicken with the sauce poured over. If you like, sprinkle some chopped parsley over the chicken to make it look pretty.

Note: the results are different but every bit as delicious if you use cider instead of wine, but it must be *dry* cider.

Chicken in the pot
(serves 4 people)

This is the 'poule au pot' associated with Henri IV of France, whose ambition was that every family in his kingdom might be able to afford to eat this dish every Sunday.

1 freshly drawn chicken with giblets, weighing about 3½ lb (1½ kg)
½ lb unsmoked streaky bacon in one piece (225 g)
3 tablespoons olive oil
4 medium-sized carrots, cut in 1 inch (2·5 cm) chunks
4 small turnips, quartered
1 clove of garlic, crushed
½ pint dry white wine (275 ml)
¾ pint chicken stock, made with the giblets (425 ml)
12 button onions
½ lb mushrooms, sliced (225 g)
1 small bunch parsley stalks
A few celery leaves (if you have them)
1 bayleaf
2 sprigs of fresh thyme (or ¾ teaspoon dried thyme)
Salt and freshly-milled black pepper
A paste made with 1 rounded tablespoon softened butter and 1 tablespoon plain flour

Pre-heat the oven to gas mark 6, 400°F (200°C)

First heat the oil in a large flameproof casserole, then cut the bacon into chunks and fry it a little with the peeled button onions. When the bacon and onions have coloured a little, remove them with a slotted spoon and keep them on one side.

Now, with the oil fairly hot, fry the chicken whole (as you would a piece of meat for a pot roast) turning it several times to brown evenly all over, then remove it from the casserole. Next fry the carrots, turnips and crushed garlic for about 5 minutes, stirring them all around so that they brown slightly. Now put the bacon and onion back in the pan. Push everything to the sides and sit the chicken in the centre. Next pour in the wine and stock, add the parsley and celery leaves tied in a bundle, plus the thyme, bayleaf and salt and pepper. Bring to simmering point, then transfer the casserole to the oven (the casserole should be without a lid, but place a piece of foil over the chicken breast) and let it cook for 30 minutes, uncovering and basting the chicken breast now and then with the surrounding stock.

After 30 minutes remove the foil, add the sliced mushrooms, then bake for another 30 minutes, again basting fairly often with the juices. When the chicken is cooked, take the casserole from the oven, remove the chicken, drain it well and put it on a warmed serving dish. Surround it with the well-drained vegetables and bacon, and discard the bayleaf and herbs.

Now place the casserole over a direct heat and boil the liquid fiercely to reduce it by about a third. Then whisk in the flour and butter paste, and bring back to the boil, whisking continuously until the sauce thickens. Now taste to check the seasoning, then carve and serve the chicken and vegetables with the sauce poured over them.

Fried mustard-and-herb-coated chicken

(serves 4 people)

This is a very good recipe for jazzing up the mass-produced chicken drumsticks or thighs that come in packets.

8 small chicken joints
1 tablespoon Dijon mustard
2 tablespoons made-up English mustard
2 egg yolks
2 tablespoons double cream

5 oz breadcrumbs (150 g) mixed with 2 teaspoons mixed dried herbs
Plain flour
Salt and freshly-milled black pepper
Groundnut or olive oil

First remove the skins from the chicken joints. Then in a small basin mix the two mustards, egg yolks, and cream until well blended and smooth. Then place the breadcrumb and herb mixture on a square of greaseproof paper and some flour on another piece. Season each chicken joint with salt and pepper and dust with flour, then dip in the mustard mixture to coat it evenly and finally, roll the joint in the breadcrumbs, and pat the coating on firmly. Chill the joints for 3 or 4 hours so that the mustard flavour can develop and the coating become firm.

Then in a very large frying pan (or two smaller ones) heat about an inch of oil to the point where a small cube of bread froths on contact. Then fry the chicken joints over a medium heat, turning them from time to time, until they're crisp and golden—about 20 minutes. Drain the chicken joints on crumpled kitchen paper and serve hot.

Chicken with lemon sauce

(serves 4 people)

This is a light, summery recipe with a sharp lemon sauce.

1 × 4 lb chicken with giblets (1·8 kg)
3 oz softened butter (75 g)
1 dessertspoon lemon juice
¼ teaspoon dried tarragon
1 lemon, quartered
Salt and freshly-milled black pepper

For the sauce:
2 oz butter (50 g)
1 tablespoon flour
¼ pint stock, made with the giblets (150 ml)
1 tablespoon lemon juice
¼ pint double cream (150 ml)

Pre-heat the oven to gas mark 6, 400°F (200°C)

Make the giblet stock as described on page 300, then reduce it down to ¼ pint (150 ml) to give a concentrated flavour.

Prepare the chicken for roasting by mixing the 3 oz (75 g) of butter with ¼ teaspoon of salt, some freshly-milled pepper and a dessert-spoon of lemon juice. Add the tarragon, then spread this mixture evenly all over the chicken. Now cut the lemon into quarters and place these inside the chicken. Next place the chicken in a roasting tin and cover the breast with buttered foil. Put the tin in the pre-heated oven to roast for 1¼–1½ hours, basting the chicken quite often with the buttery juices. Remove the foil from the breast during the last half hour.

While the cooked chicken is 'relaxing' in a warm place, make the sauce. Melt the butter in a small saucepan, blend in the flour, then gradually stir in the chicken stock and lemon juice. Bring to the boil, stirring all the time, simmer for 2 or 3 minutes, then add the cream and some of the chicken juices from the roasting tin. Now carve the chicken and serve it on a bed of rice with the sauce poured over.

Chicken in barbecue sauce

(serves 4 people)

If you can, buy fresh chicken drumsticks or thigh joints — you could use chicken breasts, but cut them in half—this is one of the easiest supper dishes I know.

8 small chicken joints
1 medium onion, chopped small
5 tablespoons dry cider (or wine)
5 tablespoons soy sauce
1 heaped tablespoon tomato purée
1 heaped teaspoon mustard powder
1 fat clove of garlic, crushed
1 tablespoon soft brown sugar
Olive oil
Freshly-milled black pepper

Pre-heat the oven to gas mark 6, 400°F (200°C)

First of all, make sure the chicken joints are absolutely dry by patting them with kitchen paper. Then rub each joint all over with olive oil and season with freshly-milled pepper (but no salt because of the sauce). Now pop them into a shallow roasting tin, tucking the chopped onion in amongst them and sprinkling them with a few drops of oil. Place the tin on the highest shelf in the oven and let them cook for about 30 minutes.

Meanwhile make up the barbecue sauce simply by crushing the garlic clove, then adding all the rest of the ingredients to it and whisking with a fork until blended thoroughly.

When the chicken has been cooking for 30 minutes, pour off any excess oil from the roasting tin then pour the barbecue sauce over the chicken and cook for a further 25 minutes, basting frequently.

This is nice served with a brown pilau rice and a salad.

Chicken with whole spices

(serves 4 people)

If you enjoyed the spiced chicken recipe on page 186, Cookery Course Part One, you'll like this one too, which is made with crushed whole spices and tastes authentically Indian.

3¾ lb chicken, cut in 8 pieces (about 1·6 kg)
2 tablespoons groundnut oil
1 tablespoon butter
2 onions, very finely chopped or minced
1 medium green pepper, finely chopped
2 dried red chillies, de-seeded and very finely chopped
2 cloves of garlic, crushed
¾ teaspoon whole cumin seeds
1 teaspoon whole coriander seeds
8 whole cardamon seeds
1 teaspoon ground ginger
2 teaspoons ground turmeric
1 bayleaf, crumbled
¼ pint natural yoghurt (150 ml)
2 fl oz hot water (55 ml)
Salt and freshly-milled black pepper

Prepare the chicken a few hours before cooking. Arrange the pieces in an oblong meat-roasting tin. In a small bowl mix together the crushed garlic, ground ginger and turmeric with 1½ tablespoons groundnut oil. Now, with a sharp knife, make several incisions in the chicken, season then coat them, as evenly as possible with the oil and spice mixture. Leave in a cool place (but not in the fridge) so that the flavour penetrates.

When you're ready to cook the chicken, pre-heat the oven to gas mark 6, 400°F (200°C). Place the tin on the highest shelf, uncovered, and cook for about 20 minutes or until the chicken pieces are a nice golden colour.

Meanwhile, prepare the whole spices by grinding them and crushing finely, either with a pestle and mortar or on a flat surface using the back of a tablespoon. Next, melt the butter and remaining ½ tablespoon of oil in a frying pan. Add the onion and green pepper, and cook for 5 minutes. Now add the crushed spices, chillies and crumbled bayleaf, stir and cook for a further 5 minutes. Take the pan off the heat, stir in the yoghurt and water and add a little salt.

Now pour this mixture all over the chicken pieces, cover the tin with a double sheet of foil and bake for 30 minutes with the heat reduced to gas mark 4, 350°F (180°C) then remove the foil and let it cook for approximately a further 10 minutes.

Serve with pilau rice and mango chutney.

Cold chicken pie
(serves 8 people)

This is a delicious centrepiece for a picnic, or any sort of lunch out of doors.

For the pastry:
2 oz lard at room temperature (50 g)
2 oz butter at room temperature (50 g)
8 oz plain flour, sifted (225 g)
Cold water
Beaten egg, to glaze

For the filling:
1 × 4½ lb chicken (2 kg)
1 lb pork sausage meat (450 g)
1 teaspoon mace
6 spring onions, finely chopped
The rind and juice of half a lemon
1 teaspoon fresh thyme (or ½ teaspoon dried thyme)

| 1 tablespoon fresh chopped sage (or ½ tablespoon dried sage) |
| 2 tablespoons double cream |
| Salt and freshly-milled black pepper |

A round, 8 inch (20 cm) diameter pie tin with rim and sloping sides which is 2 inches (5 cm) deep.

First make up the pastry, by rubbing the fats into the sifted flour till the mixture resembles fine breadcrumbs, then adding just enough water to make a dough that leaves the bowl clean. Rest the dough in a polythene bag in the fridge for half an hour, then use half the dough to line the pie-tin.

Next, with the help of a sharp knife, strip all the flesh you can off the chicken and cut the meat up into ½ inch (1 cm) pieces. Place them in a bowl, sprinkle in the mace and season well with salt and freshly-milled black pepper.

Now, in a separate bowl, combine the sausage meat with the spring onions, the thyme and sage, the lemon rind and 2 teaspoons of the lemon juice. Pour in the cream and mix everything together well to make a soft mixture (rather like a cake mix)—if necessary, add a little more cream. Next put one-third of the sausage meat mixture in the bottom of the pastry-lined tin and spread it flat. Now put half the chicken pieces on top and sprinkle in any remaining lemon juice, then add another layer of one-third of the sausage meat, followed by the rest of the chicken pieces and a final layer of sausage meat.

Roll out the rest of the pastry and use it to cover the pie—which will be well piled up, dome-like, by now. Seal the edges well, glaze with some beaten egg and bake on a baking sheet in an oven pre-heated to gas mark 6, 400°F (200°C) for 30 minutes. Then reduce the heat to gas mark 4, 350°F (180°C) and cook for a further 1¼ hours.

Chicken with grape stuffing

(serves 4 people)

Here's a nice recipe for serving in the summer, when the seedless grapes are in season.

| 4 lb roasting chicken with giblets (1·8 kg) |
| 2 oz butter at room temperature (50 g) |

Salt and freshly-milled black pepper
Giblet stock (see page 300)
4 tablespoons dry white wine
A little plain flour

For the stuffing:
3½ oz butter (85 g)
1 medium-sized onion, finely chopped
4 oz fresh breadcrumbs (110 g)
4 cloves of garlic, crushed
1 tablespoon freshly chopped parsley
½ teaspoon dried tarragon
6 oz seedless grapes, or halved and de-seeded grapes (175 g)
Salt and freshly-milled black pepper

Pre-heat the oven to gas mark 5,
375°F (190°C)

First make the stuffing. Melt ½ oz (10 g) of butter in a small
saucepan and cook the finely chopped onion for about 6 minutes or
until softened, then add the remaining butter and allow it to melt.
Now transfer the onion and the buttery juices to a bowl, add the
breadcrumbs then stir in the crushed garlic, chopped parsley,
tarragon and grapes. Taste and season with salt and pepper.

Next loosen the breast skin of the chicken a little to make a pocket
for the stuffing. Place the stuffing in the pocket but don't
overfill—if you do the skin will burst when cooking. Secure the
skin flap underneath with a small skewer. Season the chicken all
over with lots of salt and pepper, then rub it all over with the
softened butter, and cover the breast with buttered foil.

Place the chicken in a roasting tin and cook for approximately
1 hour 20 minutes, basting the meat with the buttery juices every
20 minutes or so. Remove the foil half an hour before the end of the
cooking time to brown the breast.

Meanwhile make some giblet stock (see page 300) then boil it,
without a lid, to reduce it and concentrate the flavour. To test if
the chicken is cooked, pierce the thickest part of the thigh with a
thin skewer: if cooked, the juices will run golden and clear. Drain
the chicken thoroughly and keep warm while you make the gravy.

Carefully tilt the roasting tin and pour off some of the excess fat.

Then put the tin over direct low heat and blend in a little flour. Keep stirring and allow the flour to brown before gradually adding the wine and sufficient strained giblet stock to make a thin gravy. Taste and season with salt and pepper. Carve the chicken and serve, passing the gravy round separately.

Duck

Whatever mass-produced chicken lacks in character and flavour, our duck makes up for, I think. Perhaps that's because we eat relatively little duck in this country: if demand increased no doubt we'd have another plentiful but uniform bird. In the meantime duck, though comparatively expensive, makes a superb choice for a dinner-party. In the first place you'll be serving something special; secondly duck has the advantage of needing no attention whatsoever while it's cooking; and thirdly, if your guests happen to be late, your duck will happily wait for them without being spoiled.

Buying duck

If possible, try to get a fresh duck. If you can't a frozen one will do, so long as you bear in mind one important point: ducks are very fatty birds and sub-zero temperatures do not prevent rancidity developing, So while a duck that's been frozen for three months will be perfectly good, after that it will begin to deteriorate. A duck frozen for a year will not be very good at all. (Let's hope we'll get date-stamping on poultry soon!). It is of course essential that frozen duck is completely defrosted before cooking.

The weight of a duck is very important, because to get a crisp, fat-free finish it needs long, slowish cooking—and that means the weight of the bird will be considerably reduced by the end of the cooking time. So to serve four people, buy a 5 lb or preferably a 6 lb bird (2·25 or 2·7 kg); to serve six or eight people you'll need two ducks.

Drying duck

To cook a duck to a lovely crisp finish, it has to be fairly dry before it goes into the oven. If it has been frozen (or even if it's a fresh duck which came wrapped in a polythene bag) and the skin looks damp, dry it thoroughly with a clean tea-cloth or some absorbent kitchen paper. It is also a good idea to check that the inside of the duck is dry too. Then leave the bird in a cool dry place for several hours for the air to dry it as well. The Chinese hang theirs up on lines in a draughty place and one typical 'colour supplement' article once recommended drying a duck with a hair-drier! I can assure you, you don't need to resort to such measures to get a crisply cooked duck.

Stuffing duck

Personally I never put stuffing inside a duck, because (i) duck meat doesn't need lubricating, and (ii) the stuffing tends to absorb too much of the duck fat. But if you like you can prepare some *Sage and onion stuffing* (see recipe on page 413), roll the mixture into little balls, flour them and fry them to serve with the finished duck. That's especially nice if the duck is served with an apple sauce.

Cooking times for duck

In France duck is often served pink and underdone, or sometimes the skin and bones are removed and only the breast is cooked. Also pressed duck is considered a delicacy, though it's not to my taste. In England we tend to prefer our duck cooked whole and for quite a long time, so that the high proportion of fat can be rendered down and run out, leaving moist flesh and a mahogany-coloured crisp skin (rather like crackling). 30 minutes per pound (450 g) is a general guideline. This longer style of cooking does mean that the wings and part of the legs are frazzled, but believe me, the rest is so good that it's worth the small loss. However if you prefer duck in the French manner, you can cut down the cooking time.

Roast duck

(serves 4 people)

1 duck, weighing 6 lb (about 2·75 kg)
Salt and freshly-milled black pepper
1 bunch of watercress, for garnishing

Pre-heat the oven to gas mark 7, 425°F (220°C)

The golden rule is never to put any sort of fat near a duck, because it has more than enough of its own. Just place the bird in a roasting tin, then prick the duck skin all over—going deep into the flesh—with a skewer (to leave little escape routes for the fat to run out). Season the duck quite liberally with salt and pepper, then place the tin on a highish shelf in the oven.

After 20 minutes turn the heat down to gas mark 4, 350°F
(180°C), then basically all you have to do is leave it alone for 3
hours—just once or twice pouring off the fat that has collected in
the roasting tin. Pour the fat into a bowl—don't throw it away, it
is lovely for roasting or sautéeing potatoes.

When the cooking time is up, remove the duck from the tin, first
tipping it up to let excess fat drain out of the body cavity, and
place it on a carving board. Leave it to 'relax' for 5 minutes then
divide it into portions: all you need do is cut the bird in half
lengthways (i.e. along the length of the breast and through the
backbone) with a sharp knife, then cut the halves into
quarters—you may need the help of some kitchen scissors here.
Leaving any escaped pieces of bone behind, sit the quarters up
together on a warm serving dish and garnish with watercress.

Note: it is best to place the duck on a rack in the roasting tin. If the
rack from your grill pan will fit into the oven, you can use that.

Sauces for duck
To make a gravy, simmer up some stock with the duck giblets
(as for *Chicken giblet stock*, page 300). Pour off the fat from the
roasting tin and, over direct heat, add some flour to the juices that
are left and stir it around. Now blend in the giblet stock (plus some
wine if you feel like it) and simmer gently to thicken slightly.
    Alternatively you can serve it with one of the following sauces,
which are my own particular favourites.

Morello cherry sauce

I know this sauce sounds a bit unlikely,
but it really is delicious and it takes no
time at all to make. There's one vital
point, though, and that's that the main
ingredient must be *morello* cherry jam
and no other kind (there are several
brands on the market: one made by a
Polish firm and another by an English
firm well-known for high quality jams
and preserves). The reason it's so good
is that morello cherries are bitter, and
any sharp fruit can better hold its own
when combined with the large amount
of sugar needed to make a preserve.

6 oz morello cherry jam (175 g)
$\frac{1}{4}$ pint red wine (150 ml)

Simply combine the jam and the wine in a saucepan, and simmer without a lid for 10 minutes. This is enough for 4 people and can be made well in advance and re-heated just before serving.

Bitter orange sauce

Again the bitterness of Seville oranges gives a delicious edge to this sauce. If they're out of season and you're using sweet oranges, add 1 tablespoon of lemon juice to the orange juice to give it sharpness.

2 fairly small Seville oranges
$\frac{1}{2}$ pint of stock made from the duck giblets, (275 ml) (see chicken giblet stock, page 300)
4−5 tablespoons port
3 heaped teaspoons brown sugar
1 rounded tablespoon plain flour
Salt and freshly-milled black pepper

First of all, take off the outer rinds of the oranges with a peeler or zester, then cut the rinds up finely into very thin shreds. Pop them into some boiling water and blanch for 5 minutes, then drain well. Next, squeeze the juice from the oranges and keep it on one side.

When the duck is cooked, transfer it to a serving plate to 'relax' and keep warm, then spoon out the excess fat from the roasting tin and sprinkle the flour into the juices that remain. Stir it in well to form a paste and cook over a medium heat, for a couple of minutes to brown slightly—as you do this, scrape the base and sides of the tin with a wooden spoon. Next add the stock gradually, stirring to make a smooth sauce, then add the sugar. Cook for a minute or two more before adding the orange juice and rind and a seasoning of salt and pepper. Just before serving, stir in the port, then pour the sauce over the duck and serve straightaway.

Turkey
I come from a long line of turkey cooks and, throughout my life once a year, I have enjoyed the annual ritual of feasting not just on turkey but also on all the favourites that traditionally go with it.

Fashions in cooking turkey have come and gone, but ever since kitchen foil was introduced I have stood firm and stuck to the method which, in our family, has always been a hundred per cent successful (which is to say, cooking in foil). I can honestly say we've never had a turkey that's too dry, so we've never become bored with it cold. On the contrary, our enthusiasm for turkey lasts down to the jelly and dripping—delicious on toast for breakfast—and to the beautiful soup you can make from the carcass. I offer you here the family recipe for roast turkey with all the trimmings, but first a few words about buying a turkey.

Buying turkey
Try if possible to get a fresh bird, and remember to order it in plenty of time. If you can only buy a frozen bird, or it's more convenient, try to buy one that has been frozen without added water, then don't forget to allow plenty of time for it to de-frost slowly and *completely*. Always remove the giblets as soon as you can—with a fresh bird immediately you get home, with a frozen one as soon as it has thawed.

Important points
Let the bird come to cool room temperature before you cook it (i.e. remove it from the refrigerator or cold garage, shed or wherever the night before if you plan to eat your turkey dinner in the middle of the day). Also make the stuffing the night before, but *don't* yet stuff the turkey—it is important to let the air circulate round the inside of the bird. Stuffing made in advance also needs to be taken from the fridge the night before. The point is, if everything is chilled when it goes into the oven, it upsets the cooking times. Also remove and discard the trussing strings if there are any—they are not needed (see page 394). The stuffing for the turkey and the giblet stock can be prepared the day before.

Turkey giblet stock	
The giblets (including the liver) and neck of the turkey	
1 onion, sliced in half	
A few parsley stalks	
A chunk of celery stalk and a few leaves	
1 bayleaf	
6 whole black peppercorns	
Salt	

Wash the giblets first, then place them in a saucepan with the halved onion, cover with 1½ pints (855 ml) of water and bring to simmering point. Then remove surface scum with a slotted spoon, add the remaining ingredients, half cover the pan and simmer for 1½–2 hours. After that strain the stock, and bring up to boiling point again before using to make the gravy.

Pork, sage and onion stuffing

(for a 12–14 lb turkey, about 6 kg)

As I said earlier in connection with chicken, I believe a stuffing is a good means of providing some lubrication and juiciness inside a lean-meated bird while it's cooking. Minced pork or good pork sausage meat used as a base to a stuffing provides this lubrication.

2 lb pork sausagemeat (900 g)
1 heaped dessertspoon dried sage
1 large onion, grated or chopped very finely
4 heaped tablespoons white breadcrumbs
2–3 tablespoons boiling water
Salt and freshly-milled black pepper

First combine the breadcrumbs with the onion and sage in a large mixing bowl, then stir in a little boiling water and mix thoroughly. Next work the sausagemeat into this mixture and season with salt and pepper. If (like me) you prefer your stuffing crumbly when it's cooked, leave it as it is. If you like to carve it in slices, then add a beaten egg to bind it all together.

Chestnut and apple stuffing

(for a 12–14 lb turkey, about 6 kg)

This stuffing is also delicious but Christmas, with all the extra work involved, is not the time to be peeling and skinning chestnuts—a beastly job at the best of times. As they are going to be mashed anyway, I really think a tin of whole or puréed natural chestnuts (unsweetened) will do fine.

1 × 1 lb tin of natural chestnuts (450 g)
1½ pork sausagemeat (700 g)

| 1 lb cooking apples, peeled, cored and finely chopped (450 g) |
| 1 medium-sized onion, finely chopped |
| 1 beaten egg |
| Salt and freshly-milled black pepper |

Drain the chestnuts into a large bowl, and mash them almost to a pulp with a fork. Combine them with the rest of the ingredients (except the egg) and mix thoroughly. Then add the beaten egg to bind everything together.

Now for the turkey

Size A good size of turkey for the average family is 12–14 lb (about 6 kg). This is oven-ready weight—which is equivalent to 14–16 lb (around 7 kg) New York dressed weight. But below you'll find cooking times for varying sizes of turkey.

A note for beginners Cooking a turkey for the first time at Christmas, when in-laws and other guests are probably milling around, can be quite a traumatic experience. I think the secret of success is to give the turkey a good blast of heat to begin with, and once you've got it going (i.e. the heat has penetrated right through) you can then turn the oven down and let the turkey cook through more gently. It is also a good precaution to calculate your starting time so that the bird should complete cooking at least 30 minutes before you plan to sit down to eat. That way it has a chance to 'relax' so that the flesh can re-absorb the juices that have bubbled to the surface; it also allows sufficient time to give the turkey another 10 minutes or so cooking time if it needs it.

Timing It might be helpful to beginners if I give you an account of the exact timings of my own turkey last year. The turkey (14 lb oven-ready weight) went into the oven, pre-heated to gas mark 7, 425°F (220°C), at 8.15 am. The heat was lowered to gas mark 3, 325°F (170°C) at 8.55. The foil came off and the heat was turned up to gas mark 6, 400°F (200°C) at 12.30. Then with lots of basting it was cooked by 1.15 and served by 1.45.

Here are the cooking times for other sizes of turkey:

| 8–10 lb turkey: $(3\frac{1}{2}–4\frac{1}{2}$ kg) | 30 minutes at the high temperature, then $2\frac{1}{2}$–3 hours at the lower temperature, then a final 30 minutes (uncovered) at gas mark 6, 400°F (200°C). |

15–20 lb turkey:	45 minutes at the high temperature, then 4–5
(7–9 kg)	hours at the lower temperature, then a final 30 minutes (uncovered) at gas mark 6, 400°F (200°C).

Please bear in mind that ovens, and turkeys themselves, vary and the only sure way of knowing if a bird is ready is by using the tests described in the recipe.

Traditional roast turkey

1 turkey, about 14 lb oven-ready (6 kg)
6 oz softened butter (175 g)
½ lb very fat streaky bacon (225 g)
Salt and freshly-milled black pepper
1 quantity of pork, sage and onion stuffing (or chestnut and apple stuffing)

Pre-heat the oven to gas mark 7, 425°F (220°C)

1 packet of extra-wide foil.

Begin, on the morning of cooking, by stuffing the turkey. Loosen the skin with your hands and pack the stuffing into the neck end, pushing it up between the flesh and the skin towards the breast (though not too tightly because it will expand during the cooking). Press it in gently to make a nice rounded end, then tuck the neck flap under the bird's back and secure with a small skewer. Don't expect to get all the stuffing in this end—put the rest into the body cavity.

Now arrange two large sheets of foil across your baking tin—one of them widthways, the other lengthways. Lay the turkey on its back in the centre, then rub it generously all over with the butter, making sure the thigh bones are particularly well covered. Next season the bird all over with salt and pepper, and lay the bacon over the breast with the rashers overlapping each other.

The idea now is to wrap the turkey up in the foil. The parcel must be firmly sealed but roomy enough inside to provide an air space around most of the upper part of the turkey. So bring one piece of the foil up and fold both ends over to make a pleat along the length of the breast-bone—but well above the breast. Then bring the other piece up at both ends, and crimp and fold them to make a neat parcel.

Place the roasting tin on a low shelf in the oven and cook at the initial high temperature for 40 minutes.

After that lower the heat to gas mark 3, 325°F (170°C) and cook for a further 3 hours for a 12 lb bird (around 6 kg), or 3½ hours for a 14 lb bird (around 7 kg). Then tear the foil away from the top and sides of the bird and remove the bacon slices to allow the skin to brown and crisp. Turn the heat up to gas mark 6, 400°F (200°C) and cook the turkey for a further 30 minutes. The turkey will need frequent basting during this time, so the whole operation will probably take nearer 40–45 minutes.

To test if the bird is cooked, pierce the thickest part of the leg with a thin skewer: the juices running out of it should be golden and clear. And the same applies to any part of the bird tested—there should be no trace of pinkness in the juices. You can also give the leg a little tug, to make sure there is some give in it.

Then remove it from the roasting tin (using a carving fork and fish slice) and transfer it to a warm carving dish. If you can engage someone's help while lifting it, it's a good idea to tip the turkey to let the excess juice run out. Leave the turkey in a warmish place for 20–30 minutes to 'relax' before carving: provided it's not in a draught it will stay hot for that length of time, and it will give you a chance to turn the heat up in the oven to crisp the roast potatoes (you'll find my recipe for *Roast potatoes* on page 197, in Part One).

Meanwhile to make the gravy: tip all the fat and juices out of the foil into the roasting tin. Spoon off all the fat from the juice in a corner of the tin, then work about 2 tablespoons of flour into the remaining juices over a low heat. Now, using a balloon whisk, whisk in the giblet stock (see page 412) bit by bit, until you have a smooth gravy. Let it bubble and reduce a bit to concentrate the flavour, and taste and season with salt and pepper. (And when you have carved the turkey, pour any escaped juices into the gravy.)

Goose
A breathless pause, as Mrs. Crachit, looking slowly all along the carving-knife, prepared to plunge it in the breast; but when she did, and when the long-expected gush of stuffing issued forth, one murmur of delight arose all round the board, and even Tiny Tim . . . beat on the table with handle of his knife and feebly cried, Hurrah! There never was such a goose. Bob said he didn't believe there ever was such a goose cooked . . .'
Dickens: *A Christmas Carol*

Geese are expensive and not very plentiful but a real treat for a special party or Christmas lunch. Try to get a fresh one, but if you can only get hold of a frozen one, remember to defrost it very thoroughly and dry well before cooking.

Roast stuffed goose with prune and apple sauce

(serves 8 people)

1 young goose with giblets, weighing 10–12 lb (4·5–5·4 kg)
Flour

For the stuffing:
½ lb fresh white breadcrumbs (225 g)
½ lb onion, finely chopped (225 g)
1 dessertspoon sage
1½ oz butter (40 g)
2 eggs
The goose liver, finely chopped
Salt and freshly-milled black pepper

For the sauce:
½ lb prunes (225 g), soaked in ½ pint (275 ml) dry cider for about 6 hours
½ lb cooking apples, peeled and chopped (225 g)
Half an onion, chopped
¼ teaspoon powdered cloves
2 pinches powdered mace
2 tablespoons caster sugar

For the stock:
The giblets
1 onion
A bayleaf
1 pint water (570 ml)

Pre-heat the oven to gas mark 7, 425°F (220°C)

First make the stuffing by melting the butter in a saucepan and softening the onion in it for 5 minutes, then add the chopped goose liver, stir and cook for a further 5 minutes. Now empty the contents of the saucepan into a bowl, add the breadcrumbs and sage, and mix thoroughly. Season very well with salt and freshly-milled black pepper, then bind the mixture together with two well-beaten eggs. Stuff the tail-end of the bird with this mixture, and secure the gap with a small skewer.

Place the goose in a roasting tin—on a rack if you have one—then prick all the fleshy parts with a skewer. Season well and dust it all over with flour. Put it into the pre-heated oven, cook for 30 minutes then lower the temperature to gas mark 4, 350°F (180°C) and cook for a further 3½ hours, pouring the excess fat out of the roasting tin several times during that time.

While the goose is cooking, make some stock by simmering the giblets with an onion, a bayleaf, seasoning and 1 pint (570 ml) of water for about 1 hour.

Next prepare the sauce: put the prunes and a ¼ pint (150 ml) of the cider in which they were soaked into a pan. Simmer them till they're soft, then chop them up into small pieces, throwing away the stones. Now soften the onion in a saucepan with 1 tablespoon of goose fat (taken from the roasting tin), then add the chopped apples and simmer until they're soft and fluffy. Now stir in the chopped prunes, caster sugar and spices. Taste to see if you need a little more sugar or spice, and that's it: re-heat gently just before serving the goose.

To serve the goose, lift it out of the roasting tin, drain it well and place it onto a hot serving dish. Drain off the fat from the tin and make some gravy from the remaining juices and giblet stock.

Give each person a little of the stuffing, and serve the gravy and the prune and apple sauce separately. The nicest vegetable accompaniments would be some crisp roast potatoes and spicy baked red cabbage.

Vegetarian cooking

Interest in vegetarian food has quickened considerably over the last couple of decades, hand in hand with the wholefood movement. Vegetarians used to have a crusading image, forever prophesying doom to the meat-eaters. But now—thanks to better communication, imaginative cookery books, and a number of thriving vegetarian restaurants up and down the country—the whole idea of vegetarianism seems to people much less esoteric. I'm glad of this, if only because I think that our traditional belief in this country that a main course without meat (or at least fish) isn't a main course at all is nonsense.

Personally I couldn't, and wouldn't want to, become a vegetarian, but I do have a deep interest in vegetarian food—and for two main reasons. The first is that I am convinced that the diet of the future will have to be much less meat-centred than it is at present—simply because the world's grain supply (upon which the meat supply depends) gets scarcer as the world's population gets higher. Intensive cattle farming means intensive feeding, and it takes 10 lb of grain in feed to provide 1 lb of meat. With two-thirds of the world living at or below subsistence level, while the rest suffer the effects of diseases directly attributable to over-consumption, it doesn't need a crystal ball to predict that there must be some change. And isn't it better to have a little of something really good rather than a lot of something bland and boring? Polyphosphate-injected chicken, chemically cured bacon, water-pumped ham, and barley-fed beef are all meat products that I can easily live without.

The other reason for my interest is that vegetarian cooking is challenging and stimulating. It is actually very *satisfying* to be able to produce a delicious meal that contains no meat—you discover that when people are enjoying what they're eating it doesn't occur to them that it includes no meat until you actually tell them! Vegetarian cooking opens up new horizons, and explores a whole new range of ingredients—many of them very economical.

Since the meat versus vegetarian controversy is based on a number of misconceptions on both sides, let's dispose of them first.

Vegetarians are cranky? Yes, some of them are—as in any other section of society—but the majority are not. Some vegetarian and healthfood shops do have their weird corners full of pills and potions and plant milk, but many young people now live on a healthy diet of eggs and dairy produce, vegetables, fruits, grains, nuts, seeds and plant protein quite normally and unobtrusively.

Vegetarian myths Vegetarians themselves have been known to make rash claims, such as that vegetarians are slimmer, healthier, and less aggressive than carnivores. Rubbish. I know a number of rather plump vegetarians who are subject to the same bouts of 'flu or rheumatism as the rest of us (for that matter I also know slim meat-eaters who seemingly never have a day's illness!). The facile connection between eating meat and aggression (a theory derived, I believe, from a comparison between the fierce meat-killing lions and tigers and the peace-loving, plant-eating elephants) does seem to crumble when you consider that the most aggressively-minded man of recent history, Hitler, was—guess what—a vegetarian.

The protein question The proteins in our food are essential for health, though to judge from some current advertising campaigns, which glorify products as being 'rich in protein' or 'high-protein', you might be forgiven for thinking that we need all the body-building ingredients that we can possibly push down our throats. The truth is that an average adult has a minimum protein requirement of 45 grams a day, and can do very nicely on 75 grams. This is a target that non-meat eaters can reach comfortably, with the only reservation being that they must find a *balance* of foods in their diet.

First and second-class proteins Without getting over-scientific, proteins themselves are made up of what are called 'amino acids', eight of which are essential to our health. First-class proteins contain all eight essential amino acids, and these are found in meat and fish, poultry, eggs, cheese, milk and so on. But (as some meat-eaters point out) nuts and beans are second-class proteins, which is to say they are deficient in at least one of these amino acids.

That is not to say that eating only second class protein foods cannot provide a balanced diet, however. Nature, as she usually does, has arranged things perfectly adequately by ensuring that the amino acid lacking in one plant food is supplied by another. A good example of plant foods complementing each other to provide the eight essential amino acids is beans on toast!

Should you wish to embark, full-time or part-time, on a non-meat diet what you require to eat is a balanced selection of cheese, milk, cream, butter, eggs, pulses, nuts, wholewheat bread, grains, fresh vegetables and fresh or dried fruit.

One of the positive aspects of a vegetarian diet is that it actually provides plenty of variety, whereas meat-eaters can be inclined to stick endlessly to a meat-and-two-veg routine. A typical day's meals which provides all the necessary nutrients (and amino-acids) for a vegetarian could be: breakfast of muesli with milk, wholewheat toast and coffee. Lunch something like cheeses, salad and wholemeal bread with fresh fruit to follow. And for dinner perhaps curried nut roast with vegetables, and yoghurt to follow. To me that sounds as delicious and appetising as any meat-centred diet.

But it is not the purpose of this chapter to convert anyone to vegetarianism, nor indeed to perpetuate the unnecessary distinctions between 'us' and 'them'. It is intended to offer a collection of delicious meatless main courses, which are both interesting and easy on the pocket.

Spinach pasties
(makes 6)

These are very easy to make and you can use either a packet of frozen puff pastry or the *Quick flaky pastry* given on page 90, Cookery Course Part One.

1 oz butter (25 g)
2 oz cottage cheese (50 g)
1½ oz freshly-grated Parmesan (40 g)
1 small clove of garlic, finely crushed
¼ teaspoon dried dillweed
Some freshly-grated nutmeg
Lemon juice to taste
Salt and freshly-milled black pepper
Beaten egg to glaze
8 oz ready-made puff pastry (225 g) or quick flaky pastry made with 6 oz (175 g) flour and 4 oz (110 g) margarine
8 oz cooked spinach, fresh or frozen (225 g) If you use fresh you'll need 1 lb (450 g) to make 8 oz (225 g) cooked weight

Heat the oven to gas mark 7,
425°F (220°C)

A baking sheet, lightly greased.

Cook the spinach over a gentle heat until all the excess moisture has evaporated, then remove from the heat, beat in the butter, cheeses and all the rest of the ingredients apart from the egg and pastry and season generously. Leave on one side to cool.

Right: Roast duck with Morello cherry sauce, page 409–411; Chicken with whole spices, page 404; Spiced pilau rice, page 351.

Roll out the pastry fairly thinly then, using a small saucepan lid or saucer, cut out six rounds about 6 inches (15 cm) in diameter. It will be necessary to re-roll the pastry scraps to get 6 rounds. Then put about a tablespoon of the cooled spinach mixture on one half of each pastry circle.

Brush the pastry edges with beaten egg then bring one half of the pastry circle over to cover the spinach filling on the other half, pressing the edges together to seal well and form the pasty. Repeat this with the other five circles. Glaze with beaten egg then place the six pasties on the greased baking sheet.

Make a small ventilation hole in the centre of each one and bake on the second shelf from the top of the oven for about 15 minutes or until the pasties have risen nicely and are golden brown.

Brown rice with vegetables and cheese sauce

(serves 2 people)

This is a really delicious supper dish for two people. The different textures and flavours of the vegetables, coupled with the firm 'bite' of the rice moistened with a cheese sauce all add up to proof that economy and simplicity can still come up trumps!

For the rice:

Long grain brown rice measured to the 8 fl oz level in a measuring jug

Boiling water measured to the 16 fl oz level

1 carrot, cut into $\frac{1}{4}$ inch ($\frac{1}{2}$ cm) chunks

1 large celery stalk, cut into $\frac{1}{4}$ inch ($\frac{1}{2}$ cm) chunks

1 medium-sized onion, roughly chopped

1 tablespoon oil

$\frac{1}{2}$ oz butter (10 g)

Salt

For the garnish:

4 oz cauliflower, divided into 1 inch (2·5 cm) florettes (110 g)

4 oz Chinese leaves (or white cabbage) shredded into wide strips (110 g)

Oil

Left (from top to bottom): Scallops in the shell, page 453; Marinaded kipper fillets, page 450; Dressed crab, page 457.

For the cheese sauce:
½ pint cold milk (275 ml)
1 oz butter (25 g)
1 oz flour (25 g)
½ teaspoon mustard
2 pinches cayenne pepper
3 oz strong Cheddar cheese, grated (75 g)

Start off in a thick-based saucepan by heating the butter and oil together then add the onions, carrots and celery and soften them all for about 5 minutes. Next stir in the rice and, when it's all nicely coated with fat, add salt and the boiling water. Put on a tight-fitting lid and cook gently, undisturbed, for 45 minutes.

Meanwhile make the sauce simply by placing all the ingredients (except the cheese) in a saucepan and whisking them over a medium heat until the butter has melted, the sauce has thickened and come to the boil. Simmer gently for about 8 minutes then stir in half the grated cheese and set the pan aside whilst it melts.

Next, about 10 minutes before the rice is ready, heat some oil in a frying-pan and sauté the cauliflower for 5 minutes, tossing it around to get it nicely toasted. Then add the shredded cabbage to the frying pan and sauté it for 5 minutes or until it's cooked but still with some 'bite'.

Finally, pile the rice mixture into a large heatproof serving dish, followed by the fried vegetables; pour the cheese sauce over, then sprinkle the remaining grated cheese on top. Place the dish under a pre-heated grill for just as long as it takes to get the topping golden and bubbling.

Curried nut roast

(serves 4 people)

This is the perfect recipe to serve to anyone who feels that vegetarian food might be boring—it's never failed to please. Meat eaters are always amazed that anything that doesn't contain meat can taste so good!

½ lb hazel or Brazil or walnuts, finely chopped (225 g)
½ lb fresh tomatoes, peeled and chopped (225 g)

1 medium-sized green pepper, de-seeded and finely chopped
2 medium-sized onions, finely chopped
3 oz wholewheat breadcrumbs (75 g)
1 clove of garlic, crushed
1 teaspoon dried mixed herbs or 2 teaspoons fresh mixed herbs
1 tablespoon mild curry powder (or a heaped teaspoon of hot Madras curry powder)
1 egg, beaten
Cooking oil
Salt and freshly-milled black pepper

Pre-heat the oven to gas mark 7, 425°F (220°C)

One 7 inch (18 cm) square cake tin, greased.

Begin by gently frying the onion and chopped pepper in a little oil until they're softened—about 10 minutes.

Meanwhile, mix the nuts and breadcrumbs together in a large bowl, adding the garlic, herbs and curry powder. Then stir in the onion, pepper and tomatoes, mix very thoroughly and season. Now add the beaten egg to bind the mixture together. Finally, pack the mixture into the prepared tin and bake for 30–40 minutes until golden.

This can be served hot with spiced pilau rice, yoghurt and mango chutney or with a fresh tomato sauce. It's also very good served cold with a salad.

Hazelnut and vegetable burgers

(serves 4 people)

Many of the so-called beef burgers of today taste of anything but beef—and those that include TVP (Textured Vegetable Protein) can be of a very rubbery consistency. By contrast, these made with nuts and vegetables are simple, honest and quite delicious.

2 medium-sized carrots, grated
2 celery stalks, finely chopped
1 medium-sized onion, finely chopped

2 tablespoons finely chopped cabbage
2 tablespoons brown breadcrumbs
2 oz hazelnuts, ground (50 g)
2 tablespoons wheatgerm
A couple of pinches of cayenne pepper
A pinch of ground mace
½ teaspoon dried mixed herbs or 1 teaspoon of fresh mixed herbs
1 egg
1 tablespoon tomato purée
1 tablespoon yoghurt
Salt and freshly-milled black pepper

For the coating:
1 beaten egg
About 4 oz dry wholewheat breadcrumbs (110 g)

These are quite simple to make. Having done the chopping, grating and grinding, put all the ingredients (down to and including the herbs) in a bowl and mix well. In another bowl place the egg, tomato purée and yoghurt and whisk, then add this mixture to the vegetable mixture and season to taste.

Next form the mixture into eight small patties. Cover and chill for a few hours in the refrigerator. This will help to firm up the patties and prevent them breaking during cooking.

Shortly before you are ready to cook the burgers, heat the oven to gas mark 4, 350°F (180°C). Then dip each one into the beaten egg first then into the wholewheat breadcrumbs and place on a well-oiled baking sheet. Bake for 15 minutes then turn the burgers over with care and bake for a further 15 minutes.

Serve with a home-made tomato sauce or plain yoghurt and some brown pilau rice.

Vegetarian goulash

(serves 4 people)

This is nicest made with summer vegetables.

2 tablespoons olive oil
2 medium onions, sliced
1 rounded dessertspoon wholemeal flour

| 1 heaped tablespoon Hungarian paprika |
| 1 × 14 oz tin Italian tomatoes (400 g) |
| ½ pint hot water enriched with 1 teaspoon tomato purée (275 ml) |
| ½ lb cauliflower sprigs (i.e. half a medium-sized cauliflower head) (225 g) |
| ½ lb new carrots, cut in chunks (225 g) |
| ½ lb courgettes, cut in chunks (225 g) |
| ½ lb new potatoes, cut into halves (225 g) |
| Half a green pepper, de-seeded and chopped |
| ¼ pint soured cream or yoghurt (150 ml) |
| A couple of pinches of cayenne pepper |
| Salt and freshly-milled black pepper |

Pre-heat the oven to gas mark 4, 350°F (180°C)

Start by heating the oil in a flameproof casserole, fry the onion until softened, then stir in the flour, most of the paprika and the cayenne pepper. Cook for a minute then stir in the contents of the tin of tomatoes, and the water. Bring the sauce up to boiling point, stirring all the time, then add all the vegetables. Season with salt and freshly-milled black pepper, cover then transfer to the pre-heated oven and bake for 30–40 minutes.

Finally stir in the soured cream or yoghurt, scatter the rest of the paprika on top and serve. Buttered brown rice goes well with this.

Dolmades (stuffed vine leaves)

(serves 6 people as a first course or 4 as a lunch dish)

This is one of the nicest vegetarian dishes I know. If you live in an area where there are Greek or Cypriot shops, you should be able to get hold of some vine leaves. If not, use raw spinach leaves or the blanched inside leaves of young spring cabbage.

| 12 fresh large vine leaves, approximately 2 oz (50 g) |
| Long grain rice measured to the 3 fl oz level in a measuring jug |
| 1 lb tomatoes, peeled and chopped (450 g) or 1 × 14 oz tin of tomatoes (400 g) |

2 teaspoons tomato purée
1½ teaspoons oregano
¼ teaspoon ground cinnamon
1 tablespoon chopped fresh mint
1 tablespoon chopped fresh parsley
1 small onion, chopped
3 small cloves of garlic, crushed
1½ tablespoons olive oil
1 oz pine nuts (25 g)
The juice of half a lemon
Salt and freshly-milled black pepper

Bring a frying pan of water to boiling point, then add the vine leaves all in one bunch and blanch them for about 1 minute, turning the bunch over after 30 seconds. Then empty them into a colander, rinse under cold running water and, when drained, spread out each leaf flat—vein side uppermost.

For the filling: cook the rice in double its volume of boiling salted water until tender. Heat the oil in a frying pan and fry the onion and pine nuts to colour them then tip in the cooked rice together with one-third of the tomatoes, the tomato purée, half a teaspoon of oregano, the mint, parsley, cinnamon and 2 cloves of crushed garlic. Stir well, cook for a couple of minutes then, removing the pan from the heat, add the lemon juice, salt and pepper.

Now spoon a dessertspoonful of the rice mixture onto the stalk end of a vine leaf, fold the leaf over once, squeezing and pressing the filling to a sausage-shape. Then tuck in the sides of the leaf and continue to roll up to make a tight, neat cylindrical parcel.

When all the vine leaves are filled, spoon half the remainder of the tomatoes into the base of a small flameproof casserole or heavy saucepan. Now pack the dolmades in tightly and spoon the remaining tomatoes, garlic and oregano on top. Add a seasoning of salt and pepper. Now press a suitable sized plate over the dolmades—to prevent them unrolling during cooking—cover the casserole with a lid and simmer very, very gently on top of the stove for 2 hours.

Serve the dolmades hot or cold with the juices spooned over them.

Sautéed mixed vegetables

(serves 4 people)

Kate Bush—whose performances both singing and dancing project a tremendous amount of energy—is a vegetarian. This recipe and the two that follow it are some of her favourites. They were devised by her sister-in-law Judith and make up a complete meal. It has become a firm favourite for supper in my home.

½ lb onions, roughly sliced (225 g)
6 oz green peppers, cut into ½ inch strips—approx. 2 small peppers (175 g)
6 oz carrots, sliced—approx. 3 small carrots (175 g)
½ lb mushrooms, sliced (225 g)
¾ lb tomatoes, quartered (350 g)
2½ tablespoons sunflower seed oil
Salt and freshly-milled black pepper

Begin by heating the oil in a large saucepan with a lid (or a shallow casserole). Add the onions and soften them for a minute or two before adding the carrots. Cook for a further couple of minutes, then add the mushrooms, pepper and tomatoes. Stir and season, then put the lid on and, keeping the heat fairly low, leave the vegetables to steam in their own juice for 20–25 minutes. Serve with brown rice (see page 349). The vegetables can be varied according to season.

Note: curry spices can be added to this dish while the oil is heating in the pan. A good combination is: 2 crushed cardomum pods; ½ teaspoon crushed cumin seeds; ¼ teaspoon crushed, dried chilli; 1 teaspoon fresh, chopped ginger (or ½ teaspoon dried ginger powder); 1 teaspoon turmeric; 1 chopped clove garlic.

Serve the vegetables, spiced or otherwise, with rice and the following two side dishes.

Cucumber and yoghurt salad

4 inches unpeeled cucumber, thinly sliced then cut into strips
½ pint natural yoghurt (275 ml)
The juice ½ lemon

1 large clove garlic, crushed
1 tablespoon snipped chives
Salt

Simply combine all the ingredients in a bowl. Serve with the rice and vegetables with a sprinkling of toasted seeds (below).

Toasted sesame and sunflower seeds

2 oz sesame seeds (50 g)
2 oz sunflower seeds (50 g)
1 dessertspoon soy sauce

In a shallow heatproof dish, mix the two lots of seeds together, then sprinkle in the soy sauce and mix thoroughly. Now spread them out evenly and place the dish under a hot grill to toast them for 4 minutes—shaking the dish a couple of times to even them out. When they are cool, store them in a screw-top jar.

Cabbage leaves stuffed with rice

(serves 2 people)

You can make all sorts of stuffings for cabbage leaves if you follow this basic recipe—you could use lentils or chopped nuts or whatever ingredients happen to be handy.

1 smallish head of spring cabbage
¾ lb ripe tomatoes, peeled and chopped (350 g)
1 medium-sized onion, chopped
Half a green pepper, de-seeded and finely chopped
Long grain brown rice measured up to the 5 fl oz level in a measuring jug
Boiling water measured up to the 10 fl oz level in a measuring jug
2 tablespoons olive oil
2–3 spring onions, finely chopped
Salt and freshly-milled black pepper
A pinch of cayenne

Cook the rice first of all: heat the oil in a saucepan and fry the onion and pepper in it for 5 minutes, then add the rice, give it a stir, and pour in the boiling water. Season with salt, cover and simmer for about 45 minutes or until all the liquid has been absorbed and the grains are tender. Then turn the cooked rice into a bowl and leave it to cool a little.

Meanwhile prepare the cabbage, discarding the tough outer leaves, then carefully peeling off about six or seven whole leaves. In each one of these make a V-shaped cut with a sharp knife to snip out the hard stalky bits. Next chop up the heart of the cabbage and bring a large saucepan of water to the boil. Blanch the whole leaves and chopped cabbage by cooking them in the boiling water for 5 minutes.

Then drain the cabbage in a colander, rinse in cold water and drain again. Shake off as much moisture from the leaves as you can and wrap them in a cloth or paper towel to dry.

Now heat the oven to gas mark 4, 350°F (180°C). Then add the chopped spring onions and the chopped cabbage to the cooled rice, with a generous pinch of cayenne and some salt and pepper.

Now take a heaped tablespoonful of the rice-and-chopped cabbage mixture and wrap it in one of the prepared leaves—squeezing gently until you have a neat, firm package.

Fill and roll the remaining cabbage leaves with the rest of the stuffing, then pack the parcels closely together in a casserole. Season with salt and pepper, pour the chopped tomatoes over the parcels, cover and bake for 1 hour in the oven.

Mixed vegetables à la Grecque

(serves 2–4 people)

This can be a main course if served with a brown rice salad mixed with fresh herbs, or a first course if simply served on crisp lettuce leaves.

6 button onions
4 oz cauliflower (110 g) broken into 1 inch (2·5 cm) florettes
4 oz small to medium-sized mushrooms, halved (110 g)
2 oz dry weight kidney beans (50 g), soaked and cooked as described on page 221, Cookery Course Part One
1 medium-sized onion, finely chopped
1 fat clove of garlic, crushed
2 tablespoons wine vinegar

1 lb tomatoes, skinned and quartered (450 g), or 1 × 14 oz tin Italian tomatoes (400 g)
1 teaspoon oregano
1 heaped teaspoon whole coriander seeds, crushed
8 black peppercorns, lightly crushed
4 tablespoons olive oil
Juice of 1 medium-sized lemon
2 fl oz water (55 ml) mixed with 1 heaped teaspoon tomato purée
2 spring onions (including green tops), finely chopped
2 tablespoons chopped fresh parsley
Salt and freshly-milled pepper

Heat 2 tablespoons of the olive oil in a heavy-based pan and soften the onion for 5 minutes. Then add the garlic, wine vinegar, tomatoes, oregano, coriander, peppercorns, lemon juice, water and tomato purée, and some salt. Bring to the boil and stir in the button onions. Now cover the pan and simmer for 20 minutes.

Then add the cooked and drained beans, the cauliflower and mushrooms, cover the pan again and simmer for a further 20 minutes, stirring the vegetables round once or twice during the cooking time. After 20 minutes test the vegetables with a skewer, they should be tender but still firm. Taste and check the seasoning.

Pour the contents of the pan into a shallow dish and leave to cool. I think this dish is best left overnight but a few hours will do. To serve, sprinkle the vegetables with the rest of the olive oil, then scatter the chopped parsley and spring onions on top.

Scone pizza

(serves 2 people)

This recipe was given to me on the programme *Multi-Coloured Swap Shop* by Heather Carey, then aged 12. It's very easy and quick to make and absolutely delicious.

4 oz self-raising flour (110 g)
1 oz margarine (25 g)
2 oz hard cheese, grated (50 g)
½ teaspoon salt

1 teaspoon dried mixed herbs
2 tablespoons milk mixed with 2 tablespoons water
3 mushrooms, thinly sliced
2 tinned tomatoes, drained and mashed together with 1 teaspoon tomato purée
Half an onion, very finely chopped
Salt and freshly-milled black pepper

Pre-heat the oven to gas mark 7, 425°F (220°C)

A baking sheet, well greased.

First of all sieve the flour into a bowl, add the salt then rub in the margarine. Next *gradually* add the milk and water to mix the ingredients to a soft dough—you may not need all the liquid.

Now roll out the dough to a circle approximately $\frac{1}{2}$ inch (1 cm) thick and place it on the baking sheet. Spread it with the mashed tomato, sprinkle the grated cheese on top of that, then decorate with the chopped onion and sliced mushroom, and season it with the mixed herbs and some salt and pepper. Then pop it into the oven to bake for 15–20 minutes or until golden brown and bubbling on top. A few chopped olives would make a nice addition to the topping or, for non-vegetarians, you could use a few anchovies.

'Non-meat' loaf
(serves 4 people)

This is made with split peas and lentils and is every bit as good as the meaty versions—delicious served hot with a home-made tomato sauce or cold with pickles and salad.

6 oz green or brown lentils (175 g)
4 oz split peas (yellow or green) picked over and rinsed (110 g)
1 pint vegetable stock or water (570 ml)
2 tablespoons butter or margarine
1 medium-sized onion, chopped
Half a green pepper, de-seeded and chopped
2 carrots, scraped and chopped
2 sticks celery, chopped

1 fat clove of garlic, crushed
1 egg, beaten
¾ teaspoon dried mixed herbs
¼ teaspoon cayenne pepper
¼ teaspoon powdered mace
2 tablespoons chopped parsley
Salt and freshly-milled black pepper

One 1 lb (450 g) loaf tin, well greased.

Start by bringing the stock or water to boiling point, stir in the split peas and simmer, covered, for about 5 minutes. Then add the lentils and herbs and continue to simmer, with the lid on, for a further 25–30 minutes or until all the liquid has been absorbed and the lentils and peas are soft, then take off the heat.

Now heat the oven to gas mark 5, 375°F (190°C).

Heat the butter in another pan, add all the prepared vegetables and the garlic and fry for 10 minutes or until golden. Now stir the vegetables into the lentil mixture together with the cayenne, mace, beaten egg, herbs and parsley, mix well then season to taste.

Spoon the mixture into the prepared tin, cover with foil and bake for 40 minutes. When it's cooked, slip a knife around the inside edge of the tin and turn the loaf out onto a warmed serving dish.

Provençale vegetable stew (ratatouille)

(serves 4 people)

This very famous French recipe is best made in the autumn when vegetables needed for it are cheap and plentiful.

2 medium-sized onions
3 medium-sized courgettes
2 large aubergines
4 large tomatoes (or you can use a 14 oz (400 g) tin of Italian tomatoes well drained).
2 red or green peppers
2 cloves of garlic, crushed
1 teaspoon dried basil
4 tablespoons olive oil
Salt and freshly-milled black pepper

This can be a most attractive dish—but not if it ends up mushy. So to avoid this, make sure you don't cut up the vegetables too small (they must retain their individuality), and also make sure you get rid of the excess moisture in the courgettes and aubergines by draining them at the start.

Begin, then, by wiping the aubergines and cutting them into 1 inch (2·5 cm) slices, then cut each slice in half; the courgettes should be wiped as well and cut into 1 inch (2·5 cm) slices. Now put the whole lot into a colander, sprinkle generously with salt, press them down with a suitably-sized plate and put weights (or other heavy objects) on top of the plate. Let them stand for about 1 hour— during which time the salt will draw out any bitterness along with excess moisture.

Meanwhile chop up the onion roughly, de-seed and core the peppers and chop these up too. Skin the tomatoes (plunging them into boiling water for a couple of minutes is the best way to loosen the skins), then quarter them and take out the seeds.

To cook the ratatouille: fry the onions and garlic in the oil gently in a large saucepan for a good 10 minutes, then add the peppers. Dry the pieces of courgette and aubergine in kitchen paper, then add them to the saucepan. Next add the basil and a seasoning of salt and pepper, stir once really well, then simmer very gently (covered) for 30 minutes. After that time add the tomato flesh (roughly chopped), taste to check the seasoning and cook for a further 15 minutes with the lid off.

Thick onion tart
(serves 4–6 people)

The secret of this tart, with its wholewheat cheese pastry, is to cook the onions until they almost caramelise so they form a lovely thick, brown layer over the base.

For the pastry:
2 oz self-raising flour (50 g)
2 oz wholewheat flour (50 g)
A pinch of salt
½ teaspoon mustard powder
2 oz margarine (50 g)
1½ oz grated Cheddar cheese (40 g)

For the filling:
1½ lb onions chopped fairly small (700 g)

2 tablespoons butter
2 eggs
4 fl oz milk (110 ml)
1 tablespoon grated Cheddar cheese
Salt and freshly-milled black pepper

Pre-heat the oven, and a baking sheet, to gas mark 4, 350°F (180°C)

An 8 inch (20 cm) fluted flan tin, greased.

First make the pastry by sifting the flours, salt and mustard powder into a mixing bowl, then rubbing in the margarine until the mixture becomes crumbly. Then stir in the grated cheese, and add enough cold water to make a dough that leaves the bowl clean. Wrap the dough in a polythene bag and leave to rest in the fridge for half an hour. Meanwhile you can be preparing the filling.

Melt the butter in a thick-based saucepan, then add the chopped onions, stir to get them well coated in the butter, and cook them (uncovered) over a medium heat for about half an hour until they have reduced and turned a deep brown. Give them a stir from time to time to prevent them catching on the bottom of the pan and, if at the end of the time they haven't turned almost mahogany-brown, turn the heat up and cook for a further 10 minutes.

Then roll out the pastry to line the flan tin, prick the base with a fork, place it on the pre-heated baking sheet, and bake in the centre of the oven for 15 minutes. After that remove from the oven and brush the inside of the pastry case with a little of the eggs (from the filling) beaten, and return to the oven for another 5 minutes.

Then spread the onions all over the base of the flan, beat the eggs together with the milk and some seasoning, and pour as much of this mixture over the onions as possible (depending on how much the onions have reduced, there may be a tiny spot left over — though probably not). Finally sprinkle the cheese over the top, return the flan to the oven and bake for 30 minutes till the filling is puffy and golden-brown.

Smoked fish and shellfish

Smoked Fish

Smoking fish is one thing at which the British really excel: nowhere else in the world can you get juicy kippers, smoked Finnan Haddies, or sides of smoked salmon comparable to our own. It is an ancient art but, unlike so many that have died out, this one thrives and many traditional smokehouses have survived to supply a constant demand. Smoking was one of the earliest methods developed by men to preserve the surplus of summer for the lean winter, and it was quite logical really: cooking needed fire, and fire provided smoke. The carbon in the smoke reacted with the oils in the food to create a coating which not only had a preservative effect on the fish (or ham or whatever), but also imparted an interesting smoky flavour. Sometimes resinous woods were thrown on the fire at the end of the process to give the food a final tarry layer—which helped to ward off the flies.

Smoking is in fact the last stage in the preserving process. First comes the salting or brining, which starts to extract moisture from the fish; then comes air-drying or dripping which continues to dry the fish, then smoking which completes the drying and at the same time provides that 'antiseptic' coating. Smoking is only really effective for foods containing plenty of oil, and once again nature has done her bit by supplying just such rich, oily fish as herrings, mackerel and salmon.

Before the days of refrigeration and fast transport fish was much more heavily smoked: nowadays it is only lightly smoked to create flavour rather than to improve the keeping qualities of fish. Lighter smoking also means less natural colour; dyes are often used now to make up for this and help the fish look more like the original heavily smoked product. There are two types of smoking. In cold smoking—at under 85°F—care is taken not to cook the flesh, and this is used for haddock, salmon, bloaters and herring (kippers). With hot smoking the temperature reaches 90°F and the fish is then lightly cooked at 180°F and the results—like Arbroath Smokies, mackerel, or buckling—have a stronger, smokier flavour.

While large-scale factory curing and smoking has provided a slightly blander species of smoked fish, at the same time it has put them within the reach of anyone who wants them, and this has kept up a demand. Demand, in turn, has benefited the small traditional smokehouses throughout the country. I am lucky, in this respect, to live near the Pinney family at Butley Creek in Suffolk, where people come in pilgrimage to a tiny restaurant and shop to sample their unique smoked fish. Mr. Pinney's patent process uses whole oak logs rather than the conventional sawdust (modern electric saws, he claims, can leave traces of oil in sawdust which sometimes spoils the flavour of the fish). Oak logs, too, need less attention than sawdust fires which, if unattended, have a habit of going out. Anyway the two modest looking wooden ovens provide some of the best smoked fish I've ever tasted.

Smoked salmon

To start with the king of them all. The best salmon are said to come from the coldest waters, and Scotch and Irish salmon can well claim to be the best in the world. Once smoked, prime Scotch salmon has a firmer flesh than any other, and can be carved by an expert in complete slices from head to tail, to an almost wafer-like transparency. To enjoy it at its very best (and how else can we afford to at current prices?) it should be carved to order and not pre-sliced, left to dry and curl at the edges. If you're buying it to take home, do have it wrapped carefully and eat it as soon as possible. Smoked salmon experts tend to dismiss pepper-mill and lemon wedges when sampling it and, judging from the rare occasions when I have had the opportunity to try really good smoked salmon, I rather agree.

Smoked trout

Smoked trout are delicately flavoured and therefore best served by themselves. To keep succulent, their skins (their 'mackintoshes' as Margaret Costa aptly describes them in her *Four Seasons Cookbook*) should be left on till just before eating. Serve smoked trout with lemon wedges, and a mixture of a little grated horseradish and whipped cream (not too much horseradish or you will mask the fish flavour, and certainly do not use the commercial sauces which contain turnip amongst other odd ingredients).

Smoked eel

A delicacy almost on a par with smoked salmon in my opinion. It's cheaper if bought un-filleted—and better that way because it stays moister. Skinning and filleting at home is very easy. Serve smoked eel in the same way as smoked trout.

Smoked mackerel

Ever since herring fishing has had to be controlled, smoked mackerel has really taken off commercially. It now comes dyed orange and vacuum-packed from supermarkets or, sadly, half de-frosted from fishmongers' slabs. The best smoked mackerel is unfrozen and still intact in its skin—worth hunting around for. At Pinneys (see page 440) they serve smoked mackerel with a sweet brown sauce which matches its richness perfectly. At home I like to make it into one of my favourite smoked fish pâtés, (see recipe page 445).

Smoked cod's roe
This is delicious made into the rich, pink paste which is an anglicised version of the Greek taramasalata (usually made in Greece with salted grey mullet roe). It may seem horrifyingly expensive, but a little of it goes a long way—see *Taramasalata* recipe on page 444.

The smoked herring family
Kippers A kipper is a fat, juicy herring which has been split, gutted, salted and smoked. One of the sad things in the history of kippering (a curing process invented in the 1840s by a man called John Woodger) is that since the last war—when some foods were required by weight rather than number—most kippers have been under-cured, because curing removes moisture and therefore weight. Most kippers today are also dyed: this is done to compensate for what would otherwise be their anaemic under-cured appearance. Some undyed kippers are still available from parts of Scotland and the Isle of Man, but they're rather exclusive and mainly available in the north-west.

Look for plumpness, oiliness, a silvery-golden colour and a good smoky smell in a kipper. As I've said before all fish (and meat) tastes better cooked on the bone, and kippers are no exception. I also think the best way to cook them is under a hot grill.

Grilled kippers
Pre-heat the grill, then line the grill pan with foil (which will stop any kippery smells haunting the pan) and brush the foil with melted butter. Remove the heads and tails from the kippers with scissors, then lay the fish on the foil skin side uppermost. Grill them for 1 minute, turn them over (flesh side uppermost), brush the flesh with melted butter and grill for a further 4–5 minutes until the butter is sizzling. Serve immediately with lemon to squeeze over them and perhaps a dash of cayenne. If you have an aversion to bones, you can of course buy kipper fillets: treat them in just the same way.

Jugged kippers

This is a traditional, and sometimes preferred, way to prepare kippers. All you do is remove the heads then fold the sides of the fish together and pack vertically in a tall warmed jug. Now pour in enough boiling water to cover the kippers, put a lid or plate on top of the jug, and leave them in a warm place for 6 minutes. Then drain and dry them with kitchen paper, and serve on hot plates with a knob of butter to melt over each fish.

Bloaters These are very popular in East Anglia. Instead of being split like kippers, the herrings are cured and lightly smoked whole (with guts intact!). When I bought my first bloater I thought there had been some mistake but, no, the guts are meant to provide that 'gamey' flavour. So, to cook them, split them and remove the guts, wipe them with kitchen paper and grill them just like kippers. Alternatively you can make a delicious bloater paste, by pounding the flesh together with butter, lemon juice and a pinch or two of cayenne; serve it spread on toast or in brown bread sandwiches.

Smoked buckling These are hot-smoked herrings, which need no further cooking, and are nice and juicy. Serve and eat them in the same way as smoked trout, or else separate them out into fillets (easily done with all smoked fish) and serve with thinly sliced onion rings, chopped dill-pickled cucumbers and soured cream.

Smoked sprats These are young baby herrings, cured and smoked. They're fiddly to deal with but inexpensive and delicious. Skinning and filleting them is time consuming but not difficult. They can be served plain, sprinkled with lemon juice and cayenne.

The smoked haddock family

Finnan haddock Six miles south of Aberdeen there's a village called Findon, where east coast haddock were first smoked over peat (Finnan is a derivative of Findon). Much smoked haddock still comes from the Aberdeen area, but some is also smoked in London nowadays. If you want to know the difference: in an Aberdeen cure the fish is split from head to tail so the backbone lies on the right-hand side of the tail; with a London cure the backbone lies on the left and an extra cut is made so that the flesh stands away from the bone. Finnan haddock is best cooked in the oven with a little milk to provide steam, and a generous amount of butter dotted over.

Arbroath smokies These are young haddock (or occasionally whiting) that have been beheaded and gutted but otherwise left whole. They are then smoked to a dark, almost bronze, colour and always sold in pairs. They're usually eaten hot, brushed with butter on the outside and placed in the oven with a good knob of butter pressed down inside. Or, to quote Gerald Watkin (of the Worshipful Company of Fishmongers), they can be 'placed under a slow grill, covered with bacon rashers, so as they warm the bacon fat combines with them to remedy their only deficiency'.

Smoked fillets Usually these *are* haddock, but they can be any white fish (like cod). No smoked fillets have such good flavour as fish smoked on the bone, but they're convenient if you're in a hurry or don't want to be bothered with bones. Good, I think, for poaching, buttering and popping a poached egg on top.

Golden cutlets Also known as block fillets these are small smoked fillets of haddock or whiting—too small really to be of much use, but again suitable for a poached egg topping.

Taramasalata
(serves 8 people)

This is the nicest version of this Greek smoked cod's roe pâté that I've tasted— the recipe comes from Mrs. Neil of Highbullen in North Devon and makes a really delicious first course for 8 people.

½ lb smoked cod's roe (225 g)
½ pint mild olive or groundnut oil (275 ml) —you may need an extra ¼ pint (150 ml)
Juice of half a lemon
1 clove of garlic
1 tablespoon fresh chopped parsley
A little boiling water

Before you start, the cod's roe should be soaked in cold water for at least a couple of hours, then rinse and drain it thoroughly before peeling off the skin. Now put the roe in a mixing bowl and mash it first to a pulp using a fork, then, with an electric beater, whisk it at top speed, gradually pouring in the lemon juice.

Now start adding the oil a drop at a time (still whisking as you would when making mayonnaise) and keep adding oil until the mixture becomes solid and dry—forming lumps and working its way up the sides of the bowl. At this stage you can start to beat in a little boiling water, say 2 fl oz (55 ml) or just enough to turn the mixture into a soft mousse. (Don't add the water before the mixture has become solid or it will separate.) Then stir in the chopped parsley and crushed garlic and serve straight away.

Smoked mackerel pâté

(serves 8–10 people)

There was a time when smoked mackerel was a rarity, but now it's become very popular and is almost as widely distributed as kippers. In this recipe, you only need two smoked mackerel to feed 8–10 people as a first course for a dinner party, and the pâté can be made well in advance, so there is no last minute preparation.

2 medium smoked mackerel
5 fl oz soured cream (150 ml)
4 oz cottage cheese (110 g)
Juice of half a large lemon
Salt, freshly-milled black pepper and nutmeg
For the garnish:
A large lemon, cut in wedges
1 bunch watercress
Couple pinches cayenne pepper

First, skin the mackerel then carefully remove all the fish from the bones (if the mackerel are already filleted simply scrape the flesh from the skins). Now flake the fish and place it in the goblet of a liquidiser, then add the cottage cheese, soured cream and lemon juice. Switch on and blend until completely smooth, stopping the motor and stirring the mixture half way through if you need to.

Next, spoon the mixture into a bowl, taste and season with salt and freshly-milled black pepper, a pinch of nutmeg, plus a spot more lemon juice if you think it needs it. Pack into individual dishes, cover with foil and chill for several hours before serving.

To serve, sprinkle on a touch of cayenne pepper, garnish with watercress and lemon wedges and serve with wholemeal toast.

Smoked fish pâté

(serves 8–10 people)

You can use any combination of smoked fish for this delicious first course.

1 medium-sized smoked trout
1 medium-sized smoked mackerel
¼ lb smoked eel (110 g)
¼ lb smoked salmon (110 g) (small, cheaper scraps are perfectly good for this recipe)
½ lb butter, at room temperature (225 g)
1 heaped teaspoon very finely chopped raw onion (optional)
Juice of a small lemon
Nutmeg
Salt and cayenne pepper
Watercress and lemon quarters for garnishing

To make the pâté, skin all the fish and take all the flesh from the bones—this is much easier than it sounds, and you'll find the flesh comes away quite easily. Put the trout, mackerel and eel into a large mixing bowl, and then chop the smoked salmon very finely (in fact chop it in the same way as you would chop parsley—into minute pieces). Now add the salmon to the other fish then, with a large fork, mash thoroughly until you have a fairly smooth paste.

At this point I like to add one heaped teaspoon of very finely chopped raw onion, but you can leave it out if you don't like it. Next, using a fork, mash and blend the whole lot with the butter and lemon juice. Then add about a quarter of a whole nutmeg, freshly-grated, then taste it and season with as much salt and cayenne pepper as you think it needs.

Now pack it into a dish or terrine, cover it well and chill lightly for an hour or two. Serve the pâté with baked crôutons or hot toast, plus a few lemon quarters to squeeze over and a few sprigs of watercress to make it look pretty.

Kipper fish cakes

(serves 4 people)

Kippers, I think, make better fish cakes than ordinary white fish, because they have much more character and flavour.

About 1 lb kippers or kipper fillets (450 g)
1 lb potatoes, scrubbed (450 g)

1 hard-boiled egg, chopped
2 teaspoons English mustard
2 teaspoons grated onion
2 tablespoons chopped parsley
1–2 tablespoons cream, or top of the milk
A little nutmeg and cayenne pepper
Some butter and oil for frying
Watercress and lemon quarters for garnishing

First boil the potatoes in their jackets in salted water until tender, then cool and drain them and peel off the skins. Place the potatoes in a bowl with the egg, mustard, onion, parsley and cream.

Jug the kippers (as described on page 443), then flake the fish, discarding the bones and skin, and add the flesh to the potato mixture. Beat with a fork until everything is well combined then season to taste with cayenne and nutmeg. Heat sufficient butter and oil to cover the base of a thick frying pan. Press the mixture into about 12 small cake shapes then fry for about 5 minutes on each side until they are a golden brown colour.

To serve: garnish with sprigs of watercress, lemon quarters (for squeezing the juice over the fish cakes) and have more cayenne pepper available for those who like it.

Smoked haddock with cream and egg sauce

(serves 4 people)

Smoked haddock is often served simply with a poached egg, but this recipe with chopped hard-boiled egg in a cream sauce is a delicious alternative.

1½ lb smoked haddock (700 g)
½ pint milk (275 ml)
1 bayleaf
About 2 oz butter (50 g)
1 oz plain flour (25 g)
1 small onion
3 tablespoons double cream
1 hard-boiled egg, chopped
Salt and freshly-milled black pepper

Pre-heat the oven to gas mark 4, 350°F (180°C)

First place the fish in a baking tin, season with freshly-milled black pepper and a little salt, tuck in a bayleaf and add the milk. Dot with flecks of butter and bake, uncovered, for about 20 minutes.

Meanwhile, chop the onion quite finely, melt 1½ oz (40 g) butter in a saucepan and sauté the onion very gently without colouring it. When the fish is cooked, remove it from the baking tin, keep it warm and pour the liquid in which it was cooked into a jug. Stir the flour into the butter and onion mixture, then add the fish liquid a little at a time and blend to a smooth sauce. Cook over a very low heat for approximately 6 minutes then stir in the hard-boiled egg and the cream.

To serve, pour the sauce over the fish and, perhaps, have some creamy mashed potatoes to go with it.

Smoked fish pie
(serves 4 people)

This is a lovely creamy fish pie and, with its soured cream and mashed potato topping, all it needs is a green vegetable or salad to go with it.

1½ lb smoked haddock (700 g)
4 kipper fillets, weighing a total 4–6 oz (110–175 g)
1 pint milk (570 ml)
1 bayleaf
4 oz butter (110 g)
2 hard-boiled eggs, roughly chopped
3 tablespoons fresh chopped parsley
1 tablespoon capers (these can be left out if not available)
1 tablespoon lemon juice
2 oz flour (50 g)

For the topping:
2 lb fresh boiled potatoes (900 g)
1 oz butter (25 g)
¼ pint soured cream (150 ml)
Freshly-grated nutmeg
Salt and freshly-milled black pepper

Pre-heat the oven to gas mark 6, 400°F (200°C)

Arrange the fish in a baking tin, pour ½ pint (275 ml) milk over it, add a few flecks of butter and the bayleaf, then bake in the oven for 15–20 minutes. Pour off and reserve the cooking liquid, then remove the skin from the fish and flake the flesh into largish pieces.

Next make the sauce by melting the remaining butter in a saucepan, then stirring in the flour and gradually adding the fish liquid bit by bit, stirring well after each addition. When all the liquid is in, finish the sauce by gradually adding the remaining ½ pint (275 ml) milk and seasoning with salt and pepper and simmering for 3–4 minutes.

Now mix the fish into the sauce, together with the hard-boiled eggs, parsley and capers, then taste to see if it needs any more seasoning, and stir in the lemon juice. Pour the mixture into a buttered baking dish (about 2½ pints (1·5 litre) capacity).

Next prepare the topping: cream the potatoes, starting off with a large fork, then finishing off with an electric beater if you have one, adding the butter and soured cream. Season the potatoes and add some freshly-grated nutmeg, then spread it evenly all over the fish. Bake on a high shelf in the oven—still at gas mark 6, 400°F (200°C) for about 30 minutes, by which time the pie will be heated through and the top will be nicely tinged with brown.

Potted haddock with capers

(serves 8 people)

This is good as a light lunch with some home-made wholemeal bread or toast.

1 lb smoked haddock fillets (450 g)
½ lb melted butter, unsalted (225 g)
A good pinch of hot curry powder
2–3 tablespoons lemon juice
4 tablespoons drained capers
Salt and freshly-milled black pepper
Watercress or parsley and lemon for garnish

Place the haddock fillets in a pan, cover with boiling water and poach them for about 5 minutes, then remove from the pan and drain thoroughly. Now skin the fish and flake the flesh into the goblet of a liquidiser. Add the melted butter and blend until smooth. Then empty the mixture into a bowl and season—but be sparing with the salt. Stir in the curry powder and lemon juice to taste and fill eight individual dishes with the mixture.

Chop the drained capers and scatter some on the top of each dish. Cover with foil or cling-film and put the dishes in the refrigerator so that the fish mixture becomes firm before serving. Serve with lemon quarters and sprigs of parsley or watercress.

Marinaded kipper fillets

(serves 4 people)

This dish, if you leave it to marinate long enough, puts kipper fillets in the smoked salmon class.

8 kipper fillets, approximately ¾ lb (350 g)
6 fl oz mild olive oil (175 ml)
2 fl oz wine vinegar (55 ml)
1 dessertspoon brown sugar
2 bayleaves
1 heaped teaspoon mustard powder
1 medium-sized onion, thinly sliced into rings
2 teaspoons crushed coriander seeds
Freshly-milled black pepper
Lemon slices, lettuce leaves and watercress for garnishing

Turn the kipper fillets upside down on a flat surface and, using a sharp knife to help you, take off the skins. Then in a 1½ pint (850 ml) oval dish, layer the fillets with slices of onion and a sprinkling of coriander and freshly-milled black pepper, tucking the two bayleaves here and there. Now in a screw-top jar dissolve the mustard powder and brown sugar in the vinegar and olive oil, screw on the lid and shake vigorously, then pour the mixture over the fillets. Now cover the dish very carefully, either with a lid or a double sheet of foil or cling-film. Then leave the kipper fillets to marinate in the lowest part of the refrigerator for 4 or 5 days.

To serve, place two fillets on a crisp lettuce leaf for each person. Garnish with lemon slices and watercress, and serve with thinly sliced brown bread and butter.

Shellfish
Mussels

I love the appearance of mussels: a rich saffron colour and they sit so prettily in their blue, boat-shaped shells. To me their aroma and flavour are the very essence of the sea. Some people accuse them of being dangerous to eat, but in fact mussel poisoning (unpleasant though never dangerous) is positively rare. If you know how to buy mussels and how to deal with them the risk is negligible. I would point out, however, that all shellfish is highly perishable. So you should always eat mussels (and any other type of shellfish for that matter) on the day you buy them.

Mussels are at their best in cold weather, so their season is usually from October to March. When you see them in a fishmonger's, a sign of freshness is that most of them are tightly closed: if there are a lot of 'gapers' don't bother. When buying mussels you need to allow at least 1 pint (570 ml) per person for a first course, and $1\frac{1}{2}$–2 pints (about 1 litre) for a main course. That may seem an enormous amount, but some will have to be discarded and, once they are out of their shells, mussels are very small and light.

The ritual of cleaning and preparing them *sounds* more bother than it actually is. When you get them home, dump the mussels straight away into a sinkful of cold water. First of all throw out any that float to the top, then leave the cold tap running over them while you take a small knife and scrape off all the barnacles and pull off the little hairy beards. Discard any mussels that are broken, and any that are open and refuse to close tight when given a sharp tap with a knife.

After you've cleaned each one, place it straight in another bowl of clean water. When they're all in, swirl them around in three or four more changes of cold water to get rid of any lingering bits of grit or sand. Leave the cleaned mussels in cold water until you're ready to cook them. As an extra safety precaution, always check mussels a second time after cooking —this time discarding any whose shells haven't opened.

Moules à la marinière

(serves 4 people as a first course)

This is the most popular of all mussel recipes and, for me, a real treat served with crusty French bread and some chilled white wine.

4 pints cleaned mussels (2·25 litres)
1 wine glass dry white wine
1 clove of garlic, chopped
1 onion, finely chopped
2 oz butter (50 g)

| 3 tablespoons double cream |
| 1 tablespoon freshly chopped parsley |
| Salt, freshly-milled black pepper |

In a wide-bottomed pan melt half the butter and, over a low heat, gently soften the garlic and onion. Then pour in the white wine and, when it comes to the boil, tip in the mussels—which should have been drained and dried a little first. Cover with a lid and leave on a high heat for 4–5 minutes. Then remove the lid and start lifting out the mussels as they open and place them on a warm dish—a draining spoon is best for this. Keep them warm in a very low heated oven. Throw away the empty half shells, and any mussels that haven't opened up their shells during cooking.

Have ready a sieve lined with fine muslin; strain the liquid in which the mussels were cooked through this then return it to the pan. Simmer to reduce by half then add the cream and the rest of the butter. Season with freshly-milled black pepper and, perhaps, a little salt. When the cream has heated and the butter has melted, pour the sauce over the mussels resting in their half shells, and sprinkle on the chopped parsley.

Mussels with garlic stuffing

(serves 4 people)

You *have* to like your garlic for this one and, if you do, be sure to have lots of crusty fresh bread to mop up the juices.

| 4 pints cleaned mussels (2·25 litres) |
| 4 oz butter, at room temperature (110 g) |
| 1 tablespoon lemon juice |
| 1 heaped tablespoon chopped parsley |
| 2 cloves of garlic, crushed |
| Salt and freshly-milled black pepper |

Pre-heat the oven to gas mark 8, 450°F (230°C)

Place the prepared mussels in a wide dry saucepan, cover with a lid and cook over a low heat (there's no need to add any liquid) until they all open. Now remove and discard the empty half shells and throw away any mussels that haven't opened, then arrange the remaining mussels in their half shells in four individual fireproof dishes.

Next, in a basin, combine the butter, lemon juice, parsley and garlic, season with salt and pepper and mix well. Place a small dab of the savoury butter on each mussel then put the dishes on the top shelf of the oven and cook for 5–10 minutes or until the mussels are sizzling noisily. Serve immediately still sizzling and bubbling.

Scallops

Scallops with their bright orange roes come in highly decorative shells. The fish itself sits on a flat fan-shaped shell and is enclosed by a similar concave one (the one shell scallops are traditionally served in). This curved shell has become a religious and cultural symbol: the shrine of St. James the apostle at Compostella in Spain has adopted the scallop shell at its emblem, and scallops themselves have been named after the saint—hence *Coquilles St. Jacques*. Scallops are a great delicacy, and in fact some of the best scallops in the world come from British waters off the Isle of Man, and the Cornish and Irish coasts.

When you're buying scallops, as with other shellfish, it's obviously best to buy them as fresh as possible (e.g. live in the shell); if their shells are closed you can be sure they're fresh. Don't worry if you're nervous about these things, the fishmonger will open and clean them ready for you. Some shops sell scallops already prepared, in which case you'd do well to make sure they look plump, firm and upright. If scallops look at all sad and soggy, then they've probably been prepared rather too long ago. An acceptable alternative to fresh scallops are the frozen ones—not so good of course but better than none.

Scallops cook very quickly. The corals only take a matter of seconds, so they are usually added to the cooking pan only shortly before serving.

Scallops in the shell

(serves 4 people as a first course)

I think these look very pretty served in the shells, brown and bubbly from the grill. (Ask the fishmonger for 4 deep shells to serve them in.)

8 small, or 4 large cleaned scallops
Half an onion, chopped finely
¼ lb mushrooms, sliced (110 g)
2 oz butter (50 g)

½ **pint dry white wine (275 ml)**
1½ **oz flour (40 g)**
¼ **pint double cream (150 ml)**
2 **tablespoons breadcrumbs**
A little extra butter
Salt and freshly-milled black pepper

Start by slicing the white part of each scallop into rounds, putting the corals on one side for use later. Then poach the white slices very, very gently in white wine until tender—about 10 minutes. (It's always necessary to cook scallops gently or they can become tough.) When they're cooked, strain them reserving the liquid.

Now melt the butter in a saucepan, add the onion and mushrooms and cook over a low heat for about 15 minutes. Then sprinkle in the flour, and add the scallop liquid very gradually, stirring continuously to obtain a thick smooth sauce. Add seasoning and a little more butter and cook gently for about 6 minutes.

Then remove the saucepan from the heat and stir in the white slices and the coral pieces of scallop, plus the cream. Now heat the mixture through over a very gentle heat, taking great care not to let it boil. Divide the mixture between four buttered scallop shells, sprinkle with breadcrumbs, add flecks of butter and brown under a pre-heated grill.

Scallop cream soup
(serves 4–6 people)

This is very easy and quick to prepare and cook, but tastes as though it has taken ages!

4 very large cleaned scallops (when taken out of their shells the total weight should be approximately ¾ lb or 350 g)
1 medium-sized onion, finely chopped
1 lb potatoes, diced (450 g)
2 oz butter (50 g)
1 pint fish stock (570 g) (see recipe on page 300)
½ pint cold milk (275 ml)
2 egg yolks
3 fl oz double cream (75 ml)
Salt and freshly-milled black pepper

First gently melt the butter in a fairly large saucepan, add the onion and cook it *very* gently without colouring it at all (about 10 minutes). Next add the diced potatoes, mix them in with the butter and onions, and season with salt and pepper. Then, keeping the heat very low, put the lid on the pan and leave the mixture to sweat for another 10–15 minutes.

After that pour in the hot fish stock, give it a good stir, cover the pan again and leave to simmer gently for a further 10–15 minutes.

Meanwhile you can be preparing the scallops: wash and dry them thoroughly and cut off the coral-coloured bits—chop these and keep them on one side on a separate plate. The white parts should be diced roughly, put in a saucepan with the cold milk and a little salt and pepper, then poached very, very gently for 8–10 minutes.

When the vegetables are cooked, transfer them and their cooking liquid to a blender and whisk to a purée (or else press it all through a nylon sieve). Now combine the white parts of the scallops (and the milk they were cooked in) with the potato purée. At this point the pieces of coral roe can be added and the soup gently re-heated.

Finally beat the egg yolks thoroughly with the cream, remove the soup pan from the heat, stir in the egg and cream mixture and return the pan to a *gentle* heat. Cook, stirring, until the soup thickens slightly—but be very careful not to let it come anywhere near the boil or it will curdle.

To serve, pour the soup into a warm tureen and ladle it into warm soup bowls. This really is one of the most delicate and delicious soups imaginable. *Note*: if you want to make this soup in advance, prepare it up to the egg yolk and cream stage. This final stage should only be done at the last minute, just before serving.

Prawns and shrimps
If I was ever an aspiring gourmet, time has tempered me. No longer can I be tempted to peel two pints of cooked brown shrimps (a job which used to take all afternoon) to make a tiny amount of shrimp paste—admittedly delicious but consumed, it seemed, in a few seconds. But fresh, fat and juicy prawns, *yes*, I will willingly peel to serve unadulterated—with just some lettuce, a squeeze of lemon or perhaps some home-made mayonnaise. They have to be fresh, native prawns though. For 'prawns' covers a multitude of varieties, many of them from warm foreign waters where they

grow fast and often large. Even when unfrozen these lack the firm texture and flavour of our own. If I *have* to buy frozen prawns for cooking, the best I've come across are the Norwegian prawns which the food departments of one quality chain-store sell.

Just to confuse matters, what we call prawns the Americans call shrimps. But our tiny shrimps are almost a national delicacy when potted in Lancashire with melted butter and spices (one firm in Morecambe Bay, incidentally, operates a mail-order shrimp service). At one time these potted shrimps came in prettily glazed porcelain pots, but now plastic has penetrated here too. One authority suggests that to appreciate the flavour of potted shrimps, they should be gently warmed till the butter just begins to flow. I agree, and certainly I've found that melting the shrimp butter in a saucepan with a couple of tablespoons of fresh cream makes a lovely 'instant' sauce to serve with plain grilled fish.

Scampi, by the way, is the Italian name for what we used to call Dublin bay prawns. They are not in fact prawns but a tiny member of the lobster family (yet another name for this shellfish is Norway lobster). All the meat lies in the tail and scampi are always sold headless, usually already boiled and rubbery and frozen. It seems appropriate that they end up deep-fried in bright orange 'breadcrumbs' to be served as basket meals in pubs.

How to peel prawns
Holding the prawn's head with your left hand and its tail with your right hand, uncurl the prawn and straighten it out as much as possible. Now press the head and tail towards each other in a straight line, and then pull them apart again—the shell should come away in your right hand, leaving the head and body in your left hand. Now simply separate the head from the body.

Spiced prawns with tomatoes

(serves 2–3 people)

I think fresh boiled and peeled prawns are so delicious all they need is lemon juice, seasoning and some wholemeal bread and butter. Frozen prawns, on the other hand, need an imaginative recipe like this one.

8 oz packet frozen prawns (225 g)
1 lb tomatoes, skinned and chopped (450 g)
1 large onion, halved and sliced

2 cloves of garlic, crushed
1½ tablespoons groundnut oil
¾ teaspoon coriander seeds
½ teaspoon cumin seeds
1 cardomum pod
½ teaspoon ground ginger
1 rounded teaspoon ground turmeric
½ teaspoon chilli powder
Salt and freshly-milled black pepper

In a large frying pan heat the oil, then add the onion slices and fry gently for approximately 10 minutes or until softened and golden.

In the meantime, grind the whole spices with a pestle and mortar (or this can be done in a small basin using the end of a rolling pin). Then add all the spices, together with the garlic, to the onion and stir until everything is well heated. Now add the prawns and stir them around too, so that they're evenly coated with the spice mixture, then add the prepared tomatoes and some salt and freshly-milled pepper. Bring to simmering point and cook for about 20–25 minutes, uncovered, by which time a lot of the excess liquid will have evaporated and the tomatoes will have reduced to the consistency of a sauce.

Serve with spiced pilau rice or some nutty-flavoured brown rice cooked with onion.

How to dress crab

If you're not squeamish you can buy fresh, live crab and cook it yourself. I'm afraid I am squeamish and I could no more drop a live crab into boiling water than I could stab it through the head. I'm perfectly happy to leave the boiling to the experts and to find a reliable fishmonger to choose me a good cooked crab.

A good crab full of meat should feel heavy for its size. I bought one recently which weighed just over 1 lb (450 g) and it yielded almost 7 oz (200 g) of meat. From a large 2 lb (900 g) crab you should get about ¾ lb (350 g) of meat. Together with some home-made mayonnaise and a salad, 7–8 oz (200 g) of crabmeat is plenty for two people as a main course—or you could stretch it between four for a starter.

The first thing you do is to choose and buy your cooked crab. The fishmonger will pull it slightly open so that you can see it's full of meat and not empty. Back in your kitchen you'll need a

A

B

C

D

E

chopping board, two bowls (one for the white meat and one for the dark meat), a small sharp knife, a teaspoon, a metal skewer (preferably flat), and either a small hammer or a pair of nutcrackers.

Put the crab on its back on the chopping board, so that the claws and softer body shell face upwards, then simply twist off the legs and claws (A)—they'll come away very easily—and put them on one side.

Now put your thumbs against the hard back shell close to the crab's tail, and push and prise the body section out and away from the hard back shell (B). From the body section you now remove and discard (i) the small greyish-white stomach sack, just behind the mouth and (ii) the long white pointed 'dead man's fingers'. These can be easily distinguished and it is a quick and easy job to remove them (C).

The body shell (and in particular the parts where the legs and claws joined the body) is a mass of tiny crevices, all harbouring delicious meat. Scrape and pick the meat out, dividing it between the bowls according to the colour of the meat. Remove the meat from the hard back shell in the same way (D).

Crack the claws and legs with your hammer or nutcracker then, with a skewer, poke out all the white meat into the appropriate bowl (E).

If you want to serve the crab in the hard back shell, break off the jagged, overlapping rim from all round the edge of the shell, then wash and dry it well, and smear it inside with oil (F).

Then season the white meat with salt, freshly-milled pepper, cayenne and lemon juice (chopping or shredding the

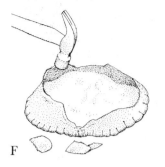

F

meat a little). Now season the brown meat in the same way. Place it down the centre of the shell, and place the white meat on either side. Finally decorate the crab with finely chopped parsley (see the photograph on page 424) and serve with a fresh crisp salad and some home-made mayonnaise.

Hot crab soufflé

(serves 4–6 people as a first course)

Crabmeat makes one of the nicest of all hot savoury soufflés.

The crabmeat from a fresh cooked crab, weighing 1 lb (450 g) or 8 oz (225 g) frozen mixed brown and white crabmeat, thawed
1½ oz butter (40 g)
1½ oz flour (40 g)
¼ pint single cream (150 ml)
¼ pint milk (150 ml)
1 tablespoon grated onion
2 tablespoons grated Parmesan cheese
½ teaspoon English mustard powder
1½ teaspoons anchovy essence
1–2 teaspoons lemon juice
3 tablespoons chopped parsley
5 egg yolks
6 egg whites
Salt and cayenne pepper

Pre-heat the oven to gas mark 6, 400 °F (200 °C) and put in a baking sheet on the shelf below centre.

First grease a 4 pint (2·25 litre) baking or soufflé dish. Then melt the butter in a saucepan, stir in the flour and cook for 1–2 minutes. Then gradually add the cream and milk, a little at a time, stirring after each addition. Bring to the boil and—still stirring—allow it to simmer for a minute or two. Now remove the pan from the heat and stir in the rest of the ingredients, except for the crabmeat and egg whites.

Next, add the crabmeat and taste the mixture—it should have quite a strong flavour. If not add some more anchovy essence, salt, cayenne and lemon juice. Now whisk the egg whites until stiff but not dry and, using a metal spoon, fold them into the crab mixture, then pour the soufflé into the prepared baking dish. Put the dish on the pre-heated baking sheet in the oven and bake for 45–50 minutes. After about 30 minutes, check to see that the top of the soufflé is not getting too brown—if it is, cover with foil. Serve *immediately* it's cooked.

Cheese

Including recipes for:

Cheese is one of the very few foods which has the distinction of providing one complete course of a meal on its own, without any other preparation or adornment. This makes it one of the best friends of a harassed hostess: an imaginative cheeseboard with a small selection of water biscuits (like Bath Olivers, if you want to be really posh), crisp celery and some fresh fruit is a very good alternative to a dessert when you're pushed for time. But a good cheeseboard can be something of an adventure too. Over the centuries the art of cheesemaking has produced an incredible range of textures and flavours, and over the last few years more and more of them have become available in our shops. So try to offer guests a good variety, say some Stilton, Cheddar, Brie or Camembert, and perhaps a goat's cheese. With a little bit of experimenting you can come up with all kinds of different combinations of your own.

In this section we are also concerned with the uses of cheese in cooking—and they are many. Cheese is used in sauces, pastry, fondues, omelettes, for toasting, gratinéing (i.e. browning the top of a dish under the grill after sprinkling with grated cheese), grating onto soups or pasta, in salads and in cheesecakes. Here, too, care must be taken to choose the right kind of cheese for the right kind of cooking. So first of all let's look at the various methods of cheese-making and the results they produce.

Cheese-making

All cheese is made from milk—mostly cow's milk, sometimes goat's and occasionally ewe's—and the basis of all cheese-making is the separation of the solids (curds) from the liquids (whey) in the milk. From then on a whole variety of processes may take place, depending on the nature of the finished cheese—cutting, stirring, scalding, salting, moulding, pressing, ripening and so on.

There are literally thousands of different cheeses, the character of each one is dependent not only on its method of production but also on unique local conditions, such as the nature of the grazing for the dairy herds. However, broadly speaking, one can distinguish certain 'families' of cheese:

Soft paste cheeses These are those with the floury (unwashed) rinds and very soft creamy centres, of which Brie and Camembert are perhaps the most famous. Slightly firmer, but similar in texture, are those cheeses whose rinds are regularly washed while they're ripening (to keep the moisture needed for fermentation): Pont l'Evêque is a well-known example. Also in the category of 'soft paste' come the goat's cheeses, although in practice the range of textures in goat's cheese is huge.

Blue-veined cheeses These are cheeses which have been injected with a penicillium mould, which creates the characteristic blue veins. Unlike other cheeses they ripen from the inside out and have to be perforated with special needles to aerate them and encourage the mould. In France, Roquefort is the prince of the blue cheeses, in England Stilton.

Pressed uncooked cheeses These cheeses are bandaged with a cloth, placed in a mould, then kept under pressure for up to 24 hours. Most of our English cheeses are of this kind, though the degree of pressing (and therefore the texture) varies. Caerphilly, for instance, is a lightly pressed cheese while Cheddar is hard-pressed.

Hard-pressed cooked cheeses To make these cheeses the curds are 'cooked' at 60°C before being put into moulds and very firmly pressed. During the maturing period (up to six months) fermentation occurs internally, creating the holes which are characteristic of such cheeses as Gruyère and Emmenthal.

In addition to these four 'families' of cheese, we can also buy processed cheese, which has little connection with the natural cheeses from which it is processed. The product is made by grinding down a cheese (e.g. Cheddar), mixing it to a paste, flavouring it then packing it into small portions—and I can't see much point in it.

Finally there is a group of cheeses generally known as fresh unfermented cheeses sometimes (incorrectly) called cream cheeses; these are soft cheeses, which are made from naturally soured milk, whole or skimmed milk, or cream. Their fat content, and their flavour, varies a great deal. They have varied uses in cooking— cheesecakes for instance, or cheese spreads or salads — but they should all be used as fresh as possible.

Cottage cheese is made from pasteurised skimmed milk. The regulations state that it must contain less than 2% milk fat, and it is therefore often recommended for those on a diet, though on its own the flavour is really rather bland.

Curd cheeses These have a more pronounced flavour, and the curds are formed by the natural action of lactic acid in milk. The fat content of curd cheese varies depending on the degree, if any, to which the milk has been skimmed.

Cream cheeses As the name suggests these are made from cream (single and double) rather than milk, and as a result they have a higher fat content. In this country cream cheeses are sold unripened; they have a buttery texture and a rich, faintly acid, flavour.

Farmhouse or factory?
Recently I spent a delightful day down on a farm—Chewton Dairy farm at Chewton Mendip to be precise—watching a real expert assessing and grading Cheddar cheese. Just by pressing his thumb on top of one and gauging the amount of 'bounce' under pressure, he could tell both the age and quality of a cheese. In his grandfather's day, he said, this test was carried out by standing on the huge cheeses and bouncing from one to the other! He then proceeded to insert a cheese iron into the Cheddar, to twist it sharply then withdraw it, extracting a small quantity of cheese from the centre. The 'bloom' on the back of the iron told him the smoothness and fat content of the cheese, and then by rubbing a small piece of the cheese between thumb and forefinger he could check the texture. A good cheese, I was informed, should 'feel like a well-nourished dairy-maid'!

This farm is one of only a few which continue to make traditional Cheddars. A small quantity of Cheshire cheese, and even less of Lancashire, is also still made on farms. Altogether about 10% of our English cheese is 'farmhouse' and it's the best you can buy. It is made from the finest quality milk that the dairy herds produce and is well-matured—always worth looking out for. The rest of our cheese is now made in factories—or 'creameries' as they prefer to be called. Modern economics have made this inevitable and even in France, where they are particularly choosy about their cheese, the same trend is happening. Factory cheese, however, is subject to the same stringent standards of classification as farmhouse, and can be excellent.

Grading In the case of farmhouse cheese, the very finest quality cheese is graded and labelled as *superfine*, and good quality cheese as *fine*. The equivalent grades for factory-made cheeses are *extra selected* and *selected*. In both cases, the rest of the cheese which is saleable in spite of having some fault is simply called *graded*.

Buying and storing cheese

Since most of us buy our cheese in relatively small quantities—
either pre-packed or sliced off a whole cheese—the complex
business of caring for a whole cheese (damp wrapping, polishing,
and humidity control) need not concern us too much, though there
are some shopkeepers and restaurateurs who could certainly do
some homework on the subject.

If you are buying portions from larger cheeses, look out for any
that are cracked or look sweaty: it means they have been exposed
to shop temperature for too long and are in the process of drying
out. In the case of soft paste cheeses, check that they are springy
to the touch and (unless you want to eat them immediately) not
too runny.

At home the best place to store your cheese is at the bottom of
the refrigerator or, failing that, some other *cool* place. At all events
wrap each piece tightly in foil, with no little tears or gaps to let the
air in. Those china cheese dishes or domes, however attractive
they may be, are not the place to store cheese since they offer no
protection from the air.

Most cheeses however have best flavour and texture if they are
brought to room temperature about 1 hour before eating.

British cheeses

There are—if you don't include the elusive Blue Vinny (said to be
made secretly in Dorset) and the very local Yorkshire cheeses—
ten major British cheeses. All are made from cow's milk, and their
very names are evocative of the dairy pastures where, for the most
part, they are still produced.

Cheddar One of the most imitated of cheeses, and understandably
so: we import Cheddars from all kinds of places like New Zealand
and Ireland, but the original English Cheddar is still the best—
and in particular Farmhouse Cheddar, which is well-matured
(anything up to nine months) and stronger than the mild, younger
Cheddars that are widely available. A good Cheddar cheese
should look amber yellow and fresh, without a greasy shine, and it
should feel firm but not hard. Its clean and mellow flavour makes
it very suitable for cooking, toasting, topping, for cheese sauces or
simply for serving with pickled onions and beer for a ploughman's
lunch.

Cheshire Said to be the oldest of English cheeses, it comes in red,
white or blue—very patriotic! The red Cheshire, which has been

artificially coloured, is milder than the white, which ideally should be flaky and slightly salty (though this will depend on its age). Both red and white Cheshire are good melting cheeses. The blue-veined variety (sometimes artificially produced, sometimes not) has a distinctive ripe, salty flavour.

Double Gloucester A bright orange (artificially induced) colour, but with a mature, creamy and delicate taste. It's best eaten, I think, just with biscuits and celery. It is called 'double' because when whole it's twice the size of a single Gloucester (which is not sold now anyway). The variety which includes chives is known as Cotswold cheese.

Caerphilly Another eating, rather than cooking, cheese. It's a quick ripener, ready for eating after only two weeks, which makes it white, mild and semi-soft.

Wensleydale From Yorkshire as the name implies, this comes in two varieties. The young white Wensleydale is mild and very slightly salty; the blue-veined Wensleydale has been allowed to mature for some six months, is soft and flaky in texture and rich, almost sweet, in flavour.

Lancashire A white mild cheese, with a fairly soft and crumbly texture which is supposed to make it 'spreadable', but certainly makes it an excellent toasting cheese.

Derby Mild, hard and honey-coloured when at its best, which is at about four to six weeks. A standard variation is the sage Derby, which is flavoured with chopped sage leaves and coloured green with spinach.

Leicester This is red and crumbly with a medium-strong flavour when it has fully matured after three months. It's good for toasting.

Stilton Named after the village on the Great North Road where it was sold to coach travellers, who spread its fame all over the country. A whole Stilton is 9 inches high and 8 inches across with a crinkly brown rind. The habit of spooning the cheese out of the centre and then pouring port in to keep it moist still persists. In my opinion this ruins the flavour and texture of the cheese, which really ought to be firm and creamy white with a clean network of blue veins. It is far better to slice Stilton horizontally and to keep it wrapped, in the fridge. At full maturity (six months) Stilton should be rich and mellow with a sharp, salty aftertaste. The young version, white Stilton, has not been left to develop a mould and is mild and crumbly.

Dunlop It might be described as the national cheese of Scotland, where indeed it is mainly found nowadays. It is a smooth, creamy white cheese with a mild, occasionally slightly sourish, flavour. It is named after the town of Dunlop in Ayrshire.

Continental cheeses
Once you could only find these—or at least a reasonable selection of them—at specialised cheesemongers or delicatessens, but nowadays many supermarkets carry quite an adventurous stock of them. They are always worth trying out for yourself, so here's a list (by no means exhaustive) of some you might come across.

France
France is *the* country for cheese-making: there are many hundreds of cheeses which are purely local specialities (and if you're ever in a particular region, do ask to sample the local cheese—it may be the only chance you ever get!). Some of course have become world famous. Of the soft paste cheeses *Brie* is widely exported in its traditional disc shape, with a downy white rind and a faintly straw-coloured interior. It should be springy to the touch, creamy and fairly mild in flavour. Rather tangier and fruitier is the famous *Camembert*, which to me is the very essence of the rich dairy lands of Normandy. Also worth trying, if you want a stronger spicy soft cheese, is its neighbour *Livarot* or, from the Alsace region, *Munster*.

The greatest of the French blue-veined cheeses (called 'bleus') is *Roquefort*, a ewe's milk cheese. To qualify for the name, the cheese has to mature only in the humid natural caves of Roquefort. Rather expensive, it's often used in recipes for quiche or salad dressing, but really deserves to be eaten on its own to appreciate its strong, distinctive taste. Other French bleus are available over here, such as *Bleu de Bresse* which is somewhat milder than Roquefort.

A proper catalogue of French pressed cheeses would be almost endless, but among those that find their way over here I'd mention *Saint-Paulin* from Brittany, mild and velvety and useful in cooking (also *Port Salut* which is a Saint-Paulin relative, made in a local monastery). *Reblochon* from the Savoy region is also mild and creamy; *Cantal* from the pastures of the Auvergne is a firm, nutty-flavoured cheese.

Goat's cheese is something of an acquired taste, I'd say, and not all that easy to find in Britain. But they can be absolutely delicious and they come in all shapes and sizes. *Saint-Maure* for example is cylindrical, firm to the touch and full-flavoured. *Valencay* is shaped like a sawn-off pyramid, its rind is dusted with charcoal, and it tastes mild and slightly nutty. *Banon* (from Provence) is disc-shaped and comes wrapped in chestnut leaves.

Switzerland
Best known of the Swiss cheeses are the hard, cooked varieties: the yellow-amber *Gruyère*, with its pock-marking of little holes, has a distinct fruit flavour. So does the ivory-coloured *Emmenthal*, which has a slightly firmer, oilier texture and rather larger holes distributed throughout it. Both are good melting and toasting cheeses, and the basis of several traditional fondue recipes.

Holland
Both the semi-hard Dutch cheeses, the firm yellow *Gouda* and the mild red-rinded *Edam*, have long been familiar over here. Both look good on a cheese-board and are useful in recipes.

Italy
The Italian repertoire of cheeses is extensive, and the Italians make good use of their cheeses in cooking. *Parmesan*, a hard brittle cheese, is indispensable for grating over soups, pasta and other dishes. It is widely sold here ready-grated, which means it has lost a good deal of its flavour: do try to get hold of a whole piece of it and grate it yourself when needed—it keeps very well. *Mozzarella*, a very white soft cheese (occasionally found made from buffalo's milk) comes in little plastic bags which should be stored in water. It is the traditional cheese for cooking on pizza, with a nice elastic texture, and when really young and fresh it is delicious with a little olive oil in a salad. For the end of a meal creamy *Bel Paese* and pungent, almost runny blue *Gorgonzola* make a good contrast.

Greece
Greek cheeses, unfortunately, are usually only to be found in Greek or Cypriot shops in Britain, but *Feta* (soft ewe's milk cheese) is delicious, when very fresh, in a salad; and the hard salty *Kefalotyri* is excellent fried.

Cheese and onion quichelets

(makes 10)

The name sounds odd but it describes these little cheese tarts perfectly. Serve them on picnics or car journeys or at buffet parties when you need food that can be picked up easily.

For the pastry:

---

2 oz wholewheat flour (50 g)

2 oz self-raising flour (50 g)

1 oz margarine (25 g)

1 oz lard (25 g)

Salt and freshly-milled black pepper

For the filling:

---

1 large egg, beaten

3 fl oz milk (75 ml)

$\frac{1}{4}$ teaspoon mustard powder

$1\frac{1}{2}$ oz strong Cheddar cheese, grated (40 g)

1 onion, finely chopped

$\frac{1}{2}$ oz butter (10 g)

Cayenne pepper

Pre-heat the oven to gas mark 4, 350°F (180°C)

First make up the pastry: combine the flours and add some seasoning, then rub in the fats until the mixture is crumbly; add enough cold water to make a dough that leaves the bowl clean. Place the dough in a polythene bag and leave to rest in the fridge for 30 minutes. Then roll out the dough and, using a $3\frac{1}{4}$ inch (8 cm) plain cutter, cut out rounds. Use the rounds to line a patty tin.

Next, for the filling, melt the butter in a small saucepan and soften the onion in it over a low heat for 10–12 minutes. Leave to cool then put a little onion in the base of each tartlet and put a little grated cheese on top. Now whisk together the milk, egg and mustard powder and season to taste, then spoon some of the liquid carefully into each tartlet.

Bake in the centre of the oven for about 30 minutes, then top with a light sprinkling of cayenne pepper. These little tarts can be served hot or cold.

Pan-fried pizza

(serves 4 people)

This is an extremely quick and easy way to make a pizza, without having to bother with making a bread dough.

8 oz self-raising flour (225 g)
½ teaspoon salt
Freshly-milled black pepper
4–5 tablespoons olive oil
4 generous tablespoons tomato purée
1 × 14 oz tin Italian tomatoes, drained and chopped (400 g)
About 5 oz Saint-Paulin or Port Salut cheese, cut into small cubes (150 g)
1 dozen black olives, pitted and chopped
1 teaspoon dried mixed herbs
1 × 1¾ oz tin anchovy fillets in oil (45 g)

First sieve the flour, salt and freshly-milled black pepper into a bowl. Make a well in the middle and pour in 2 tablespoons of olive oil, then 4 tablespoons of water. Now mix to a soft, though not sticky, dough—you may find you have to add a further tablespoon or so of water to get the right consistency. Prepare a floured surface, turn the dough out onto it and knead lightly. Now roll out a round to fit the base of a 9–10 inch (23–25 cm) frying pan.

Next heat 1 tablespoon of olive oil in the pan, place the circle of dough in the pan and cook over a low heat for about 5 minutes or until the base is lightly brown.

Have ready an oiled plate and turn the pizza base out onto it. Then, after heating a further 1 tablespoon of oil in the pan, slide the pizza base back in, and cook the reverse side for 5 minutes.

During this time, spread the tomato purée over the surface of the pizza base, together with the drained tomatoes. Next scatter over the cubed cheese, chopped olives and herbs. Finally, arrange the anchovy fillets on top in a criss-cross pattern and drizzle on the oil from the tin.

To see if the underside of the pizza base is cooked you can lift up a corner with a palette knife and have a look. When it's cooked, transfer the pan to a pre-heated grill for 2 or 3 minutes to melt the cheese and heat the topping.

Serve straight away with a mixed salad.

Cheese and herb sausages

(serves 3–4 people)

This is adapted from a traditional Welsh recipe called *Glamorgan sausages*. They really are lovely—we like them served with fried broccoli and red tomato chutney.

5 oz fresh breadcrumbs (150 g)
4 oz strong Cheddar cheese, grated (110 g)
1 medium-sized onion, grated
1 egg yolk
1 teaspoon dried mixed herbs or 2 teaspoons fresh chopped mixed herbs
¾ teaspoon mustard powder
Salt and freshly-milled pepper

For coating and frying:
½ oz breadcrumbs (10 g)
½ oz grated Parmesan cheese (10 g)
1 egg white, lightly beaten
Oil

Place the breadcrumbs in a large mixing bowl together with the grated onion, Cheddar and herbs; add the mustard powder and a seasoning of salt and pepper. Then add the egg yolk and stir to bind the mixture together. Now divide it into 12 or 14 small portions and, using your hands, roll each piece into a sausage shape squeezing it to hold it together.

Before frying them mix the breadcrumbs reserved for coating with the Parmesan cheese and dip each sausage first into the egg white and then into the breadcrumb and cheese mixture and coat evenly.

Fry in hot shallow oil till crisp and golden. Drain on crumpled kitchen paper before serving.

Roman gnocchi

(serves 3–4 people)

These are little fingers made with cheese and semolina, then baked in the oven with butter. Simple, inexpensive but really good. They *can* be served with a fresh tomato sauce, but I don't think they necessarily need it.

½ **pint milk (275 ml)**
5 oz semolina (150 g)
3 oz butter (75 g)
2 eggs, beaten
Freshly-grated nutmeg
5 oz freshly-grated Parmesan cheese (150 g)
Salt and freshly-milled pepper

Put into a saucepan the milk, semolina and ½ pint (275 ml) of water together with a good grating of nutmeg and a little salt and pepper, and bring it all to the boil, stirring all the time. Let the mixture boil for about 4 minutes (still stirring) until it is thick enough to stand a spoon up in. Then remove the pan from the heat and beat in 1 oz (25 g) of butter, 3 oz (75 g) of the Parmesan cheese and both the beaten eggs. Check the seasoning, then spread the mixture in a small Swiss roll tin or something similar (approximately 11 × 7 inches, 28 × 18 cm), lined with oiled greaseproof paper. Leave to cool or refrigerate—overnight if possible.

When you're ready to cook the gnocchi, pre-heat the oven to gas mark 6, 400°F (200°C).

Then cut the cheese and semolina mixture into 'fingers' (you should get about 24–27) or use a pastry cutter for round shapes (see photograph, page 389) and peel away the greaseproof paper. Place them, slightly overlapping, in a shallow buttered baking dish, then dot the top of the gnocchi with the remaining 2 oz (50 g) of butter and bake for 10 minutes.

Then baste the gnocchi with the melted butter and sprinkle the remaining 2 oz (50 g) of Parmesan over them. Replace the dish on an upper shelf of the oven and bake for a further 30 minutes or until the whole thing is golden brown and bubbling nicely.

Spinach and cream cheese quiche

(serves 4–6 people)

Fresh spinach would be best for this quiche, but 1 lb (450 g) of frozen spinach (so long as it's well drained) would do as an alternative.

2 lb fresh spinach (900 g)
1 oz butter (25 g)
½ **lb cream cheese (225 g)**

3 eggs, beaten
¼ pint milk (150 ml)
Freshly-grated nutmeg
2 tablespoons grated Parmesan
A squeeze lemon juice
Salt and freshly-milled pepper
Wholewheat shortcrust pastry made with 3 oz wholewheat flour (75 g) and 3 oz self-raising flour (75 g) (see recipe page 78, in Part One)

Pre-heat the oven to gas mark 4, 350°F (180°C) and pop in a baking sheet.

First make the pastry and use it to line a 10 inch (25 cm) flan tin. Prick the pastry base all over with a fork, and bake on the pre-heated baking sheet for 15 minutes. Remove the flan tin from the oven and brush the pastry all over with some of the beaten egg from the filling ingredients. Return the flan tin to the oven and cook for a further 5 minutes to allow the egg to set.

Set the flan tin on one side, but leave the baking sheet in the oven and increase the heat to gas mark 5, 375°F (190°C).

Now prepare the filling. First wash the spinach, discarding any coarse stalks or damaged leaves. Drain the leaves thoroughly and place them in a heavy-based saucepan together with the butter and some salt and pepper (there is no need to add any water). Cover and cook the spinach for about 7 minutes, giving the pan a shake occasionally, until the spinach collapses down into the butter.

Then drain the spinach thoroughly in a colander, pressing out any excess moisture. Now place the cream cheese in a bowl and beat it, gradually adding the milk followed by the remaining beaten eggs, Parmesan cheese and a seasoning of salt, pepper and nutmeg. Chop up the drained spinach with a sharp knife, and stir it into the cream mixture, adding a squeeze of lemon juice and (if it needs it) a little more seasoning.

Pour the whole mixture into the flan case and place the flan tin on the hot baking sheet in the upper part of the oven. Bake for 40 minutes, or until the filling is puffy and golden on top.

Note: this is also very nice made with a cheese shortcrust pastry, using 3 oz (75 g) each of wholewheat and self-raising flours, 3 oz (75 g) of fat and 2 oz (50 g) grated Cheddar cheese.

Toasted cheese with ale

(serves 4 people)

This is a lovely sort of toasted cheese, good for a really speedy supper.

8 oz strong Cheddar cheese, grated (225 g)
2 oz butter (50 g)
4 tablespoons brown ale
1 tablespoon mustard powder
Salt and freshly-milled black pepper
Cayenne pepper
4 thick slices of bread

First melt the butter in a saucepan. Then add the mustard, brown ale, grated cheese and some seasoning and, with a wooden spoon, stir continuously until the mixture looks creamy and the cheese has almost melted—but it's important that you don't let the mixture boil.

Then remove the saucepan from the heat and quickly toast the bread slices on both sides until they're nice and crisp. Pour the cheese mixture over each piece of toast, sprinkle with cayenne pepper then place them under the grill until hot and bubbling. Serve immediately with, perhaps, some more brown ale to drink with it.

Welsh rarebit soufflé

(serves 3 people)

This, if you've got the time, is a Welsh rarebit with a difference. It's rich golden brown, light and puffy.

$\frac{1}{2}$ **oz butter (10 g)**
$\frac{1}{2}$ **oz flour (10 g)**
6 tablespoons milk
1 teaspoon French mustard
A dash of Worcestershire sauce
A little cayenne pepper
2 eggs, separated
1 oz strong Cheddar cheese, grated (25 g)
1 oz Parmesan cheese, grated (25 g)
6 slices white bread (cut medium thick) from a small loaf
Salt and freshly-milled black pepper

First melt the butter in a small saucepan, blend in the flour and cook for a minute or two before adding the milk very gradually, stirring all the time. Let the mixture bubble for 2 minutes, take the saucepan off the heat and stir in the mustard, Worcestershire sauce, a little cayenne, some salt and freshly-milled pepper. Next beat the egg yolks, stir them into the sauce and leave it on one side to cool for a minute.

Now toast the bread on one side. Then beat the grated cheeses into the sauce mixture. Whisk the egg whites until stiff and, using a metal spoon, carefully fold them into the cheese mixture. Cover each slice (on the untoasted side) liberally with the cheese mixture. Pop the slices under a medium grill and when the tops are golden brown, light and puffy, serve at once.

Fillets of sole gratiné

(serves 4 people as a starter or 3 as a main course)

This, like all the best recipes in the world, is unbelievably simple and tastes really good. You can use Dover sole, lemon sole or even plaice fillets.

6 fillets of sole
8 oz stale breadcrumbs (225 g)
3 oz grated Cheddar cheese (75 g)
2 tablespoons fresh chopped parsley
4 oz melted butter (110 g)
6 lemon quarters
Salt and freshly-milled black pepper
A little extra melted butter

Pre-heat the grill to its highest setting.

Mix the breadcrumbs, grated cheese and parsley with 4 oz (110 g) of melted butter. Line the grill pan with foil and paint the foil with melted butter. Lay the sole fillets on it and season them with salt and freshly-milled black pepper, cover them with the breadcrumb mixture and pour over a little more melted butter. Cook under the hot grill for about 5 minutes until the crumbs have turned a rich brown and the fish is cooked. Serve garnished with lemon.

Greek salad

(serves 2–3 people as a lunch dish)

This should, authentically, have crumbled pieces of Greek Feta cheese mixed in with the salad ingredients, but white Stilton would be an alternative.

6 oz Feta cheese, chopped in small pieces (175 g)
6 ripe, firm tomatoes cut in quarters then in eighths
Half a small young cucumber or a whole ridge cucumber cut into ⅛ inch (3 mm) thick slices, the slices then halved
1 medium-sized onion cut in thin rings then the rings halved
2 oz small firm black olives (50 g)
4 tablespoons olive oil
1 small lemon, quartered
Salt and freshly-milled black pepper

Simply mix the cheese, tomatoes, cucumber, onion and olives together in a salad bowl. Season with salt and freshly-milled black pepper then pour the oil all over everything just before serving. Garnish with lemon quarters for squeezing over the salad.

Dutch omelette

(serves 1 person)

This is an omelette made with Dutch Gouda cheese, which is placed in the centre then melted under a hot grill so that the omelette itself is finally wrapped round a lovely, creamy, stretchy mass of cheese.

2 large fresh eggs
2 oz Gouda cheese (50 g)
1 tablespoon snipped chives (or very finely chopped spring onion tops)
1 oz butter (25 g)
Salt and freshly-milled black pepper

Pre-heat the grill to a high heat.

Break the eggs into a small basin and, using a fork, mix them lightly together, season, and add the snipped chives. Now cut the cheese, with a sharp knife, into thin slices.

Then over a fairly high heat melt the butter in a 7 inch (18 cm) frying pan. When the butter starts to froth, swirl it round so that the pan base and sides are well coated, then pour in the eggs. Now quickly lay the slices of cheese all down the centre of the omelette and, after cooking the base of the omelette for a few seconds, transfer the pan to the hot grill. Leave it there until the cheese just melts (it will over-cook if left too long).

Have a hot plate ready and fold the omelette into three: tilt the pan, flip the edge of the omelette nearest you over the centre part, then roll that over the far side of the omelette and turn the whole lot over again and out onto a plate.

Eat the omelette absolutely immediately with some crusty bread and a garlicky salad.

Broccoli cheese soufflé

(serves 4 people)

This always looks so beautiful. It's a pale green colour with a golden brown crust on top.

1 lb fresh broccoli (450 g)
2 large eggs
2 extra egg whites
2 oz Cheddar cheese, grated (50 g)
1 oz butter (25 g)
2 tablespoons plain flour
5 fl oz milk (150 ml)
A pinch of cayenne pepper
Freshly-grated nutmeg
1 tablespoon grated Parmesan cheese
Salt and freshly-milled black pepper

Pre-heat the oven to gas mark 6, 400°F (200°C)

A 1¾ pint (1 litre) soufflé dish, well buttered.

If you've never made a soufflé before, don't worry because this is a fairly easy one, and no soufflé is ever *all that* difficult once you've mastered the art of whipping egg whites to the right stage and, having got them to the right stage, the art of folding them in properly.

Having turned on the oven, take a large meat-roasting tin, big enough to hold the soufflé dish, then fill it with 1½ inches (4 cm) of hot water and put that in the oven to pre-heat as well.

Now start to prepare the broccoli by trimming off the very stalky bits, then place the rest in a saucepan with a little salt and about 6 fl oz (175 ml) of boiling water. Put a lid on and simmer it gently for about 10–15 minutes or until the broccoli has softened and most of the water has disappeared.

Now drain the broccoli well, then transfer to a largish mixing bowl and, using a large fork, mash it to a pulp. Get it as pulp-like as possible, but don't worry too much about getting rid of all the fibrous pieces of stalk.

Next melt 1 oz (25 g) of butter in a saucepan and stir in 2 level tablespoons of flour. Then when it's smooth gradually add the milk, stirring vigorously after each addition. When all the milk is in you should have a thick glossy paste and now you can mix in the cheese, keeping the pan over the lowest heat possible. After that, empty the cheese mixture into the bowl containing the broccoli pulp, then mix everything together thoroughly. Do a bit of tasting, add salt if it needs it and also some freshly-milled pepper, a pinch of cayenne and about a quarter of a whole nutmeg freshly-grated.

Now for the egg bit. Separate the eggs, add the two yolks to the broccoli mixture and mix them in fairly thoroughly. (All this, by the way, can be done well in advance.) For the whites, take a very large mixing bowl—making sure it's completely dry and free from grease, and you'll need a whisk which is the same. Whisk the egg whites until they stand up in peaks when you lift the whisk, but be careful not to overdo it, or they'll start to flop a bit and go watery.

As soon as they're ready carefully fold the egg whites into the broccoli mixture, using a metal spoon. Turn the bowl round as you fold, adding about a quarter of the mixture at a time. (When you're folding the egg whites in, the most important thing to remember is that you don't want to lose all the air you've whisked into them.)

Now spoon the mixture into the prepared soufflé dish, sprinkle with a dusting of Parmesan cheese, place the dish in the roasting tin, and cook the soufflé for 30–35 minutes. When it's done, it should be nicely risen and beginning to crack on the surface—but be careful not to overcook; it should be soft and moist inside. And, needless to say, serve immediately.

Note: this is equally good made with 1 lb (450 g) cooked cauliflower or courgettes mashed to a pulp.

Alpine eggs

(serves 3 people)

This is a recipe I have given many times before, but I don't apologise for including it here again because it never fails to please and is the quickest supper dish for any number of people — including one.

6 large fresh eggs
¾ lb grated Cheddar (or Lancashire) cheese (350 g)
1 oz approximately butter (25 g)
Salt and freshly-milled black pepper
1 dessertspoon freshly-snipped chives, if available

Pre-heat the oven to gas mark 4, 350°F (180°C)

Butter a shallow oval baking dish quite generously, then cover the base with half the grated cheese. Now carefully break 6 eggs onto the cheese, season well with salt and freshly-milled black pepper, then sprinkle the rest of the cheese over the eggs, covering them completely.

Dot with a few flecks of butter here and there, then bake in the centre of the oven for 15 minutes, by which time the cheese will be melted and bubbling, and the eggs just set. Just before serving sprinkle the chives over, and serve with crusty fresh bread and a crisp green salad.

Note: for a special occasion serve Alpine eggs as a first course. Use individual dishes (buttered) with 1 egg per person and 2 oz (50 g) grated Gruyère cheese per person. Prepare and cook in exactly the same way as above.

Cheese tartlets with mushroom pâté

(makes about 24)

These are made with a really crisp cheese pastry and filled with a mushroom and onion pâté.

For the pastry:
4 oz wholewheat flour (110 g)
4 oz self-raising flour (110 g)
1 teaspoon mustard
Pinch of salt

2 oz margarine (50 g)
2 oz lard (50 g)
3 oz Cheddar cheese, grated (75 g)
Some cold water to mix

For the filling:
1 oz butter (25 g)
6 oz flat mushrooms, finely chopped (175 g)
1 small onion, finely chopped
2 eggs
4 fl oz milk (110 ml)
1 tablespoon grated Parmesan cheese
Nutmeg
Salt and freshly-milled black pepper

Begin by making the pastry: sieve the flours, salt and mustard into a large mixing bowl, add the bran remaining in the sieve, rub in the fats until the mixture is crumbly, stir in the cheese, and add sufficient water to make a dough that leaves the bowl clean. Wrap the pastry in a polythene bag and chill it in the refrigerator for about 30 minutes.

Now melt the butter in a small pan and sauté the onion in it until soft—about 5 minutes. Then stir in the mushrooms and continue to cook gently, uncovered, for 30 minutes, stirring occasionally. The mixture should now have formed a sort of paste. Taste it and season.

Pre-heat the oven to gas mark 5, 375°F (190°C) and put a baking sheet in near the top.

Next, on a floured board, roll out the pastry fairly thinly and use a 3 inch (7·5 cm) cutter to cut out pastry rounds. Ease these into greased 2½ inch (6 cm) patty tins, prick the bases then put on the baking sheet in the oven and cook for 5 minutes. Now beat the eggs lightly, take the pastry out of the oven and brush each tart with a little egg, then return to the oven for a further 5 minutes.

Now whisk the milk, some seasoning and nutmeg into the beaten eggs. Put a little of the mushroom and onion mixture in the base of each tartlet and, very carefully, pour on some of the egg mixture. Sprinkle with Parmesan, return to the oven for 30 minutes until the mixture is set.

Finally, leave in the patty tins to cool for about 15 minutes.

Orange cheesecake

(serves 8 people)

This is unbelievably easy, it doesn't need any cooking and can be made well in advance.

4 oz wheatmeal biscuits, crushed to fine crumbs with a rolling pin (110 g)
2 oz butter (50 g)
1½ lb cream cheese (700 g)
3 fl oz concentrated orange juice, thawed (75 ml)
2 oz caster sugar (50 g)
The grated zest of 1 orange, boiled in water for 5 minutes, then drained

Begin by melting the butter in a saucepan, but do not let it brown. Then stir in the biscuit crumbs and mix well. Now press the mixture into a lightly oiled 8 inch (20 cm) cake or flan tin with a loose base and leave in a cool place, or in the refrigerator, to harden a little.

When it has firmed, beat the cream cheese, orange zest and sugar together very thoroughly, add the thawed orange juice and continue beating until you have a smooth mixture, then pour it into the biscuit-lined tin. Cover with foil and chill thoroughly.

If you wish, the cheesecake can be decorated with segments of fresh orange (carefully peeled, skinned and well drained) or, in the summer, whole strawberries make it particularly delicious — but don't decorate with either fruit until just before serving.

Curd cheesecake with fruit topping

(serves up to 12 people)

This is a large cheesecake which will serve up to 12 people. The fruit you use can be whatever is in season — in summer I think the nicest topping of all is a mixture of ½ lb (225 g) strawberries and ¼ lb (110 g) each of redcurrants and raspberries.

1½ lb curd cheese (700 g)
8 oz sugar (225 g)
3 eggs
1 teaspoon vanilla essence

For the base:

8 oz wheatmeal biscuits (225 g)

4 oz butter (110 g)

For the topping:

½ pint double cream, whipped (275 ml)

Icing sugar

Fresh fruit (as above)

Pre-heat the oven to gas mark 2, 300°F (150°C)

A 9-inch (23 cm) cake tin about 2–3 inches (5–7·5 cm) deep with a loose base.

Gently melt the butter in a small saucepan, without letting it brown. Crush the biscuits to fine crumbs with a rolling pin, then stir them into the melted butter. Transfer the biscuit mixture into the cake tin and press it down evenly all over to form a base. Now combine the curd cheese, eggs and sugar together in a mixing bowl and beat to form a smooth, thick cream—an electric mixer is best for this. Then mix in the vanilla essence and pour the mixture over the biscuit base, smoothing it out evenly.

Cook the cheesecake for 30 minutes on the centre shelf, then turn the oven off and leave it to get quite cold in the oven. It should then be chilled for at least 2 hours, or preferably overnight. To turn the cheesecake out of the tin, rinse a clean dishcloth in hot water: hold it around the tin for a few seconds, then push up the base very gently. Just before serving, top the cake with the whipped cream, the fresh fruit and a dusting of icing sugar.

Fresh lemon cheesecake with frosted grapes

(serves 6–8 people)

This is fresh-tasting and lighter than the other cheesecake recipes given in this book, and looks attractive with clusters of frosted grapes on top.

4 oz digestive biscuits, crushed into crumbs (110 g)

2 oz butter (50 g)

For the filling:

2½ oz caster sugar (60 g)

12 oz cottage cheese (350 g)

2 large egg yolks

The grated rind and juice of 2 lemons

¼ oz powdered gelatine (10 g)

5 fl oz double cream (150 ml)

To decorate:

4 oz seedless grapes (110 g)

1 egg white

Caster sugar

An 8 inch (20 cm) flan tin or sponge tin with a loose base, lightly oiled.

First prepare the base of the cheesecake by melting the butter in a small saucepan, then mix the melted butter with the biscuit crumbs in a bowl. Spoon the mixture into the prepared tin and press it well down all over as evenly as possible.

Now put the gelatine, along with 3 tablespoons cold water, into a small cup and stand this in a small saucepan of barely simmering water. Leave it for about 10 minutes or until the gelatine looks clear and transparent. Then put it on one side.

Now put the egg yolks, sugar and cheese in a liquidiser, blend for about one minute, then add the lemon juice and rind plus the gelatine (pour the gelatine through a strainer). Blend again until everything is thoroughly mixed and the mixture absolutely smooth. Now whip up the cream until you get a 'floppy' consistency, pour this into the liquidiser and blend again for just a few seconds. Next pour the whole mixture over the biscuit base, cover with foil and chill for a minimum of three hours.

Meanwhile whisk up the left-over egg whites. Break the grapes into little clusters of 2 or 3 grapes each and dip each bunch first in the egg white, then in a saucer of caster sugar. Leave them spread out on greaseproof paper for a couple of hours before using them for decoration.

Cœur à la crème
(serves 4 people)

This lovely cream mixture—ideal for serving with soft summer fruits—was originally served in heart-shaped dishes (hence the name). But small ramekins will do for the less romantic!

8 oz unsalted cream cheese (225 g)
½ pint soured cream (275 ml)
2 level tablespoons caster sugar
2 large egg whites
4 tablespoons double cream

Quite simply combine the cream cheese, soured cream and sugar thoroughly in a mixing bowl. Then whisk the egg whites until they are stiff and fold them carefully into the cream mixture. The whole lot now needs to be drained—overnight—in a cool place, and this is done by placing the mixture in a suitably-sized square of muslin, and placing this in a sieve over a bowl. When it has drained completely, pile the mixture into small dishes or ramekins, arrange your fruit on top, then pour a tablespoon of cream over each serving.

Index